How Empire Shaped Us

How Empire Shaped Us

Edited by

Antoinette Burton
and
Dane Kennedy

Bloomsbury Academic India
An imprint of Bloomsbury Publishing Plc

BLOOMSBURY
NEW DELHI • LONDON • OXFORD • NEW YORK • SYDNEY

BLOOMSBURY INDIA
Bloomsbury Publishing India Pvt. Ltd
Second Floor, LSC Building No. 4, DDA Complex, Pocket C–6&7,
Vasant Kunj, New Delhi 110070

BLOOMSBURY, BLOOMSBURY ACADEMIC INDIA and the Diana logo are
trademarks of Bloomsbury Publishing Plc

First published in India 2024
First published 2016

This edition published with permission from Bloomsbury Publishing Plc,
50 Bedford Square, London, WC1B3DP, UK

British Library Cataloguing-in-Publication Data
A catalogue record for this book is available from the British Library

Library of Congress Cataloging-in-Publication Data

ISBN: 978-93-93715-64-7

Typeset by RefineCatch Limited, Bungay, Suffolk
Printed at Manipal Technologies Limited, Manipal
To find out more about our authors and books
visit www.bloomsbury.com and sign up for our newsletters

CONTENTS

NOTES ON CONTRIBUTORS

Shigeru Akita is Professor of British Imperial History and Global History at Osaka University, Japan. He specializes in the economic international order in Asia in the nineteenth and twentieth centuries, with a special focus on the British Empire, and, more recently, global history from an Asian perspective. His Japanese language books include *Igirisu Teikoku no Rekishi* (*The History of the British Empire*), which won the Yoshino Sakuzo Prize in 2013. He also edited *Gentlemanly Capitalism, Imperialism and Global History* (2002) and, with Nicholas White, *The International Order of Asia in the 1930s and 1950s* (2013). He is one of the founders of *The East Asian Journal of British History*, a joint Japanese/Korean initiative.

Clare Anderson is Professor in the School of History, University of Leicester, UK. She has an undergraduate degree in History and Sociology, and a doctorate in History from the University of Edinburgh. She worked previously in the Department of Economic and Social History at the University of Leicester, and in the Department of Sociology at the University of Warwick. She has published widely on empire in the Indian Ocean, Australia and Asia, and is currently editor of the *Journal of Colonialism and Colonial History*. You can follow Clare on Twitter @sysgak. Her website is located at: https://www2.le.ac.uk/departments/history/people/canderson

Tony Ballantyne is a Professor of History, Head of the Department of History and Art History and the Director of the Centre for Research on Colonial Culture at the University of Otago in Dunedin, New Zealand. Born and raised in Dunedin, his undergraduate education was at the University of Otago and his PhD was from the University of Cambridge. He has also taught at the National University of Ireland, Galway, the University of Illinois, Urbana-Champaign and Washington University in St Louis. He has published extensively on colonial knowledge productions, the networks and forms of mobility that shaped the British Empire, and on the connections between religion and colonialism.

Bridget Brereton is Emerita Professor of History at the St Augustine (Trinidad) campus of the University of the West Indies. She has served as Head of the Department of History, as Deputy Campus Principal and as Interim Campus Principal, all at St Augustine. She has been a Visiting Professor at Johns

Hopkins University, Baltimore. She has served both as Secretary-Treasurer, and later as President, of the Association of Caribbean Historians, and is a past Editor of the *Journal of Caribbean History*. In 1996 she won the cross-campus Vice-Chancellor's Award for Excellence in Teaching, Research and Administration, the first woman to do so. She has been Chair of the Board of the National Library and Information System Authority (NALIS), Trinidad & Tobago, and also chaired the Committee appointed by Cabinet to consider the nation's highest award (the Trinity Cross) and other national symbols and observances. She has served on numerous university and campus boards and committees. She is the author of several books, including *Race Relations in Colonial Trinidad, 1870–1900* (1979), *A History of Modern Trinidad, 1783–1962* (1989), *Law, Justice and Empire: The Colonial Career of John Gorrie, 1829–1892* (1997) and *From Imperial College to the University of the West Indies: A History of the St Augustine Campus, Trinidad & Tobago* (2010), as well as many journal articles and book chapters. She is the editor of Volume V of the UNESCO *General History of the Caribbean, The Twentieth Century* (2004) and the co-editor of several other books. She has been a teacher for over forty years, and pioneered courses at St Augustine in the history of Trinidad & Tobago, and in women and gender in the history of the Caribbean. She has also authored two school texts, *Social Life in the Caribbean, 1838–1938* (for CXC) and *An Introduction to the History of Trinidad and Tobago* (for Forms 1 to 3 in secondary schools).

Caroline Bressey is a Reader in Historical Geography at University College London. Her research focuses upon the historical and cultural geographies of the black presence in London, alongside Victorian theories of race and anti-racism which was the focus of her first monograph, *Empire, Race and the Politics of Anti-Caste* (2013), and the links between contemporary identities and the diverse histories of London as represented in heritage sites in Britain. Her work on the black presence has mainly focused upon black women and their experiences in four arenas of life: institutions, imperial elite society, work and anti-racist politics. Her latest book is *Empire, Race and the Politics of Anti-Caste* (2015).

Antoinette Burton is Professor of History and Bastian Professor of Global and Transnational Studies at the University of Illinois, Urbana-Champaign. She has written widely on women and feminism and empire with a focus on Indian women and diaspora. She also teaches and writes about world history. She has just edited a collection of documents entitled *The First Anglo-Afghan Wars* (2014). Her latest book, *The Trouble with Empire*, is forthcoming from Oxford University Press.

Catherine Hall's research focuses on re-thinking the relation between Britain and its empire in the nineteenth and twentieth centuries. She is particularly interested in the ways in which empire impacted upon metropolitan life, how the empire was lived 'at home', and how English identities, both masculine and feminine, were constituted in relation to the multiple 'others' of the empire. *Civilising Subjects* looks at the process of mutual constitution, both of colonizer and colonized, in England and Jamaica in the period between the 1830s and the 1860s. Her recent book, *Macaulay and Son: Architects of Imperial Britain* (2012), focuses on the significance of the Macaulays, father and son, in defining the parameters of nation and empire in the early nineteenth century. She was Principal Investigator of the 'Legacies of British Slave Ownership' (2004–12) project funded by the Economic and Social Research Council (ESRC), and of 'The Structure and Significance of British-Caribbean Slave-Ownership, 1763–1833' (2013–16) project funded by the ESRC and the Art and Humanities Research Council. A resulting publication is *Legacies of British Slave-Ownership* (2014), co-authored with Keith McClelland.

Dane Kennedy is the Elmer Louis Kayser Professor of History and International Affairs at George Washington University, where he teaches British, British imperial and world history. His publications include *Islands of White: Settler Society in Kenya and Southern Rhodesia, 1890–1939* (1987), *The Magic Mountains: Hill Stations and the British Raj* (1996), *The Highly Civilized Man: Richard Burton and the Victorian World* (2005) and *The Last Blank Spaces: Exploring Africa and Australia* (2013). He was President of the North American Conference of British Studies from 2011 to 2013.

Marilyn Lake is Professor in History and Australian Research Council Professorial Fellow at the University of Melbourne, where she convenes a public lecture and seminar series called 'Australia in the World'. She has published widely on citizenship, nationalism and internationalism and campaigns for sexual and racial equality. Her books include *Getting Equal: The History of Australian Feminism* (1999), *FAITH: Faith Bandler Gentle Activist* (2002), *Connected Worlds: History in a Transnational Perspective* (edited with Ann Curthoys, 2005), *Drawing the Global Colour Line: White Men's Countries and the International Challenge of Racial Equality* (co-authored with Henry Reynolds, 2008) and the multi-authored *What's Wrong with Anzac? The Militarization of Australian History* (2010). She is a Fellow of the Academies of Humanities and Social Sciences and is serving her second term as President of the Australian Historical Association.

Philippa Levine is Mary Helen Thompson Centennial Professor in the Humanities and Co-Director of the Program in British Studies at the University of Texas at Austin. Her work has focused principally on gender, race and empire. She is at present working on a book on nakedness.

Wm. Roger Louis holds the Kerr Professorship in English History and Culture at the University of Texas. He has written or edited more than thirty books, including *Imperialism at Bay* (1977) and *The British Empire in the Middle*

East (1984). His edited publications include *The End of the Palestine Mandate* (1986), *The Transfers of Power in Africa* (1988), *Suez 1956* (1989), *The Iraqi Revolution* (1991) and *Churchill* (1993). Louis is the past President of the American Historical Association and the founding Director of the AHA's National History Center. He is Editor-in-Chief of *The Oxford History of the British Empire*, and the former Chairman of the Historical Advisory Committee, US Department of State.

John M. MacKenzie is Professor Emeritus at Lancaster University and Honorary Professor at St Andrews, Aberdeen and Stirling Universities, and Honorary Fellow at Edinburgh University. He is a Fellow of the Royal Society of Edinburgh. He has published books on popular and cultural imperialism, as well as aspects of environmental history. He has also written about Scottish migration and the development of museums around the world. He founded the 'Studies in Imperialism' series at Manchester University Press.

Thomas R. Metcalf is Professor Emeritus at the University of California, Berkeley. He is the author of numerous books on British India, including *The Aftermath of Revolt: India, 1857–1870* (1964), *An Imperial Vision: Indian Architecture and Britain's Raj* (1989) and *Ideologies of the Raj* (1995). His most recent book is *Imperial Connections* (2007).

Adele Perry is Professor of History at the University of Manitoba. She is the author of *On the Edge of Empire: Gender, Race, and the Making of British Columbia, 1849–1871* (2001), a number of works on Canadian women's history, Western Canadian history and nineteenth-century British Columbia. Her latest book is *Colonial Relations* (2015), a study of an elite Creole-Metis family in the nineteenth-century imperial world. She is doing new research on the fur trade and liberal humanitarianism.

Richard N. Price is Professor of History at the University of Maryland, College Park where he has taught since 1982 and has served in various administrative positions, including twelve years as Chair of the Department. He was awarded the D.Phil from the University of Sussex in 1968. He is the author of several books in both working class and imperial history, including *An Imperial War and the British Working Class* (1972), *Masters, Unions and Men* (1980), *Labour in British Society 1780–Present* (1986), *British Society 1680–1880: Dynamism, Containment and Change* (1998) and *Making Empire: Colonial Encounters and the Creation of Imperial Rule in Nineteenth Century Africa* (2008) which won the 2009 Albion Prize for the best book in British History since 1750 awarded by the North American Conference on British Studies. He has served on the editorial board of various journals, including *Victorian Studies*, *International Review of Social History*, *History Compass* and the *Journal of British Studies*. He is a frequent presenter at international scholarly conferences. His current research is on the relationship between liberalism and empire.

Jonathan Saha specializes in the history of nineteenth- and twentieth-century colonialism in South and Southeast Asia, focusing particularly on British Burma. His research to-date has been into the history of corruption within the colonial state, exploring how the state was experienced and imagined in everyday life. This has recently been published as a monograph entitled *Law, Disorder and the Colonial State: Corruption in Burma c.1900* with Palgrave Macmillan. As well as corruption, he has published on crime, medicine and 'madness' in colonial Burma. Increasingly he is interested in the history of animals, particularly the ways in which they shaped, and were shaped by, the colonization of Burma.

Mrinalini Sinha is a historian of the British Empire and of colonial India. She has written on various aspects of the political history of colonial India, with a focus on anti-colonialism, gender and transnational approaches. She has recently become interested in the different forms of political imaginings, beyond the nation-state, that animated anti-colonial thought in India at least until the inter-war period. Her current project, with the title 'Complete Political Independence: The Curious History of a Nationalist Indian Demand', will explore the contingency of the development of the nation-state form in India.

Introduction:

The Autobiographical Pulse in British Imperial History

Antoinette Burton and Dane Kennedy

Few historical subjects have generated such intense and productive debate in recent years as the history of empires, particularly the British Empire. This was not the case in the period immediately following decolonization: interest in the subject then waned, and it became something of an historiographical backwater. But it has since undergone a remarkable revival and transformation. Historians have once again turned their attention to the British imperial experience – its institutions, ideas and impact on peoples around the world – though they now do so from multiple vantage points, drawing on widely varied sources and bringing previously neglected perspectives to bear on what had hitherto been a history too often implicated in the imperial enterprise itself. What accounts for this renewed if reshaped preoccupation with empire by historians? How has it gained such purchase on the imaginations of so many of us? And how have we sought to reconcile our engagement with empire with what for many of us is a deep ambivalence towards – if not outright disavowal of – imperial history as an affiliating label for our work?

In seeking to answer these questions, historians of empire would do well to reflect on what inspired or impelled us to study the British imperial past in the first place. This is the purpose of the present volume. It brings together a number of scholars whose work covers various geographical regions and has addressed the problem of empire from various frames of reference. Our contributors are historians of different generations, different nationalities, different methodological and theoretical perspectives, and, no doubt, different ideological persuasions. Each of us addresses the relationship between our development as historians who were drawn to imperial themes both for personal intellectual reasons and the broader set of forces that have shaped our lives. Our aim, then, is to investigate the connections between the past and the present, the private and the public, the professional practices of historians and the social and political environments within which they have taken shape. We ask ourselves how the events we observed and experienced in our own lives may have informed or inflected how we have engaged with the British imperial past. And we offer readers a rich sampling of the impact of the British Empire on the lives, careers and imaginations of those who have chosen to become its historians.

Providing an intellectual genealogy of the recent historiography of empire that acknowledges the role of the personal and the political in its production necessitates an approach that goes beyond the standard historiographical survey. Such surveys are plentiful, and we have no desire to add to this literature.[1] Rather, we want to bring a collective form of 'life-writing' to bear on the subject. Such an approach requires a critical self-examination of the role of the historian's own subjectivity in the shaping of his or her historical concerns.[2] It should come as no surprise that the questions we ask about the past, the methods we employ to answer them and a great many other aspects of our historical practices besides, are informed by our personal experiences as subjects of forces at play in our own time and place. The autobiographical impulse is not only compelling, it offers insights into the stuff of history that are not available by any other means. Among other things, the self-reflection it entails challenges the notion that history is objective or disinterested. And it reminds us that historians produce situated knowledge, conditional on a variety of factors – including the untold or unacknowledged experience of historians themselves. By bringing these issues to the fore, we believe that much can be learned about how the British imperial past has exerted such influence on the Anglophone historical imagination during an extended moment when Western empires have been on the wane. Taken together, the essays that follow offer an intergenerational, transnational archive of the origins of contemporary British Empire history-writing in the wake of decolonization.

It scarcely needs stating that each of us is heir to an historiographical tradition that goes back many generations, and that our work as historians has occurred both within and against that tradition. Our terms of engagement with the imperial past are entangled with earlier generations of historians' ways of thinking about empire. One strand of this heritage can be traced to John Seeley, Thomas Babington Macaulay and other historians who contemplated the empire as foundational to a Greater Britain.[3] Another strand consisted of critics such as J. A. Hobson and John Strachey, who highlighted the militaristic, exploitative and politically corrupting effects of empire. For several of the contributors to this volume, the most direct and powerful influence has come from Ronald Robinson and John Gallagher, whose scholarship and guidance had a profound impact on Oxbridge-trained historians of the British Empire. Robinson and Gallagher provided an interpretive framework that simultaneously emphasized the persistent presence of a vast informal empire, which was economic in nature, and the catalysing consequence of political crises in this informal empire, which precipitated colonial conquest and rule. Their primary preoccupation, however, was with the strategic considerations of British statesmen who shaped imperial policy, a line of inquiry they referred to as 'the official mind'.

Other historians of empire have drawn on very different intellectual traditions. If decolonization marked a rupture from a world of empires, so too did it mark a rupture from historiographical perspectives and practices that took that world for granted. Many of our contributors have found intellectual inspiration less from the conventional strands of imperial historiography than from sources that this historiography sometimes labelled as products of the 'periphery'. These historians have come to the subject from the bottom up, as it were, grappling with an imperial heritage that obliged them to make sense, for example, of the expropriation of indigenous lands by settlers in Canada, Australia and New Zealand or the challenge of nation-building in ex-colonial states in South Asia, Africa and the West Indies. The number of contributors who reference Edward Said, Stuart Hall, Ranajit Guha and the Subaltern Studies Collective and other non-Western intellectual influences in their essays speaks to this shift of orientation.

So who are we? Who comprises the collective 'us' announced in the title of this volume? All of us are historians whose scholarship has focused either on Britain's imperial influence or on events, people and societies shaped by the long reach of imperial power and colonial settlement. If this plurality of historical subjects and approaches reflects the diverse backgrounds and experiences of imperial historians more generally, it also speaks to the shifting demographic nature of the field since the 1950s. Some of our contributors grew up in the British Isles; some came of age in ex-colonial societies; still others, the co-editors included, possess no personal connections to the British imperial world by birth or upbringing. Yet all of us were drawn in one way or another to that world, discerning in it something that spoke to circumstances that have shaped our own lives, whether consciously or unconsciously. We have pursued our shared subject in varied ways, by adopting diverse historical methods, drawing on a mix of theoretical stances, and relying upon different forms of empirical evidence. Some of us are political historians, others economic or social or cultural or intellectual or gender historians – or, as is more often the case, some combination of these categories. Some of us have devoted ourselves to the study of a specific region of the world, while others have ranged across wide swaths of the British Empire. Our academic training and careers have occurred in various geopolitical locations and they have been informed by those locations' specific contexts. This variation is itself a kind of testimony to the global scope and scale of empire and its various institutional legacies.

Our volume seeks to show that debates about British imperialism have ramifications that extend well beyond the cloistered walls of academia: we argue that by understanding where historians have come from we see more clearly how their work engages the debates of the day, both then and now. As historians of empire, we grapple, perforce, with issues of contemporary import, confronting concerns that are very much a matter of public debate in a world where decolonization and postcolonial states are recognized facts, if not the *sine qua non* of the global order in the last century. The impact of the decolonized world on contemporary geopolitics is, in fact, a crucial reason why British imperial history has resonated so powerfully beyond the mere confines of academic scholarship in recent decades.[4] To understand how and why this should be so, we must appreciate the role the afterlife of empire played in making British imperial historians who they are.

In order to take up this challenge, we invited contributors to address some of the following questions: How did you come to study imperialism? Who were your teachers, interlocutors, reading communities, imagined audiences? What has the impact been of events in the twentieth and twenty-first centuries on your approach to the subject, whether in your written work or your classroom experiences? Has your engagement with empire history changed over the decades? What personal and/or political experiences – including family history, institutional locations and research opportunities – have shaped your intellectual trajectory as a historian of empire? Though we expected that the answers our contributors gave to these questions would engage and intrigue, the essays we received in response to these questions have, frankly, far exceeded our expectations. Thoughtful, insightful and even lyrical in places, they provide windows into family lives, schooling and politics both local and global. Most intriguingly perhaps, they reveal the imprint of local space and place on the making of historical sensibilities and often on the very desire to do imperial history. Some of the contributors set out to become historians; others stumbled into their careers. Some were born, literally, into empire; some were colonials by design or by ascription; still others found themselves in the middle of post-imperial landscapes that shocked them into the realization of their vocation and their craft. One way or another, they all relate stories of finding themselves in the grip of empire histories they needed to tell in order to understand the significance of the archives they encountered or the big questions they wanted to answer. The ins and outs and ups and downs of that quest make for positively fascinating reading, not least because each contributor offers glimpses into the times in which s/he lived along the way. In this sense, *How Empire Shaped Us* is as much a repository for social, cultural and political histories of the profession and its practitioners as it is the backstory of imperial history-writing per se.

We urged our contributors to write accessibly and to keep a variety of readers in mind. One important audience we anticipate is our undergraduate students, who all too rarely have the opportunity to hear first-hand how the personal experiences and perspectives of historians impact the histories they are reading to fulfil requirements or complete modules. All of us know from direct experience that students' intellectual breakthroughs often occur as a result of an encounter with an especially inspiring teacher, someone who is able to bring a subject to life through his or her passion and personal example. This was certainly true of all the historians in this volume. Yet depending on generation, temperament and institutional location, the personas historians adopt in their scholarship may exclude the personal on the grounds that it is incompatible with their professional claims of objectivity or their authority as truth tellers. We believe these essays will provide undergraduates with some insight into the ways the histories we write are informed by our own experiences and enthusiasms.

We hope, too, that this collection of autobiographical reflections will attract the interest of history graduate students, who may gain greater understanding of the circumstances that have shaped the professional and intellectual development of their predecessors and, in turn, may look more deeply into the reasons they are pursuing their own chosen field of study. At a time when doctoral degrees in history are under all kinds of financial pressure, it is arguably critical for aspiring historians to appreciate that they are not the first generation to feel buffeted by circumstance or to be held in the grip of historical forces beyond their control. These essays obviously also speak to our colleagues, most particularly other historians in the field of imperial history, but to historians more generally, who do not as a rule tend to think autobiographically.[5]

Last but not least, this volume is intended for a broader audience of readers who may have no interest in the sometimes arcane historiographical debates that preoccupy members of the profession, but who read history for the sheer pleasure of learning more about the past. We hope they will find this volume of value for the light it sheds on how, why and in what circumstances the vagaries of personal experience have given rise to the empire histories they are drawn to. Like empire itself, all imperial histories are the consequence of the collision of individuals with historical forces large and small. Empire leaves its mark, in other words, on histories and historians alike.

We are acutely aware, of course, that this volume is not as representative of the range of scholars who currently work on various aspects of the British imperial world as we would like. Though we have sought to give as much generational, geographical, gender, historiographical and other forms of diversity to this collection as possible, gaps obviously exist. We have no contributors, for example, who work from African or South Asian academic institutions. Ireland is conspicuously absent as well, whether as a subject of study or as the location of the historian. Several of our contributors had to withdraw from the project for personal reasons. Another, the great South African historian Jeff Guy (1940–2014), tragically died before he was able to complete his essay. His passing is a poignant reminder of how fleeting are the memories we seek to capture. So, too, is the equally sad loss of Christopher Bayly, who had declined our invitation to contribute to the volume because he felt he had said his autobiographical piece elsewhere.[6] We want to stress, then, that for all kinds of reasons, this volume is at best a partial account of how empire has shaped the field of British imperial historiography. We intend to start a conversation about the relationship between historians and their subjects rather than close it off with claims to comprehensiveness. Indeed, we hope it generates a real dialogue about the stakes of recognizing not just how empire shapes us, but how all histories are made in and through the wide variety of historical circumstances that shape those who chronicle them.

Empire certainly left its mark in indelible ways on the lives and careers of the historians gathered here. Among the most common flashpoints are the Suez Crisis, the Falklands War, the Troubles in Ireland, the expulsions of South Asians from Africa, events in Rhodesia and South Africa and, if we think of empire more expansively, Vietnam, Iraq and Afghanistan as well. Of Suez Tom Metcalf writes: '[The British] people I met left me in no doubt about their bitter feelings of betrayal when President Eisenhower forced the British to call off the invasion. Some of their animosity was even directed at me as an American – the only time this ever happened. The trauma of Suez seemed also to validate my own commitment to the study of imperialism.' For Roger Louis, who found himself in Egypt as the event unfolded, the impact was even more consequential for his scholarship and for his lifelong view of the stakes of imperial history. For Richard Price, however, it was Mau Mau. He vividly recalls an exchange with a schoolteacher, who told him 'well . . . [the Africans] never asked us to go there in the first place, you know'. From that moment forward, he claims, 'I always read news on the empire in a different, more questioning and reserved light.'

Such touchstones are generation-specific, of course. The essays of Metcalf and Louis and Price cluster around memorable events at the front end of decolonization, whereas Dane Kennedy has vivid memories of Rhodesia in the 1970s as 'a colonial society in its death throes', an experience that shaped his dissertation and first book on comparative settler societies. John MacKenzie, for his part, is unequivocal abut the impact that debates about the Central African Federation had on his generation's views of what empire history could and could not be. As events in Africa unfolded against the backdrop of his training as an empire historian, he realized that 'we were witnessing a reaction against the notion that empire had provided the central meaning and moral force of British history, promoted by T. B. Macaulay, Sir John Seeley and such later historians as Sir Reginald Coupland. Such a position was scarcely sustainable in an age of decolonisation.' Those born after Bandung (1955) are more likely to have lived empire vicariously, whether through their parents' experiences of national independence, as Mrinalini Sinha recounts, or via the slow but accelerating trickle of postcolonial immigrants into the urban neighbourhoods of their childhood, as Philippa Levine documents. And those born after 1960 – such as Caroline Bressey and Jonathan Saha – tend to frame their empire histories through the lens of post-imperial British social and political history, where they have felt and feel more or less visible because of their mixed race families and the challenges to their ready legibility as 'British' that such origins have generated.

Yet even these generalizations are necessarily tentative and subject to debate. For despite commonalities of generation or location, empire did not intrude evenly or self-evidently. In fact, empire may have seemed remote or non-existent even to those growing up in post-war Britain. Clare Anderson's essay is evocative in this regard. She speculates that empire was not especially apparent to her as a child 'because of the difficulties of finding a vocabulary to talk about the discomfort of the loss of imperial dominions and possibly the erosion of national distinction or pride, in the aftermath of the war'. Growing up in Canada, Adele Perry observes, 'the British Empire, as a formal political structure, was mainly gloss', the remnants of racial thinking in the national anthem and the image of the Queen on the currency notwithstanding. In Australia and New Zealand, as Marilyn Lake and Tony Ballantyne are at pains to show, the presence of indigenous populations – and their struggles for inclusion in the settler colonial nation-state – mark the limits of awareness of empire, which was present but eclipsed by the particularity of racial politics in those contexts.[7] For that matter, the empire history that Roger Louis has produced over his long career may be said to have been shaped as deeply by growing up in segregated Oklahoma as it was by the fact of Suez. What Price calls the 'filaments' of empire were often like gossamer, and they moved in mysterious ways.

We have chosen to arrange the essays in this volume by birth order, precisely to showcase the historicity of empire's impact and to dramatize the differences across generations. Yet to our great surprise, there are many commonalities at work across these historians' lives as well. The vast majority of contributors record the impact of school and/or university days on their views of empire and history, noting the influence of teachers on their hearts and minds. For Marilyn Lake, it was Michael Roe and Kay Daniels; for Tony Ballantyne it was Chris Bayly; for Richard Price it was Ranajit Guha; for John MacKenzie it was the indomitable Glaswegian, Miss Cruikshank: his 'wonderfully radical classics teacher . . . who invited a notable missionary from Malawi, the Rev. Tom Colvin, to come to speak about the iniquities of the Federation and of the need for Malawian freedom'. Not all such encounters were salubrious. It was the antagonism of Emmet Larkin that shaped Antoinette Burton, while for Caroline Bressey it was that apparatus of national-imperial pedagogy, the BBC mini-series, that shaped her. Those Sunday night broadcasts taught her about the absences that a post-imperial culture might guarantee and, over time, about the thrill of the black British actor on screen that greater multicultural awareness might deliver.

Interestingly, many of the contributors here remark on how little empire intruded on their formal education. In many places across the empire before the 1980s, imperial history was not, apparently, much of a proper subject. That meant that one's empire education happened elsewhere – and that those who became empire historians might need to leave home to get it. For Clare Anderson, the Girl Guides were a very particular kind of classroom. She reports that working for her commonwealth badge and choosing Antigua shaped her view of the wider British imperial world, albeit through her mind's eye as a child.

Family contexts also loom large. They figure in particularly striking ways in the intellectual trajectories of Jonathan Saha and Caroline Bressey, both of whom found themselves struggling to navigate a path through the liminal, racialized spaces produced in part by their family backgrounds. For Tony Ballantyne, Catherine Hall and Bridget Brereton, their families of birth brought them into direct and indirect contact with imperial legacies and influences. In Brereton's case, the encounter was vivid, and in her account it is almost palpable: 'Granny's house, a Victorian semi-detached in a pleasant suburb on the Firth of Forth, was full of Indian relics. The so-called library contained weapons and other bits and pieces from Nagaland, where the people, we were told, had been head-hunters, and other bric-a-brac from the Raj were scattered around the house. And our Aunty Cass, the widow of the war profiteer, lived with us, a different kind of Indian relic.' As with Hall, Brereton's marriage resulted in a mixed race family of her own. And in both their cases, that shaped their career interest in the Caribbean, their choice of method and audience, and their sense of their own racial position and privilege at home and away. That they were both born in the same year – 1946 – is striking.

Feminist perspectives on empire figure significantly in the work of some of the contributors, as do the structural challenges of navigating what has been, until quite recently in historical terms, a male-dominated profession. Marilyn Lake details the impact that debates about women's history and aboriginal history had on her intellectual formation, debates that helped shape her collaborations (especially the multi-authored *Creating a Nation*) and her career trajectory as well. But as startling is her simple observation that early on, 'little children kept me close to home'. Recounting the entanglement of feminist and left politics on her intellectual formation, Catherine Hall remarks, 'by 1968 not only was I heavily involved in student politics but I had my first child – an event which turned my life upside down'. There is much history yet to be written in the space occupied by that en-dash. Hall goes on to note that while her husband, the acclaimed critical race theorist Stuart Hall (1932–2014), was 'thinking about a new moment in race politics and had embarked on the collective work that was eventually to become *Policing the Crisis*, I was deeply preoccupied with the women's movement, motherhood, childcare and what kind of history it might now be possible to discover, teach and write'. Her memories remind us how race, class and gender are bound up, and of how their entangled pasts have shaped some decolonizing histories. The relative silence on similar matters – the 'private', the 'intimate', the 'domestic' – across most of the rest of the essays speaks volumes, too, about the selectivity of all autobiographies and the limits of this book as anything other than a very patchy history of how imperial historiography, at any rate, made and unmade us.

As we indicated above, space and place recur as key forces in the shaping of the imperial historians gathered here. Those places might only acquire meaning over time, often through serendipitous means, as was the case with Catherine Hall's discovery of the Jamaican village of Kettering, a simulacrum of the Northamptonshire town where she was born, or as in Lake's memory of the 'Black Station' at Oyster Cove, Tasmania, her childhood swimming spot.[8] Or they might be places of institutional significance in the intellectual journey of the contributor, as was the Royal Commonwealth Society library for Dane Kennedy – or the Institute of Historical Research, London, for Shigeru Akita. For Mrinalini Sinha it was the Jawaharlal Nehru University library canteen that proved the most consequential training ground, a home to the 'multi-generational bubble' which so powerfully shaped her apprehensions of both Indian and empire history. Such spaces could be large or small, mirroring the multiple scales at which empire functions and at which historians have tried to imagine it. Lake reminds us what it has meant to think the British Empire from Melbourne, in the context of an Asian Pacific century and in the shadow of Asian migrations dating from the high noon of Victorian imperialism. For Tony Ballantyne, the cramped quarters of the senior common room culture of Cambridge proved stultifying, especially in contrast to the lure of the cricket pitch – a contrast whose impact he traces on his dissertation and several projects beyond it as well. Roger Louis brings alive for us the melodrama of the Oxford seminar – and mentions, almost as an aside, the 55 annual visits he has made to that most impactful of sancta sanctorum, the Public Record Office (now the National Archives). For Antoinette Burton the Fawcett Library was an equally important space, buried as it was in the basement of a struggling London polytechnic but full of untapped riches that helped her to unlock feminist imperial history. Meanwhile, for Philippa Levine it was the variety of London neighbourhoods, together with her first experience of life in Australia, that shaped her education as an empire historian.

As readers will quickly discover, there are some real gems to be found in these empire stories. Who could invent the conversations Dane Kennedy recalls with his Rhodesian acquaintances, Dickie and Beryl? Certainly not Kennedy, who draws on the diaries he kept during his field research. Tom Metcalf also returns to letters he wrote while studying at Cambridge in the 1950s. He seemed to comfort himself at the thought that the research he was doing 'does throw light on the present situation' – in this case, the Suez crisis. Little did they know they would be drawing on their own archive decades later. Meanwhile, the house Catherine Hall grew up in was full of books. Her future subject of study, Macaulay's *History of England,* sat on the shelf between G. M. Trevelyan's *Our Island Story* and Sellar and Yeatman's *1066 And All That*: the serious and satirical side by side. These are rare and remarkable glimpses into the social and cultural fabric of working- and middling-class life in the late twentieth century Anglophone world. Such is the tale of Jonathan Saha's first, wordless encounter with his Indian grandmother and his female Indian relatives, an episode that dramatized for him – and now for us – the cultural distance between himself and his family of origin. We leave it to readers to think about the impact of these affective dramas on Saha's theatrical take on the colonial state in Burma. And we challenge students to dig up the state-sponsored development film which so enraptured Philippa Levine at the age of nine, or to research the kinds of Great Lives lessons – Livingstone, Rhodes, Cavell, Nightingale – that were apparently the bedrock of the 1960s northwest suburban London curriculum, whence schoolchildren might imbibe 'gender norms alongside imperial patriotism'.

What is perhaps most striking is the variability with which the contributors identify with the very rubric that guides this book. Some, like Tom Metcalf and Roger Louis, have no doubt about it and take considerable pleasure in mapping the highways and byways by which they have earned the label of imperial historian. Metcalf, for his part, takes a certain pride in having lived through the transformations the field has undergone as well. Bridget Brereton and Marilyn Lake prefer to keep their distance from the label of empire historian rather than reject it altogether. Tony Ballantyne has an ambivalent relationship to it in part because his loyalties are as much to New Zealand national frameworks – and Maori political and cultural ones – that allow him to explore local and regional histories that lie 'underneath' the nation proper. In the end, he admits his family and by extension his career has been 'embedded in the dynamics of colonization', a description with which Lake and Adele Perry might agree. Perry in fact calls herself 'a kind of accidental or at least a sideways historian of empire' who nonetheless recognizes the tremendous staying power of the imperial narrative in a postcolonial nation. Yet that is not quite the same as joining the ranks of empire historians. Antoinette Burton too has always kept her distance, with the qualifier 'feminist' imperial historian ever in view. Caroline Bressey is a cultural geographer with a historical sensibility and black British women always in her sights, which distances her in some ways from the appellation as well.

Shigeru Akita's career illustrates with particular vividness how bound up the identity of the imperial historian has become with that of global history. The irony is that the sort of economic history he was inspired to practice in part by imperial historians like Tony Hopkins lost much of its influence in the Anglo-American academy due to the cultural turn among historians and the migration of economic historians, especially in America, to economics departments, where their work became divorced from other historians'.

Alone among the contributors to this volume, Akita has investigated the economics of empire, a line of inquiry that has led him in turn to a far broader inquiry into global history. In the age of transnational flows and global capital, his experiences look quite prophetic.

In the end, then, the memories collected here both reaffirm and challenge the very parameters of the category of imperial history. As Jonathan Saha aptly puts it at the close of his essay, 'We might be shaped by empire, but through our studies we are striving to find our way out.' Empire made its way quite circuitously through the lives of those who sought to write about it, and even when its impact has been direct, it could, and did, have centripetal effects. Empire was something to wrestle with, either because it was an appealing puzzle or because it was the third rail: a highly charged subject whose geopolitics put pressures on people differently depending on their origins, generation, gender or racial identity. Hardly inclusive, imperial history has nonetheless had to make room for new interlocutors and new subject matter as well. Meanwhile, it is not perhaps enough to say that empire shaped us in dynamic, fluid and contested ways or that we cannot easily generalize its impact across time and space. Rather, we might conclude by insisting that for students of imperial history, the empire is never done. For all those who wish to appreciate what imperialism is and has been must acknowledge that like anything with a history, how we understand it grows in part out of the lives and experiences of those who write about it. Those entanglements are not peripheral to what British imperial history is. At this uncommonly volatile moment in the history of global empires, when the geographies of the decolonized world seem to be up for grabs, the question of who writes about – who even sees – the impact of empire itself on imperial history-writing has arguably never been more significant. What will a volume like this look like, half a century on? Will it too address the issue of empire in terms that remain essentially national in orientation, with the United States or perhaps China replacing Britain as the empire of note? Or will the ambivalence that some of the contributors exhibit towards the British Empire as their frame of reference become even more pronounced, pointing to a shift of orientation to a world where the power differentials that undergird empires will come to be understood in more fluid, transnational, even global terms? We cannot plot the possible trajectories of the future. At this juncture, we can only do what historians do: look forward to the past for clues about what is to come.

Notes

1 Notable examples include Andrew S. Thompson, ed., *Writing Imperial Histories* (Manchester: Manchester University Press, 2013); Catherine Hall and Keith McClelland, eds, *Race, Nation and Empire: Making Histories, 1750 to the Present* (Manchester: Manchester University Press, 2010); Robin W. Winks, ed.,

The Oxford History of the British Empire: Vol. V, Historiography (Oxford: Oxford University Press, 1999).

2 For an insightful examination of this issue, see D. L. LeMahieu, '"Scholarship Boys" in Twilight: The Memoirs of Six Humanists in Post-Industrial Britain', *Journal of British Studies*, 53, 4 (October 2014): 1011–31.

3 Theodore Koditschek, *Liberalism, Imperialism, and the Historical Imagination: Nineteenth-Century Visions of a Greater Britain* (Cambridge: Cambridge University Press, 2013).

4 This point is developed by Dane Kennedy, 'The Imperial History Wars', *Journal of Imperial Studies*, 54, 1 (January 2015): 5–22.

5 For an interesting exception, see Laura Lee Downs and Stéphane Gerson, eds, *Why France? Historians Reflect on an Enduring Fascination* (Ithaca: Cornell University Press, 2009).

6 See C. A. Bayly, 'Epilogue: Historiographical and Autobiographical Note,' in his *Origins of Nationality in South Asia* (Oxford: Oxford University Press, 1998), pp. 307–22.

7 The impact of these indigenous/settler politics can also be seen in Adele Perry's chapter.

8 Ketterings abound in this archive; there is one in Marilyn Lake's history as well.

1

From Empire to India and Back:

A Career in History

Thomas R. Metcalf
b. 1934

The first course I ever taught, as a graduate student at Cambridge University, was 'The Expansion of Europe'. My task as a tutor during the academic year 1956/7 was to prepare undergraduates for their year-end tripos exams. The last full course I taught was the 'British Empire', as a seminar for graduate students and as a lecture course for undergraduates, during the spring semester of 2007 at the University of California, Berkeley – exactly fifty years later. The intervening fifty years encompassed a professional career in which, as the historiography flowed first in one direction and then in another, and then back again, the British Empire, and above all the Raj in India, defined my enduring scholarly engagement. An account of this career, as one individual threaded his way through it, may help illuminate the larger shifts and turns of imperial history in the latter half of the twentieth century. At its core are my two years at Cambridge University, where I studied with Ronald Robinson and experienced first hand the tumult of the 1956 Suez Crisis. These were followed over the subsequent decade by a struggle to secure regular university employment in the new environment of the 1960s as the US began to engage with the 'Third World' and scholars disparaged Britain's imperial past.

Empire

As a youth growing up in a small city in upstate New York, with a father who was an engineer, and a mother who, despite having a college degree, was a homemaker, I was in no obvious way drawn to the study of history. My schooling, even in high school, was bland and uninspiring. History was taught only tangentially under the label 'civics', and even then, for fear of McCarthyism, anything that might be controversial was adroitly skirted. I have no recollection of India's independence in 1947. What did engage me, from at least the age of ten, was collecting postage stamps. I still have, on a shelf above my desk, the albums that contain my collection. At its heart are the stamps of the British Empire. I was drawn to them I imagine in part because of my parallel youthful fascination with geography. There were just so many British colonies scattered all around the globe, and the stamps were often decorated with colourful local scenes. At the same time, during those years I closely followed the battles of the Second World War, and watched from a distance as my father, dodging German bombs, worked on the development of Britain's radar network and then in the Pacific on the deployment of the atomic bomb. Poring over a map was for me as a youth never only an academic exercise. In high school I joined local chapters of the World Federalists and the United Nations Association. By the early 1950s I was fully aware of America's growing world predominance, and I supported such actions as the Korean War. Yet I was anxious that this power be contained within a larger world order. 'We' would not issue stamps from numerous colonies!

From high school I went on to Amherst College in 1951. Here I first encountered history taught as a serious academic subject, and was soon drawn to it. I wrote a senior honours thesis on 'The Development of Liberalism in the Thought of William Ewart Gladstone, 1831–1868'. Why did I care about liberalism? Perhaps as an enthusiastic liberal myself – I had stood in the crowd at the railway station when Harry Truman came to my town on his 'whistle-stop' tour in 1948 and a few years later I supported the doomed candidacy of Adlai Stevenson – I wanted to see where the ideas of liberalism had come from, and how and why they had flourished. For this purpose it made sense to me on completion of my Amherst degree to pursue British history in Britain itself. I enroled at Cambridge University with the aim of pursuing a second BA (as was the case for overseas students in those days when separate Master's programs did not exist). By a serendipitous chance – a wartime friend of my father's was a graduate – I joined St Johns College, and was assigned Dr Ronald Robinson as my supervisor. Two years before, in collaboration with John Gallagher next door at Trinity, he had published a path-breaking article on the 'Imperialism of Free Trade'; and he was then engaged in the writing of what would become *Africa and the Victorians* (1961).

When I appeared at Robinson's door, I had already begun to wonder why empire had made no appearance in my senior thesis. I had included such topics as Peelite free trade and church disestablishment, but the historiography that I had unquestioningly accepted spoke of the mid-Victorian era as a time of 'anti-imperialism', especially among liberals such as Gladstone. Yet I could plainly see that the empire was expanding during the 1840s and 1850s in India and South Africa, that British overseas trade was growing dramatically as the country made itself into the 'workshop of the world', and that Britain, from the 1850 Don Pacifico affair to the two Opium Wars, was unhesitatingly asserting its power around the globe. None of these events could plausibly be explained under any theory of mid-Victorian 'anti-imperialism'.

Hence, I quickly fell under Robinson's spell. With his encouragement I decided to compress the usual two-year course into one year, and to devote the second year to research. Unfortunately, when I came up for the Expansion of Europe tripos examination at the end of my first year, I found myself confronted with questions that my studies with Robinson had left me unprepared to answer. What was I to make of a question such as, 'To what do you attribute Portuguese success in Brazil?' (I still have the exam paper.) I was not surprised when I did not receive a 'first class honours' degree from Cambridge.

But it did not matter, for I now had a year in which to devise a doctoral project. Robinson was himself a historian of Africa. So I assumed that, as his student, I should work on Africa as well. To my surprise, he replied, 'I am doing Africa. You do India.' I protested that I knew nothing about India and had no topic in mind. (My initial thoughts had been directed either to Sierra Leone or the Chinese treaty ports.) He then gave me a research topic: the 1857 revolt. Again, I protested that I knew nothing about it. But that did not alter his opinion. So, as my research year began, every morning I bicycled to the Cambridge University Library, and set about methodically going through its voluminous holdings, reading everything on the mid-Victorian empire to see what I might come up with for a topic. I knew I would focus on the ties between liberalism and empire, but there existed almost nothing in print to guide me. (Eric Stokes's magisterial *The English Utilitarians and India* only appeared three years later, in 1959.)

My ideas took shape gradually during that autumn of 1956. In weekly letters to my parents I sought to describe the process. Initially, in early October I wrote simply that I would 'of course be having regular meetings with my supervisor Dr. Robinson to discuss my reading and try to get a project in motion'. Naively, I continued, 'The main problem in doing a thesis is that of defining the topic; once you know what you are trying to do, actually doing it is relatively easy.' A month later, with the Suez crisis raging outside, I was closing in on a topic. I had decided to study, as I wrote on November 11, 'the conflict between the mid-Victorian ideology – of free trade and liberalism and the moral superiority of England and of Christianity – and the practical results of their experience in ruling India'. The Mutiny, I continued, was the 'key point' that forced Britain to realize that its policy and attitude to India must be changed, 'because India could not be made into a copy of 19th century England'. Here, in a nutshell, was the argument of my dissertation, and subsequently of *The Aftermath of Revolt: India 1857–1870*, published in 1964.

To undertake the necessary archival research, I soon discovered, was no 'easy' matter. During the 1950s, the India Office records were still housed in the old India and Foreign Office Building off Whitehall, constructed in the 1860s, with a looming statue of Clive at the end of King Charles Street. While it was exciting to 'hob nob' with diplomats, as I wrote in mid-December when I first ventured in, 'There are so many documents in the India Office I do not know where to start.' Overwhelmed, after a week I abandoned the enterprise 'until I know what I am trying to do'. In the end sustained archival research had to await my return to Britain, and then on to India, some three years later.

Much else besides my work with Robinson shaped my engagement with the empire during my years at Cambridge. Many of my friends were, at least initially and perhaps not wholly by chance, fellow 'colonials', from Australia, New Zealand, even Mauritius. My roommate one year was from Malaya, just then gaining its independence. Man Mohan Singh, later prime minister of India, was also a classmate at St Johns. What were they all doing at Cambridge, I often asked myself? From them I gained some sense of what the empire meant, as it shaped the lives of its former colonial subjects. Though keen on taking advantage of an English education – my Malayan roommate subsequently became a prosperous lawyer in Singapore – they were not, as I saw it, what Homi Babha later would call 'mimic men', seeking unsuccessfully to become English.

Then too, above all, there was the Suez crisis. As a naive American liberal, I was unprepared for the storm that burst over Britain in the fall of 1956. I could not fathom how Anthony Eden could join a conspiracy to invade Egypt, nor could most of my Cambridge friends. I participated in a number of anti-war protests, and several heated discussions. Only later, when I visited friends' families in the countryside over the winter holidays, did I come to realize how much the empire meant to Britons across wide sections of the public. Indeed, people I met left me in no doubt about their bitter feelings of betrayal when President Eisenhower forced the British to call off the invasion. Some of their animosity was even directed at me as an American – the only time this ever happened. The trauma of Suez seemed also to validate my own commitment to the study of imperialism. My work, as I wrote in a letter at the height of the crisis, 'does throw light on the present situation'. After Suez I came to realize that the study of empire was a project worth undertaking, and further that imperialism would not simply disappear without a trace. Did I take up the study of the British Empire so that I could better understand the growing world power of the United States? I cannot say. But, clearly, as an American of the mid-twentieth century I could not escape complicity in it.

From Empire to India

Upon my return from England, I enroled at Harvard to complete my PhD. Using only published library sources, and building upon the work I had done at Cambridge, I finished the dissertation in two years. I then secured a position as instructor at the University of Wisconsin in Madison, where I was hired to teach both British and Indian history. This dual position suited me, but by 1960 the academic world was beginning to shift beneath my feet. Above all, with the collapse of the empire, imperial history fast went out of favour. In Britain, the subject became prey to nostalgia, regret and general indifference among scholars. E. P. Thompson, for instance, took up the study of the English working classes rather than that of the Raj of his childhood, while Eric Hobsbawm sought 'primitive rebels' in Europe not in the empire. In the United States, propelled by the Cold War, and then by the enthusiasms of the Kennedy era, scholars turned first to study of the nation's antagonists, the Soviet Union and 'Red China', and then to the newly freed states of South Asia and Africa. America now required knowledge of the so-called 'Third World'; the lens of empire no longer sufficed. Hence scholars sought, by studying such topics as rural social change and political mobilization, to make sense of the histories of former colonial societies from within and from below. In the United States this new style of research, which informed work in the social sciences more generally, came to be known as 'area studies'. Much of this, of course, under the label 'development studies', advanced American interests in encouraging capitalist economies and political stability. Still, from the early 1960s, the government began an extensive programme of supporting language and area studies by creating research centres and fellowship programmes. Ancillary organizations, partly foundation funded, such as the American Institute of Indian Studies, grew up alongside these government programmes, so that over the last fifty years almost all American scholars of countries such as India have secured research support during their careers.

My position at Wisconsin was among the earliest casualties of this new scholarly turn. In 1960 Wisconsin's newly hired African historian, Philip D. Curtin, though himself schooled in imperial history, established a graduate training programme called Comparative Tropical History. This programme sought to comprehend the histories of Latin America, Africa, India and Southeast Asia under a single rubric that would enable these formerly colonized regions to be studied together, and – most importantly – apart from Europe. Students were expected to master the history of one region and become knowledgeable in the others. Though imaginative in its formulation, this programme, one might say, in effect turned imperial studies on its head by excluding the colonial connection. To introduce his new programme Curtin had my appointment terminated in favour of a 'properly trained' historian of India. I taught at Madison for but one year.

I had at that point little choice but to make of myself an historian of India. Fortunately I secured one of the first new 'area studies' grants, in this case funded by the Ford Foundation. That enabled me to spend a year in India. As well as completing research for my book *The Aftermath of Revolt*, I could on my return credibly claim some knowledge of that country. In part by simply presenting myself at the department chairman's door, I managed to secure an appointment as an assistant professor at UC Berkeley. I was the first regular faculty member ever hired at Berkeley to teach the history of India. As the campus had been the beneficiary of one of the new government-funded South Asia Centers, it became my task to develop a programme in South Asian history and to train graduate students in the field. My PhD students took up for their research a diverse array of topics reflecting their own varied interests. Throughout my career at Berkeley I continued to train students in modern Indian history. Over time, however, ethnic and gender identities underwent a dramatic shift. My first three students, in the 1960s, were named John, Richard and Kenneth; my last, forty years later, were Nita, Amita and Kavita.

But there remained the question of my own research. I decided to stay with the mid-nineteenth century Raj but to shift my focus from the making of policy to its consequences for rural society in what is now the state of Uttar Pradesh. This was not a difficult transition. The upper Gangetic valley had been the heart of the upheaval of 1857, and it had been the central focus of the new land policy the British introduced after the suppression of the rebellion. Further, study of land tenures and relations among those on the land had begun to attract the attention of younger scholars in the United States as part of the new area studies approach. In the summer of 1964 I organized a major conference on Indian land tenures at Berkeley; the subsequent year and a half I spent in India undertaking research in archives in Lucknow and Allahabad. The focus on land was not at all surprising. The British, like their Mughal predecessors, had built an agrarian empire that derived the overwhelming bulk of its revenue from the land; of necessity they had to regulate the assessments and tenures of those they ruled over. I soon realized that, to come to terms with the working of the Raj, the land was the place to start. Though my research had a larger scope, what fascinated me was the fate of the landlord class in the province of Avadh (Oudh). Their estates confiscated when the British annexed Avadh in 1856, these men promptly joined the uprising the following year – only to find their properties returned to them after 1858. Yet the conditions under which these men held their estates under the Raj were dramatically different from the days of the Nawabs. They lost their forts and retainers but they gained novel proprietary rights over their estates. What did this transformation mean for the working of the agrarian order? How did the landlords fare? What kinds of struggles took place with their newly disenfranchised tenants? The outcome was eventually the book *Land, Landlords, and the British Raj*.

This research strategy did not, however, put an end to the suspicion that I was in some way not fully an Indian historian. The problem arose to some extent from my continued interest in the Raj, but in large part it had to do with language. When I was a graduate student, modern Indian languages were not taught at either Cambridge or Harvard. The only historian of India in the entire United States in the 1950s was Holden Furber at the University of Pennsylvania. As a result neither I, nor my contemporaries, were a beneficiary of the language and area studies training secured by subsequent generations of graduate students – among whom, I might note, was my wife Barbara, who studied at Wisconsin in Curtin's programme and whose work was subsequently supported by government grants at Berkeley as she shaped her own research, built upon the study of Urdu, on Islamic reform movements. As a result my appointment to tenure was delayed as the senior members of the department debated my future. Opposition was apparently strongest among historians of China and Japan, for whom mastery of the local language was essential to work in the field. Though I always insisted that my own graduate students learn an Indian language, there existed an endless abundance of English language archival materials on the India of the Raj. Doubters may have been convinced when my *Aftermath of Revolt* won the Watumull Prize of the American Historical Association – no longer awarded – as the best book on the history of India published in the preceding two years. When I told him of the prize, the department chairman told me to attend the annual meeting to collect the prize, but not to apply for another job.

My work on the history of rural India did not entirely displace my earlier engagement with the history of the larger British Empire. Indeed, when informing me of my promotion, the department chairman smiled, and said, 'Now you can teach the British Empire.' Although I did so, throughout the 1970s the subject remained deeply out of favour, both among scholars and students. Although I eventually induced my department to offer a graduate field in Modern Imperialism and Colonialism, few students enroled. (Among the hardy few was one of the editors of this volume.) The Vietnam War, oddly, generated little student interest in the larger issues of imperialism; what mattered was the war itself and, above all, the military draft. With the ending of the war, Berkeley students turned their attention to issues of ethnicity and identity. The outcome was the establishment of politicized departments of African-American and Ethnic Studies.

As I sought to formulate a new project on India, with my landlord study nearing completion, I encountered only frustration. In Indian history the 1970s was the era of the Cambridge School. Inspired by Namier's detailed studies of mid-eighteenth-century British political alignments, this school deprecated idealism and insisted upon the importance of local-level factions, patronage and self-interest as the driving force of Indian nationalism. Although an important contribution to historical studies, I did not find its approach attractive. Similarly, I did not find congenial that school's successor in the 1980s, the influential 'Subaltern Studies Collective'. That school, while it successfully challenged conventional interpretations of India's colonial history and ultimately helped shape the historiography of colonized territories around the world, was closely tied to its founder Ranajit Guha and his Marxist focus on movements of autonomous popular resistance to colonialism. In the mid-1970s I spent six months in Pakistan undertaking research on the history of Karachi city; I thought of it as a study of urban social history to complement my earlier work on rural society. Shortly afterwards, sensing that the project was going nowhere, I abandoned it. I was ready for something fresh.

From India to Empire

That 'something' was Edward Said's *Orientalism*, published in 1978. Almost overnight the study of empire and of the colonizer was revitalized. Empire, I discovered to my delight, once again mattered. Though exaggerated and even tendentious at times, Said's contention that the 'Orient' was an artefact of European knowledge – constructed to control the 'East' – rapidly radiated out from Said's initial concern with the Middle East to encompass the entire colonized world. Above all, it raised fundamental questions about the nature and meaning of imperialism and colonialism, and forced scholars to examine their own preconceptions. An 'Orient' described as the West's 'Other', as Said argued, enabled the colonial ruler to justify the subjugation of 'Oriental' peoples and helped structure colonial governance. Much in this way of thinking had already been anticipated in the work of Bernard S. Cohn, whose studies of colonial ritual and the 'invention of tradition' opened up exciting new approaches to the history of the Raj. About 1980 I began research into British colonial architecture in India.

My turn to architecture was not as abrupt a break with my past as might seem apparent. I had always been intrigued by colonial architecture, above all of course such grand monuments as Lutyens' New Delhi. In the mid-twentieth-century heyday of architectural modernism, however, the ornately decorated buildings erected by the Raj, with their historicist references, were beneath contempt. The study of India's architectural heritage ended, so it was assumed, with the buildings of the great Mughals, and then leapt ahead to the excitement of Le Corbusier's much-admired Chandigarh. One day, idly walking the streets of Madras while waiting, frustrated, for materials to be delivered for a possible project at the local archives, I suddenly realized that my new project was before my eyes. Here were extraordinary public buildings – law courts, banks, post offices, railway stations – constructed by the British in a flamboyant architectural style known as 'Indo-Saracenic'. Why would the British erect buildings in this style, especially in the far south of India? What did the use of this style say about the nature of the Raj? No one knew, because these buildings had never been studied. Putting aside

Lutyens' Delhi, I decided to make late-nineteenth-century architecture the focus of my research.

Such a topic was still at the time unfamiliar to mainstream scholarship. When I took these questions from Madras back to Delhi for a lecture before the history department of a major university, the assembled scholars – Marxist and nationalist in their approach to history – looked upon me with disbelief, unable to discern any purpose in such a talk. But Said's insights, which propelled the growth of what came to be known as 'postcolonial studies', provided historians with a new vocabulary, and a new way of reading colonial 'texts'. By the end of the decade even the 'subaltern' group had adopted a 'culturalist' style of analysis. For myself I saw British building in India as a kind of 'text' that could be 'read' in the same fashion as the printed documents of the census and gazetteers. Architectural styles and forms, that is, could reveal much about the ways the British conceived of India, and the 'Orient' more generally.

As cultural studies flourished during the 1990s, I refused to follow the ever-growing tribe of 'postcolonial' theorists down the path to ever more intricate arguments and jargon-filled prose. To be sure, much of this outpouring of ideas was stimulating and provocative. But that was not my style of scholarship. At the same time, I was determined to escape what Wm. Roger Louis, in the new *Oxford History of the British Empire*, called 'the shadow of the reshaping of Imperial history by Robinson and Gallagher', in which, he claimed, 'we live today'.[1] Responding to an invitation from the Cambridge University Press, I decided to revisit my earlier studies of liberalism and empire. Incorporating the new Saidian-inflected historiography, I wrote a volume for the New Cambridge History of India series entitled *Ideologies of the Raj*. In this book I endeavoured to define a liberalism that, on the one hand, retained at its core the Macaulay-ite vision of an India transformed, yet, on the other, had after 1858 been caught up in what I called the 'creation of difference'. Liberalism, that is, was more than simply an 'alibi of empire' (as a recent critic has put it), but it was still inextricably bound up with empire. The ties of liberalism and empire remain hotly contested to the present day.

By the late 1980s the flourishing women's movement had begun to make its presence felt in the historical profession. Its contributions I appreciated in principle but I found much of it too political for my taste. About 1992 I was invited to attend a conference on 'imperialism and feminism' at Cincinnati. I had just written a section on 'gender and empire' for my forthcoming *Ideologies of the Raj*. Researching this work, I had come to realize that gender was a crucial analytical concept – right up there with race and class – that helped structure all kinds of larger patterns of history and thought. At the conference, to my surprise, I discovered that I was almost a solitary male among a group of some fifteen women. This was a novel experience for me – though not an unpleasant one! Towards the end of the session, a lively discussion arose about what projects 'we as feminists' might next undertake as a group. Somewhat awkwardly, I interjected that 'I am not a feminist'. The organizers hastened to reassure me that I was, but some distance still remained between myself and the others. Two years later, when I offered a graduate seminar on gender and empire at Berkeley, again I discovered that the students who enroled were all female. Much fortunately has changed in the decades since those initial encounters. The young scholars I met at Cincinnati (several of whom are contributors to this volume) are now leaders in the field, while women and gender as research topics belong to all of us.

What was soon called the 'new imperial history' grew rapidly during the 1990s, until it appeared at times almost to overshadow domestic British history. For myself, much as I was pleased with this new historical turn, still I grew increasingly dissatisfied with examining colonial territories only as distinct units in relation to the imperial centre. Surely, it would be useful to look at the British Empire as an integral system, and at the circulation of ideas and peoples within it. In particular, I conceived that India could, to some degree, be portrayed as an imperial 'centre' itself, dominating the Indian Ocean. Such a study, too, made sense in an era when, with Indian workers spread across the Gulf and a fast growing global economy, the country's regional predominance was being renewed for the first time in over half a century. Further, my project complemented exciting new studies that focused on oceanic rather than land-based linkages across the globe. Initially this involved study of the 'Atlantic World'. In recent years, however, a promising subfield of Indian Ocean Studies has emerged. My contribution took the shape of a volume, *Imperial Connections: India in the Indian Ocean Arena, 1860–1920*. Increasingly nowadays, the imperial history of the 1990s is being superseded by, and at the same time incorporated into, these exciting new approaches to comparative and global history.

The invasion of Iraq in 2003 prompted me to think again about America, and its role in the world. Looking back a century to the American conquest of the Philippines, I wondered whether Americans, as they came to terms with their new imperial status, saw the British Empire as a model for themselves. One newly appointed official, passing through London, even stopped at the Colonial Office, and asked if the British 'had any colony where the people were similar to those of these islands'. Nevertheless, I quickly discovered, even those engaged in the work of colonial governance on the ground, several Michigan and Berkeley professors among them, adamantly disavowed any comparison. America's aims in the Philippines, as later in Iraq, they insisted, were limited, and directed only to education and training for self-government. My reflections produced a short article entitled 'From One Empire to Another: The Influence of the British Raj on American Colonialism in the Philippines', for a Russian journal, *Ab Imperio*.

A half-century allows a career to take many shapes. Mine surely did so as I moved from one research topic to another, from empire to India and back again. Serendipity, with simple intellectual curiosity, surely played a role. Larger currents of ideas, from the work of Ronald Robinson to that of Edward Said, mattered a great deal. So too did the influence of contemporary events, from the 1956 Suez crisis to the Iraq war a half century later. Always, America's late twentieth-century global predominance encouraged me to reflect on the present as well as the past. Underlying everything I did, however, was one impelling question: what is empire, what it does it mean and how does it function, for colonizer and colonized alike?

Note

1 Wm. Roger Louis, 'Introduction', in Robin W. Winks, ed., *The Oxford History of the British Empire, Volume V: Historiography* (Oxford: Oxford University Press, 1999), p. 41.

2

Seven Pivots Towards Empire

Wm. Roger Louis[1]
b. 1936

In thinking about 'pivots', I asked myself about antecedents to my connection with empire. Perhaps in childhood? There is indeed a tenuous link in the sense of domination, white over red (and black). My mother was born in Indian Territory. It did not take me long to learn that relations with Indian tribes and individuals were better there than in the neighbouring states, especially Kansas. In Oklahoma City, I grew up with a friend nicknamed Choctaw. His father once explained to me that the state's name derived from the Choctaw words *okla* and *humma*, meaning 'red people'. Indians were treated as equals at the local YMCA, where I swam and played handball. During summers in high school, I served as a counsellor at a YMCA camp in the Arbuckle Mountains. Special permission allowed me one summer to stay on through the extra session held for blacks only. Oklahoma was as segregated as any of the neighbouring states. Relations between blacks and whites were sometimes tense, as they had been at least since the time of the Tulsa race riots of 1921. I do not think that my mother or father relished my participation in a black summer camp, but the experience left a lifelong imprint.

My education through high school did not amount to much, because my interests were in sports (swimming and tumbling) and music (French horn in the high school orchestra). But my twelfth-grade English teacher compelled students to memorize lines of poetry, including Kipling. There was never a doubt that I would go to the University of Oklahoma. I joined a fraternity, Sigma Alpha Epsilon (SAE), known locally as 'sleep and eat'. It was because of SAE that I played a microscopic part in the civil rights movement of the 1950s. As president of the local chapter, I attended a national meeting to become acquainted with other presidents. Some of the more prominent were from southern states. No one needed to tell me about the 'good ole boys'.

Entirely on my own initiative (some at the time believed my own stupidity), I stood up to move that the fraternity be integrated nationwide. Someone actually supported me, but we were drowned out in a torrent of abuse. When I returned to the SAE house in Norman, I was greeted merely with incredulity. I later wrote that the civil rights movement and decolonization were like two streams flowing into the same river.[2]

One of my college years I spent abroad, one semester in Freiburg, the other at the Sorbonne – *Pivot One*. Critical to my later studies on empire, I became fairly fluent in German (or so I thought at the time). I began to learn about the German colonial empire. I remember discussing with fellow German students the renowned commander in East Africa during the First World War, Paul von Lettow-Vorbeck – though mainly because of his anti-Hitler stance in the 1930s.[3] I was later glad that my book on the German colonies during the First World War was sufficiently interesting to German academic readers to merit translation.[4] In Paris, I lived in a workers' district where the words '*cessez-le-feu en Algérie*' were inscribed on the pissoir near the metro stop, Pantin. Among my few French friends, one (who became a journalist) distributed pamphlets against the war; another (who became a banker) had served in the army and said he would not hesitate if necessary to use force, including torture. I hung out mainly with an expatriate group of rather bohemian students on the Left Bank at the Café Danton, including Nancy Maginnes (now Mrs Henry Kissinger). The one book everyone had in common was Henry Miller's *Tropic of Cance*r (1934), perhaps because of the combination of erudition and sexual vulgarity. While in Paris, I became much aware of the 'assimilated natives', as they were then called, especially those from North Africa but also from tropical Africa and the Caribbean. For my later work, the significance of my student days in Paris can be summed up in one word: *Algeria*.

During one of the vacations, I travelled to Algiers. Along the way I read *Le Mythe de Sisyphe* (1942), simply because many of my friends were reading Camus.[5] I took in as much as I could of the early stage of the Algerian War. I eventually made it to Egypt. By pure luck, I was in Cairo on 26 July 1956, when Nasser nationalized the Suez Canal Company. Nasser was in Alexandria, but loudspeakers were rigged to lamp-posts in Cairo. An Egyptian friend translated parts of Nasser's passionate, melodious speech, which went on and on, as I recall, well past midnight. I believed that I caught the spirit of Arab nationalism; in any event, I witnessed an historic event. A little over three months later, the British, French and Israelis attacked Egypt. The Suez crisis became a permanent part of my life. I would return again and again to try to understand Nasser, Eden, Mollet and Ben-Gurion, or, in other words, the collision of national and imperial aims – *Pivot Two*.[6]

At the University of Oklahoma, I was a Letters major, an honours programme in history, English, and philosophy, along with ancient and modern languages. I remember mainly my English courses, which took me to Joseph Conrad, Somerset Maugham, Graham Greene and Evelyn Waugh. But I was interested also in history and economics. In 1959, I won a Woodrow Wilson Fellowship to Harvard – I suspect because the selection committee needed someone from such a place as Oklahoma to demonstrate that the fellowships were not entirely for the Ivy League. At Harvard, I enrolled in the joint PhD programme in economics and government – *Pivot Three.*

My supervisor was the Australian economist Arthur Smithies. He was a critical admirer of Joseph Schumpeter and encouraged me to study *Imperialism and Social Classes*, which became a landmark in my reading. Yet my interests developed in a slightly different direction, largely because Harvard in the early 1960s had a magnificent faculty. Merle Fainsod's course on the Soviet Union caused me, briefly, to believe that there was such a thing as totalitarianism. Stanley Hoffmann's unsurpassed lectures on France turned me to the work of the French anthropologist Germaine Tillion, a member of the Resistance and author of *L'Algérie* (1957), a perceptive and most remarkable book that has had a lasting influence on me. The sociologist Barrington Moore systematically and sympathetically discussed Marxism.[7] Rupert Emerson's seminar on empire and nationalism produced some of the leading scholars of decolonization.[8] But it was because of Ernest May that I decided to become an historian. He left a lasting impression on how to pursue original research and to conduct a seminar. To my mind, he remains the model of a teacher and writer, making the connection between historical events and present-day problems.[9] When I explained my changing interests to Smithies, he said, 'If you are actually interested in African and Asian nationalism, then you had better go somewhere where they know something about it' – which was not, he added, Harvard. Ernest May agreed. Both helped me win a Marshall Scholarship to Oxford – *Pivot Four.*

I landed in St Antony's College, founded in 1950 – I was thus in the first generation of students. I had in effect two supervisors. A. J. P. Taylor, one of the great radical historians, took me on, I believe, out of curiosity about my rather complex proposal for a DPhil thesis dealing mainly with German East Africa. He had written a book entitled *Germany's First Bid for Colonies* (1938).[10] He read my thesis chapters one by one, giving me not only rigorous suggestions on substance but also on style, with an emphasis on clear, concise, crisp sentences. He once introduced me to the President of Magdalen College by saying, 'He's an American, but never mind. He's all right.'

My other supervisor was Margery Perham – 'Miss Perham', as she was always known in Oxford. She was the foremost Africanist of her generation. She took an interest in my thesis because it involved the German, British and Belgian colonial empires in the north-western part of German East Africa – the two countries then known as Ruanda and Urundi. In Usumbura (at the northern tip of Lake Tanganyika), I had the good luck of discovering the local records of the German colonial administration, which proved to be the basis of my Oxford thesis.

Miss Perham had taken a courageous public stand after the fall of Singapore in February 1942 by stating that the British Empire would have to be reconstructed after the war by eliminating the 'colour bar'. Reform of the colonial system and 'race relations' (the terminology at the time) remained one of her preoccupations.[11] She would occasionally introduce some of her visitors – many of whom were, or had been, District Officers – to her students. When I later edited, with Ronald Hyam, a few of the volumes in the *British Documents on the End of Empire*, I discovered, I believe, one of the best descriptions of the duties of a District Officer, the cornerstone of the empire and a redoubtable symbol of its mystique:

> The District Officer . . . sits in court . . . and sees the old procession of clerks and petition writers . . . He inspects gaols and pursues smugglers, runs hospitals and builds roads . . . He decides fishing disputes, negotiates blood-money, examines boundaries, manumits slaves . . . He exempts, pardons, appeases, exacts, condemns, ordains. Over a large but undefined field he in effect rules. All this will pass one day and . . . when it does it will indeed be the end of a very auld sang.

The writer of those lines was a Scot named Sir James Craig, later Ambassador to Saudi Arabia, at present an Honorary Fellow of St Antony's, and known as the best Arabist of his time.[12] Partly because of his inspiration, in the summer of 2014 my wife, Dagmar, and I went to Oman, where I took an intensive course in Arabic.

In the autumn of 1960, in one of my first seminars in Oxford, Miss Perham invited the Labour politician John Strachey to speak on his recent book *The End of Empire* (1959). After giving the gist of the book, he launched a lengthy, well-argued Marxist attack on the British colonial system. David Fieldhouse was the first to respond. With machine-gun-like rapidity and a finger-snap grasp of economic logic and detail, he utterly demolished Strachey's complicated argument point by point, detail by detail. It was a brilliant performance. Fieldhouse was on his way to becoming the paramount economic historian of the British Empire.[13] Decades later, he dedicated a book to me.[14] I regard it as one of the great compliments of my life.

A. J. P. Taylor gave me valuable advice from the beginning. 'Write your thesis as a book', he told me, 'then you won't have the bother of having to revise it for publication.' I submitted my thesis to the Clarendon Press in 1962, and it was published in the following year.[15] During the rest of the decade, or most of it, I wrote *E. D. Morel's History of the Congo Reform Movement* (1968), with Jean Stengers, and *British Strategy in the Far East* (1971). Stengers holds a place of his own among twentieth-century historians for exhaustive research and balanced judgement, but alas, his works on the Congo are not widely read in the English-speaking world.[16] Geoffrey Hudson of St Antony's clarified, indeed salvaged, my interpretation of British imperialism in China. He remains to me the epitome of a gentle scholar of vast and complex learning made comprehensible by graceful writing.[17]

I taught at Yale from 1962 to 1970, rising to the rank of associate professor. I owe the variety of my teaching interests to Edmund S. Morgan, then chairman of the History Department. I said to him shortly before my first semester there that in addition to my two-semester course on the expansion of Europe, I wished to teach a course on India and another on the Middle East. 'But Roger', he said, 'you don't know anything about India or the Middle East.' I impertinently replied: 'That's the point. I want to learn about them.' After a couple of moments of silence, he said, 'OK, the best way to master a subject is to teach it.' During my time at Yale, Prosser Gifford and I edited a four-volume set on colonial Africa, each linked with a major conference, each with about twenty authors, and each with a gargantuan number of pages.[18] The archival records on decolonization from the 1950s onward were still closed, but the volumes remain useful, above all because of the quality of interpretation by such authors as Henri Brunschwig, Leonard Thompson and John Hargreaves.[19]

I returned to England each year. In London, I worked at the Public Record Office (now The National Archives). I have now completed my fifty-fifth annual visit.[20] In Oxford, I became friends with Jack Gallagher, who had been one of my examiners. He held the Beit Chair in the History of the British Commonwealth, 1963–70. Ronald Robinson was his successor, 1971–87. I have written about Robinson and Gallagher elsewhere.[21] Here I emphasize only some of the main points.

I am a recidivist. I believe that the Robinson and Gallagher argument still carries punch. In 1953, they published 'The Imperialism of Free Trade', and eight years later *Africa and the Victorians*. In both, they emphasize the continuity of British expansion. They summarize the main point about exercising imperial sway: 'informally if possible and formally only if necessary'. Decades later, Robinson and I wrote an article entitled 'The Imperialism of Decolonization'.[22] It merely extends the argument to the post-1945 era: after the end of formal empire, the British attempted to retain as much control as possible by reverting to informal influence and indirect pressure.

In *Africa and the Victorians* (1961), the two historians emphasize indigenous resistance. An empire cannot exist without 'native cooperation'. Yet in 1882 it was African resistance that sucked the British into Egypt, to stabilize the government and protect European investments. The cause of the Scramble was therefore to be found in Egypt rather than England. Robinson and Gallagher turned away from the predominant view that European expansion had its origins, motives, and worldwide reach in industrialization, and that European rivalries were a cause of the partition of Africa.[23]

Shortly after *Africa and the Victorians* was published, I detected a curious feature in their description of Arabi Pasha, whose 'proto-nationalism' precipitated the Scramble. I am sure I was not alone in detecting this detail, but I thought so at the time. In the book, Arabi Pasha bears a curious resemblance to Gamal Abdel Nasser. *Africa and the Victorians* was written during and immediately after the Suez crisis.

In 1970, I moved to the University of Texas, where for forty-five years I have taught a course on the history of the British Empire. In 1975, with the assistance of Harry Ransom and others, I began the British Studies seminar. It has met every semester since then, without ever cancelling a Friday-afternoon session. Philippa Levine has been the Co-Director since 2010. The participants have included John Darwin, who in 2006 gave a lecture entitled 'Gallagher's Empire'. Together with a half-dozen graduate students, he and I concocted a list: '100 Top Hits of Imperial History'.[24] Drawing on the Friday-afternoon lectures, British Studies has published more than a half-dozen volumes in the *Adventures with Britannia* series with the latest – *Resplendent Adventures with Britannia* – published in 2015.

In the 1970s, I worked through the Second World War archives in South Africa, Australia, New Zealand, Britain and the United States, eventually publishing *Imperialism at Bay* (1977). One of the themes is the expansionist ambition of the colonial powers *and* the United States. While writing the book, I kept in touch with Sir Keith Hancock, then at the Australian National University.[25] When *Imperialism at Bay* appeared, Hancock saw for the first time the full documentation of American expansionist aims in the south-western Pacific. He had followed my argument and evidence by reading some of my draft chapters, but nevertheless was taken aback at what he regarded as the naked territorial designs of the United States. He wrote a lengthy, impassioned two-part review in the *Canberra Times*, concluding that he and his fellow Australians should 'keep our powder dry'.

In the 1980s, I turned my full attention to the Middle East – *Pivot Five*. I had the advantage of belonging to the Middle East Centre at St Antony's. I thus knew the legendary Director, Albert Hourani, who was one of the truly creative social and intellectual historians of the Middle East.[26] He read my draft of *The British Empire in the Middle East* line by line. Oxford University Press published the book in 1984. I argued, with what I believed at the time to be a flicker of originality, that non-intervention could become intervention by other means, thereby indirectly sustaining the empire.

In the 1980s and 1990s, I continued working in collaboration with colleagues in Middle Eastern history. Among other books, I edited, with Robert Stookey, *The End of the Palestine Mandate* (1986); with James Bill, *Musaddiq, Iranian Nationalism, and Oil* (1988); with Robert Fernea, *The Iraqi Revolution of 1958* (1991); and with Roger Owen, *A Revolutionary Year: The Middle East in 1958* (2002).

In the early 1990s, Lord (Robert) Blake and I organized a conference that brought together many of the leading authorities on Churchill. We subsequently published *Churchill: A Major New Assessment of his Life in Peace and War* (1993). A few years later, Sir Michael Howard and I convened a conference and then published the *Oxford History of the Twentieth Century* (1998). I wrote the chapter on the dissolution of the European colonial regimes as well as the concluding chapter – the latter at Michael Howard's insistence, because, he said, I had a style that resembled that of *The Economist*; in fact, I did so because we could find no one else to write it. I concluded in 1998: 'For many living in the closing years of the twentieth century . . . the decade may well appear at a later time to have been a golden age.'

Pivot Six: in 1992, Oxford University Press appointed me Editor-in-Chief of the *Oxford History of the British Empire*. It was a collective effort: five other editors, five volumes and some 125 historians. The series begins with the origins of the empire, carries on with a volume for each century since the eighteenth, and ends with a volume on historiography. In retrospect, I think it drew too much from an Oxford–London–Cambridge authorship. I should have tried to recruit more authors from such places as Japan, India and the United States. But I was especially wary of loading the project up with Americans – a sensitive point. Articles appeared in the *Spectator*, the *Daily Telegraph* and the *Sunday Times* in which the following question was typical: 'How is it that the Oxford University Press has appointed an American to a position so vitally important to our national heritage?' This view and similar ones were so ridiculous that they collapsed under their own weight. If followed to its logical conclusion, British historians would not be able to write about the American Revolution. The five volumes were published in 1998–99 – a pretty good track record in view of the old *Cambridge History of the British Empire* taking a quarter of a century to complete. Queen Elizabeth in 2001 appointed me Commander of the British Empire (CBE).[27]

We knew we would face criticism for sins of omission and for failing to project present-day trends into the future. But our purpose was simply to produce as well as we could the history of the British Empire by our generation of historians. I did to some degree try to anticipate criticism by creating a Companion Series, making it clear that the contributors would be entirely free to criticize the five volumes in whatever way they might like. There are now close to a dozen Companion volumes covering areas such as gender, Ireland and the environment.

I served as President of the American Historical Association in 2001. I was a reformist President, managing to found, with the help of many others, the National History Center, for the purpose of making the work of historians more visible to the American public – for example, with sessions in partnership with the Council on Foreign Relations.[28] There are at least two programmes of the National History Center that I hope will have an enduring influence. The Washington History Seminar, which meets weekly at the Woodrow Wilson Center in Washington, DC, brings together historians with those in the US government for whom it is useful to have historical perspective on current problems. It thus resembles the purpose that Ernest May and Richard E. Neustadt had in mind with *Thinking in Time*. The other programme is the Decolonization Seminar, which each summer for the last ten years has brought fifteen young historians with recent PhDs to Washington. They study decolonization from African, Asian and Caribbean perspectives as well as

Portuguese, Dutch, Belgian, French and British. They come from all parts of the world, Indonesia as well as Jamaica, Ghana as well as India. With funding from the Mellon Foundation, the seminar has met for the month of July since 2006 at the Library of Congress. The seminar completed its tenth and final year in July 2015, with an overall total of 150 'seminarians' now reinforcing the relatively new field of decolonization.

Pivot Seven: in 2002, the Oxford University Press (OUP) appointed me Editor of Volume III of the *History of the Press*, covering 1896–1970. I wrote two of the chapters and edited twenty-five others, along with a chronology, colour plates, illustrations and figures, maps, tables and graphs – all in only 876 pages (writing about the Press sharpened my sense of irony). I found myself in the world of rags pulped for Bible paper, of printing presses presided over by a tyrant, and of a committee of inquiry trying to figure out the enigmatic relationship of the Press to the University. OUP is the largest university press in the world. By the 1960s, it was producing 850 titles yearly (as compared with 250 by its nearest rival, Cambridge University Press), keeping 17,000 titles in stock, and distributing 17 million books annually. How to explain the development of this phenomenon?

One underlying explanation was my discovery that OUP resembled the old British Empire. OUP delegated authority and responsibility, for example, to OUP New York and OUP India. By 1970 there were some thirteen branches around the world, from Tokyo to Toronto to Cape Town to Canberra. Each branch eventually created its own list, finding a balance between importing OUP books from Oxford and London, and publishing its own scholarly and other books.

I visited as many OUP branches as possible. In Karachi, the OUP Pakistan staff put me up in a small, inconspicuous hotel, fearing I might be kidnapped. I gradually discovered an historic point that would provide the volume with one of its themes – the preparation of books overseas, in particular books for English-language teaching. By directing their attention to education, officers of the Press over a period of decades developed a paternal sense of racial equality – and helped ensure the global dominance of English. The ideals of OUP developed in parallel with those of the British Empire and Commonwealth.

I have commented at such length on my research, writing and editing that it may give a misleading impression overall. I devote as much time, and probably more, to teaching – every semester two courses, one for undergraduates, and another for graduate students. In one way or another, the British Empire as a theme finds its way into virtually all my teaching. In one of my classes, students choose a book to read each week; by the end of the semester they have read some thirteen or fourteen books that often have an imperial theme (*Yes!* – students in honours programmes can rise to the challenge of a book a week). Some of the lists drawn up by the students might include Lytton Strachey's *Eminent Victorians*, especially the chapter on General Gordon at Khartoum (1918); Elizabeth Monroe's *Britain's Moment in the Middle East* (1963); and Caroline Elkins's *Imperial Reckoning: The Untold Story of Britain's Gulag in Kenya* (2005). Another student might include the four volumes of Paul Scott's *Raj Quartet* (1966–75). Biographies that have proved to be favourites are Hermione Lee's *Virginia Woolf* (1996) and John Mack's *Prince of Our Disorder: The Life of T. E. Lawrence* (1976) – the last significant because it brings together the fields of psychology and history.

Students in my classes come from a wide range of majors, including, in the last decade, Asian studies, Middle Eastern studies, economics, physics, theatre and dance, journalism, and comparative literature as well as history, English, and government. The students are at the centre of my life. I sum up my teaching experience simply by stating that I rejoiced a few years ago when the 50,000 students at the University of Texas chose me Professor of the Year.

Much of this chapter has dealt with seminars, which suggest a way of life and help to explain the way in which the discipline of history has shaped my career. The English intellectual and politician Richard Crossman once said that his idea of paradise was a good academic seminar. I remember his words every Friday afternoon when students mix with faculty members at the British Studies seminar.

Notes

1 I have written two previous autobiographical accounts: 'Hinges of Fate', *Burnt Orange Britannia* (London: I. B. Tauris, 2005); and 'Historians I Have Known', *Perspectives* (May, 2001). My pivots towards empire were brought about by ideas and personalities probably as much by time, place and education – and later pivots were specific turns to particular projects. I cite myself by my initials and refer mainly to books that have had an enduring influence on me. Quotations are from memory.

2 WRL, 'The Dissolution of the British Empire in the Era of Vietnam', *American Historical Review*, 107 (2002). The phrase about the two streams belongs to Brian Urquhart, which he uses in *Decolonization and World Peace* (Austin: University of Texas Press, 1989) and *Ralph Bunche: An American Life* (New York: W.W. Norton, 1993).

3 The joke in Freiburg at the time was the question, did von Lettow actually tell Hitler 'to go fuck himself'? The answer was yes – 'but less politely'.

4 WRL, *Great Britain and Germany's Lost Colonies, 1914–1919* (Oxford: Clarendon, 1967), translated as *Das Ende des deutschen Kolonialreiches* (1971).

5 As I often still do whenever possible with German or French books, I was reading the original in one hand and the English translation in the other. The works of Albert Camus have been of permanent interest to me, especially *L'Homme révolté* (*The Rebel*, 1951).

6 See WRL and Roger Owen, eds, *Suez 1956* (Oxford: Clarendon, 1989), which brings together former participants in the crisis (for example, Sir Harold Beeley and Mordechai Bar-On) as well as scholars.

7 See Barrington Moore, *Political Power and Social Theory* (Cambridge, MA: Harvard University Press, 1951), which attacks the anti-Marxist methodology of the social sciences. In view of the climate of the Cold War, his course was quite remarkable, perhaps unique.

8 Rupert Emerson, *From Empire to Nation: The Rise to Self-Assertion of Asian and African Peoples* (Cambridge, MA: Harvard University Press, 1960). One of the members of Emerson's seminar was Crawford Young; see his seminal work, *The African Colonial State in Comparative Perspective* (New Haven: Yale University Press, 1994).

9 Ernest May, *The World War and American Isolation 1914–17* (Cambridge, MA: Harvard University Press, 1959), *Imperial Democracy: Emergence of America as a Great Power* (New York: Harcourt Brace and World, 1973) and *Strange Victory: Hitler's Conquest of France* (New York: Hill and Wang, 2000). On historical perspective and contemporary affairs, see May and Richard E. Neustadt, *Thinking in Time: The Uses of History for Decision-Makers* (New York: Free Press, 1986).

10 His masterpiece is *English History, 1914–1945* (Oxford: Clarendon, 1965). On his most controversial work, see WRL, *Origins of the Second World War: A. J. P. Taylor and His Critics* (New York: John Wiley, 1972).

11 See especially Margery Perham, *Colonial Reckoning* (New York: Knopf, 1962).

12 Minute by Craig, 27 September 1964, in *British Documents on the End of Empire, 1964–1971* (London: HMSO, 2004), #116. For Hyam, see especially *Britain's Declining Empire: The Road to Decolonization, 1918–1968* (London: HMSO, 2006).

13 See especially *Economics and Empire* (London: Weidenfeld and Nicolson, 1973), *Black Africa, 1945–80: Economic Decolonization and Arrested Development* (London: Allen and Unwin, 1986) and *The West and the Third World* (New York: John Wiley, 1999).

14 *Western Imperialism in the Middle East, 1914–1958* (Oxford: Oxford University Press, 2006).

15 *Ruanda-Urundi, 1884–1919* (Oxford: Clarendon, 1963). I was startled about a decade ago to see it selling for £35 in a rare-book catalogue.

16 See especially Jean-Marie Duvosquel, Alain Dierkens and Guy Vanthemsche, eds, *Jean Stengers: Belgique—Europe—Afrique* (Brussels, 2005), and Vanthemsche, *Belgium and the Congo, 1885–1980* (Cambridge: Cambridge University Press, 2012).

17 See *The Far East in World Politics* (Oxford: Oxford University Press, 1936). A former Fellow of All Souls, Hudson possessed comprehensive and analytical knowledge of China and Japan; but unfortunately, his great book remained in draft (now vanished). I later became especially interested in the history of Hong Kong; see WRL, 'Hong Kong: The Critical Phase, 1945–1949', *American Historical Review*, 102 (1997).

18 *Britain and Germany in Africa* (New Haven: Yale University Press, 1967), 824 pp.; *Britain and France in Africa* (New Haven: Yale University Press, 1971), 989 pp.; *The Transfer of Power in Africa* (New Haven: Yale University Press, 1982), 654 pp.; and *Decolonization and African Independence* (New Haven: Yale University Press, 1988), 651 pp.

19 See, for example, Henri Brunschwig, *Mythes et réalités de l'impérialisme* (Paris: Colin, 1960); Leonard Thompson, *Unification of South Africa* (Oxford: Clarendon, 1969); John Hargreaves, *The End of Colonial Rule in West Africa* (New York: Barnes and Noble, 1979).

20 I once gave a talk entitled 'Five Reasons Why I Am Not an Anglophile'. The list begins with 'The District Line to Kew Gardens'.

21 WRL, *Imperialism: The Robinson and Gallagher Controversy* (New York: New Viewpoints, 1965); see also my foreword to the new edition of *Africa and the Victorians* (London: I. B. Tauris, 2015).

22 The article was rejected by the *American Historical Review*. It eventually appeared in the *Journal of Imperial and Commonwealth History*, 22 (1994).

23 For my own interpretation, see 'The Scramble for Africa', *English Historical Review*, 81 (1966).

24 In *Ultimate Adventures with Britannia* (London: I. B. Tauris, 2009), along with Darwin's lecture.

25 See WRL, 'Sir Keith Hancock and the British Empire: The *Pax Britannica* and the *Pax Americana*', *English Historical Review*, 120, 488 (2005); and WRL, *Oxford History of the British Empire*, V (Oxford: Oxford University Press, 1999), p. 30: 'There would probably be a consensus among the . . . historians involved in the *OHBE* that he was far and away the greatest historian of the Empire and Commonwealth.'

26 *A History of the Arab Peoples* (London: Faber and Faber, 1991) is his most famous work, but I find it unreadable. His collected essays are clearly, perceptively and powerfully stated; see, for example, *A Vision of History: Near Eastern and Other Essays* (London: Constable, 1961).

27 The full title is Commander of the Most Excellent Order of the British Empire.

28 Ernest May was the first NHC speaker at these meetings.

3

Empire From Above and From Below

John M. MacKenzie b. 1943

For me, it started with ships. If you were brought up, as I was, in the Scottish city of Glasgow in the 1940s and 1950s, ships were all around you. They were being built on the stocks of the many shipyards of the River Clyde as the post-war rebuilding of the merchant fleet proceeded apace. They were also arriving and departing on the quays within walking distance of my home. My primary school was near the docks and sometimes we were marched out in a long snake of children to see a dramatic launching from the Harland and Wolff yard across the river in Govan. It was an inspirational sight, calculated to provide unforgettable images for a small boy – ships everywhere; tugs and other smaller boats busily fussing about in the river; multiple ships' sirens providing a celebratory cacophony; workers scrambling over the hulls and decks of vessels. My truly striking memory – apart from the sights and sounds of those yards and the constant hooting of the different registers of sirens (some summoning workers to work or releasing them at the end of the day) – is of the freedom we felt. For some reason, there were few constraints on the movements of myself and my friends. From the age of ten, I would say, we roamed at will. We found every quayside gate wide open, even the entrances to shipyards and to dry docks. The days of Health and Safety and of tight security were yet to dawn. My childhood explorations were therefore in a real adventure playground of shipyards and quays, constantly crossing and recrossing the river on the free ferries of the Clyde Navigation Trust, designed to transport workers quickly from one bank of the river to the other. This, after all, was the river which built twenty per cent of the world's shipping in the late nineteenth/early twentieth century. It was the river that had been dredged in order to make Glasgow a great city of empire, initially connected to the Atlantic trades, starting supremely with tobacco in the eighteenth century, later to more global patterns of commerce. The most important dock for me was Yorkhill Quay. It was the mooring place of the Anchor Line and, astonishingly, the early 1950s still saw a direct connection from there to Bombay by Anchor passenger and cargo vessels with exotic and ancient imperial names such as *Circassia* and *Cilicia*. I would watch the cranes loading these vessels in the days of 'break bulk' cargoes and sometimes I would see crew and passengers ascending the gangway shortly before departure. I was envious.

That all sounds highly romantic, yet it ultimately translated into studies of empire. I was fortunate enough not to have to wait long to walk up such a gangway, not in Glasgow, but in Southampton. I sailed on a Union-Castle ship with my parents for Cape Town in 1955, thence to drive (an eight-day journey in the rainy season with flooded rivers) to Ndola in Northern Rhodesia (Zambia) where my father worked in the Public Works Department, the PWD, a classic department of empire. At school there I became friendly with the son of the local District Commissioner. I visited their home and it was one of the grandest in town. I heard something of the DC's work. For an impressionable boy, scarcely into secondary school, it sounded intriguing and I formed an ambition to be a district commissioner myself one day. That may seem like a rather startling confession, but given the place, time and my age, it is perfectly comprehensible. But other influences were asserting themselves. First, Africa itself. It was the start of my attraction to the continent – and also to its peoples. I was young enough, I think I can say, to have no racial feelings and, although we slotted into the social and racial hierarchies of a colonial society, albeit one only a few years from independence, I genuinely valued my contacts with Africans. I was a loner and my parents provided me with a dog for company. Every afternoon after school, my dog and I went out to explore the bush paths that were close to our home. Indeed, I mapped them, together with villages, cultivation patterns, streams, and much else. I used to meet and talk to people in villages and was always struck both by the dignity and the friendliness, as well as the relative poverty, of the people I met. Then one day I had a strange experience. I walked into a sort-of village I had never been to before. I noticed that the houses were rather superior to African ones. Next I observed that the women seemed to be black, but that any menfolk around seemed to be either white or of mixed race. I had stumbled into the place to which such apparently unacceptable relationships were banished. Although I was only about twelve, such experiences lodged in corners of my mind, making me aware of some of the social and racial realities of colonial rule, a situation in which it is true I was a privileged observer, intruder even, using (though I scarcely realized it then) my status as a member of the white ruling group to move and gaze at will. Strangely enough, our next-door neighbour was one who used his professional position to legitimise his observations. He was a distinguished anthropologist, A. L. Epstein, who came to see us, and who was at that time working on a book I would rediscover some years later. A connection was formed because he came from Manchester, as did my mother.

The book was called *Politics in an Urban African Community*, published in 1958, and I found it in the library of the University of British Columbia (UBC). In the years leading to that moment, I had become increasingly politicized. In Zambia, I had been well aware of the Central African Federation and of the passions it aroused among both whites and black nationalists. At my secondary school in Glasgow, there was a wonderfully radical classics teacher, Miss Cruickshank, who invited a notable missionary from Malawi, the Reverend Tom Colvin to come to speak about the iniquities of the Federation and of the need for Malawian freedom. The Church of Scotland, to which we adhered, was also becoming increasingly radicalized and my own minister took me to Edinburgh in 1959 to hear the great debate on the Central African Federation at the General Assembly of the Church. There, the celebrated Reverend George MacLeod famously delivered his passionate speech against the Federation. I can still remember the tension and excitement in the Assembly Hall as the Church, in effect, positioned itself in an anti-Government stance. It remains an iconic moment, much commented upon in all histories of the decolonization of that Federation.

My university education in Glasgow, however, was wholly conventional, with historical training which linked me to ideas and modes of research and thinking which seem to me now to have been strikingly old-fashioned. Having graduated with a four-year Scottish degree in 1964, I set out for new adventures in Canada. Finding Epstein's book was a second African epiphany. I read it and resolved to study African labour migration, returning to Central Africa for much of 1967, working in the magnificent archives in Salisbury (Harare). I returned in 1970, 1973–4 (spending a year teaching in the university which was experiencing straitened times) and again in 1976, appalled by the activities of the Smith regime and following closely the development of the nationalist guerrilla campaign. By this time I had become an oral researcher and spent many hours conducting interviews in what the white rulers patronisingly named 'tribal trust lands'. My contacts with elderly African men and women, with their villages and their environments, left a lasting impression. My admiration for my 'informants' knew no bounds. Their recounting of their personal and kin pasts – in the context of lives that were so different from my own – provided much inspiration. When historians work in the field, it is impossible not to be influenced by environmental contexts, not to consider the changes in landscapes, flora and fauna, as well as agricultural and stock-rearing practices. I asked all my interlocutors (many in their 90s and in two cases over 100) about the changes in the landscape they had seen in lifetimes which had covered the whole era of colonial rule since 1890. That was in addition to my questions about labour migration, pre-colonial iron working, and much else.[1] I was beginning to be an environmental historian even before the category was fully invented. I also visited a number of mission stations and many African schools, often speaking to the pupils.

Such African experiences were transforming, although my research took a new turn. From 1968 I had been lecturing at Lancaster University. My teaching ranged widely and in the late 1970s I became aware of a worrying dichotomy. I read some of the British historians of the time and was mystified. It seemed to be conventional to separate domestic history from the imperial experience and when empire did intrude, its significance was generally dismissed. Even theories of imperialism, which I had studied at UBC, seldom seemed to be interleaved with domestic British history. It later occurred to me that the 'new amnesia' about empire was inseparably bound up with the contemporary era of decolonization. We were witnessing a reaction against the notion that empire had provided the central meaning and moral force of British history, promoted by T. B. Macaulay, Sir John Seeley and such later historians as Sir Reginald Coupland. Such a position was scarcely sustainable in an age of decolonization. The end of empire and the period of post-Second World War guilt led some historians to suggest that imperialism might have been something that happened out there, with some economic consequences, but for the British public and British politicians empire had been only marginal to British concerns. The evidence apparently lay in the fact that both Europe and the United States were more significant in British investment and trade than empire while imperial matters invariably cleared the floor of the House of Commons. Of course there had been major migrations in the direction of the territories known as Dominions, but even here the United States constituted a much more significant destination. In any case the highly detailed research on migration developed in recent decades still lay in the future. As the British cast off almost all of their empire in the years from 1947 to the 1960s it could be safely dismissed by historians, consoling themselves that it had never been particularly important in the first place.[2] As one would later put it, echoing Seeley, the British had indeed been absent-minded imperialists,[3] imperialists caught up in and swept along by tides of history which they neither fully controlled nor indeed understood.

But such an idea conflicted with my own experiences. The Glasgow of my childhood seemed to me to have been steeped in empire. Some of the street names, many of the statues, the architecture, the shipyards, the locomotive works, the iron foundries (like the great Saracen) and some of the city's manufactures seemed inseparably bound up with empire. As a boy attending the Church of Scotland, we still had missionaries on furlough visiting to talk of colonial places (and of course raise money for their endeavours). Then there were the memories of the great exhibitions of 1888, 1901, 1911 and 1938. I knew an elderly lady who never ceased to regale me with stories of the grandeur of the first three, all notably imperial and located in Kelvingrove Park, near my home, and they were certainly among the most dazzling experiences of her life. As for the Glasgow Empire Exhibition of 1938, my own father had worked at that one and had been similarly impressed by the manifestations of empire built and displayed in Bellahouston Park to the south of the city. Each day on my way to secondary school and then to university I passed the astounding equestrian statue of Field Marshal Lord Roberts of Pretoria and Kandahar, the plinth of which had exotic relief sculptures of the various regiments and indigenous opponents associated with him from the Indian Revolt to the North West frontier, Afghan wars, and the Anglo-Boer War. It is still located on one of the most striking sites in the city, a high promontory projecting from Park Circus looking out over the university. David Livingstone seemed to be but one of a number of imperial heroes associated with the city. I thus began to confront the question why were historians writing up a past which seemed to have no relevance to my experience? Was it not the case that the imperial presence was deeply embedded in the fabric of Britain, in its culture – including working-class culture – in its intellectual life and in its collective consciousness? The more I thought about this during the mid to late 1970s, the more it seemed to me that historians had been too obsessed with the document. I had spent many hours myself in the old Public Record Office in London's Chancery Lane working on the records of the British South Africa Company, but I had been helped in my distrust of documents by an extraordinary encounter with a former colonial governor who impatiently told me that the trouble with historians was that they actually believed what they read. 'When I was a governor', he said, 'don't imagine that I told my masters in the Colonial Office the truth – I told them what they wanted to hear.' In any case, it seemed to me high time to get away from the 'official mind' of imperialism and seek out the popular psychology. We surely needed to explore what the possession of empire had done to us and such an exploration required different types of sources – programmes of exhibitions, school textbooks, popular publications and literature (including that written for juveniles), records of various entertainment forms, the press, visual materials, institutions charged with projecting empire and societies that took up this particular challenge, not to mention even ephemera. This project would not involve the total abandonment of records (for example the London Imperial Institute had left copious documentary evidence lodged in the National Archives at Kew), but the sourcing net would be thrown as widely as possible. Throughout this project, I was influenced by two key colleagues: Stephen Constantine, whose interest in migration and aspects of imperial culture was a considerable stimulus, and Jeffrey Richards, with his staggeringly wide knowledge of film, media and literature.

The book was already well advanced when suddenly the popular imperialism of the nineteenth century seemed to be recreated before my very eyes. A colonial war, involving a group of almost forgotten islands off the coast of Argentina, broke out. A prime minister took on Churchillian airs, wrapped herself in the Union Jack and set about a remarkably distant war of re-conquest. The press and all other media became obsessed, tabloids in a manner as jingoistic as 1878, 1884/5, 1898 or any of the other climacterics of an earlier imperialism. The British public seemed enthralled. Huge crowds turned out to wave off troops and naval vessels. Even larger ones turned up for the triumphant returns. Thatcher engineered a sort of Roman triumph in the streets of London. Vast acres of newsprint, as well as thousands of hours of radio and television time, were expended on this extraordinary phenomenon – not a war of national survival, but a Palmerstonian war to protect the Britishness of the lives of a few thousand islanders at the other side of the globe. It seemed like an amazing modern laboratory for a historic phenomenon. *Propaganda and Empire* was published two years after this Falklands War. It seemed to strike an immediate chord, was widely (and not always favourably) reviewed, and has remained in print ever since.

Scholars often embark on research projects imagining that they are on their own. Invariably they quickly find that they are not. The publication of this book very agreeably unveiled the numbers of people working in related fields. That had two effects – the founding of the 'Studies in Imperialism' series just a few months after the publication of the original book, and then the follow-on edited collection, *Imperialism and Popular Culture* in 1986. After a relatively slow start, perhaps in common with many other series, the number of books began to accelerate and it became apparent that a cultural approach to empire, one which (as I had put it) dealt with the centripetal as well as the centrifugal effects of imperialism, had become a major concern of modern scholarship. It seemed that it would be difficult to disentangle British domestic history and the imperial experience again. Those books also demonstrated the inevitable gaps in *Propaganda and Empire*. It had given far too little prominence to the press, for example, or the full significance of gender, and it had also omitted sufficient understanding of the role of the churches and of missionaries in the dissemination of an essentially imperial message. There was also far too little on the development of academic disciplines within the context of imperialism. These and other defects were progressively repaired by the wave of books which came to the series (as well as the many important works appearing from other publishers). As I write this in 2014, the series has over 110 published books and many more are in the press or have been commissioned under the new general editor, Andrew S. Thompson. For thirty years I thoroughly enjoyed writing introductions to each of those works.[4]

Historians are very fortunate, for they are generally free to follow the twists and turns of their intellectual development. After *Propaganda and Empire*, I was anxious to return to Africa, but again I hoped to create an entirely new approach, one that set out on fresh explorations, not least of the African environments that I had visited in extensive travels in Uganda, Kenya, Tanzania, Malawi, Zimbabwe and elsewhere in southern Africa. Throughout my career I had been reading widely in works of African exploration and travel, memoirs, anthropological materials and related publications, originally considering their evidence for nineteenth-century African societies. But another theme seemed to run through them all, namely the hunting of wild animals. It seemed to me that it was a vast and important field which had been largely ignored. I set out to read as widely as possible and to flesh out these sources with an exploration of colonial hunting law, of taxidermy, natural history and museums, and the development of conservation ideas together with further imperial dominance of land usage through the creation of game reserves, controlled hunting areas and national parks. I was of course also concerned with the dimensions of race dominance and exclusion, of dispossession and displacement that ran through these themes. I soon came to the conclusion that Africa had been conquered on the backs of its animals. This was transparently true of the exploitation of the huge resource of ivory which had not only led European hunters into the interior, but had also served to fund the activities of missionaries and others, even at one stage the travels of David Livingstone. Then there was the fact that all white travellers in Africa moved with large retinues of porters, guards and other helpers. They all had to be fed and Africa's animals supplied a massive protein supplement. This was soon taken up by engineers building railway lines, bridges and roads, while early settlers fed their workers and asset-stripped their lands by shooting game, securing a significant temporary income through the sale of horns, hides, skins and other materials. In the process, African traditional hunters were largely excluded. Whereas hunting was significant in many societies, notably in times of crop failures, colonial game law now excluded them from the hunt. Moreover, hunting had developed the ritual overtones of empire, of dominance of the environment, as well as the transfer of social and racial hierarchies into the depths of the continent. Since the great ritual hunt was also a highly significant visible expression of power and the ruling presence in Mughal India, taken over in dramatic ways by the British, I could not resist a chapter that examined this Indian parallel. In any case, hunting in Africa was often prosecuted by military officers from India while on leave. This revealed yet another aspect of the hunt, that it was a training for war, the use of techniques in pursuing campaigns against animals which could readily be turned against humans – as they were for example in the suppression of the Shona-Ndebele revolt in Zimbabwe in 1896–7. *The Empire of Nature* (I was fortunate in finding the perfect title) was published in 1988 and was soon followed by the collected essays of *Imperialism and the Natural World* (1990). Whatever their defects, these took their place as early expressions of the great wave of environmental publications then underway. Of course they were limited by their period and by the particular focus adopted and it has been inevitable that they have been much revised since.

In 1991, I was invited to deliver an inaugural lecture in association with my chair of imperial history. Having spent a number of evenings considering what I might speak about, I suddenly had a Eureka moment. My fresh turn emerged from the realization that an inaugural should contain a touch of autobiography. My life had embraced Scotland and the Empire. Why not pursue that theme, not least because few publications had appeared in the field. The lecture was divided into two parts, 'Scotland and the Empire' and 'The Empire and Scotland'. Reciprocation remained my primary focus. Later published, it has been (gratifyingly) much quoted. A new field opened up, for I quickly realized that the so-called 'British' Empire could only be fully understood in terms of the ethnic differences of the metropolitan state. The British had often suggested that peoples in Asia and Africa were fractured, that ironically one of the purposes of empire was to create new nations. Yet they too were ethnically diverse, something long conveniently forgotten. In the Scottish case, the Act of Union of 1707 had ensured the survival of a distinctive Scottish civil culture, in its legal and banking systems, its national church and its educational practices, including its universities. Moreover, the Scottish Enlightenment, albeit in contradictory ways, had had untold effects upon the theorization and practices of empire. Scots had emerged as particularly dominant in certain professions, which I characterized as mercantile, marine, medical and missionary. In addition, they had been significant in key imperial environmental professions, embracing surveying, engineering, botany, geology and forestry. Throughout they had brought distinctive skills and ideas to bear, not to mention relationships with particular environments and indigenous peoples, all to be analysed if the 'British' could be fully understood. It was an easy step to realize that the 'British' Empire could only be comprehended in terms of the 'four nations' idea pioneered by Pocock and others. Ireland was then becoming a significant focus for imperial studies. Soon Wales was added to the picture and only studies of England, to a certain extent, lagged behind.[5] Once again, these were fields that expanded mightily in the succeeding decades, producing something of a revolution in imperial studies.

More historical paths beckoned. I became involved in debates about Edward Said's striking Orientalist ideas, in developments in studies of the press, missionaries, maritime history, intellectual history, in the diaspora of the Scots, and the history of institutions (such as museums) relating to empire. Many of these seemed yet again to loop back to my early experiences. But most important, I have been in awe of the significant work done in more recent times in rendering some of the research I had touched on in much more sophisticated forms. The concept of the penetration of British culture and politics by the imperial experience seems to have been carried backwards in ways I could never have anticipated in the remarkable work of Kathleen Wilson, David Armitage, Sarah Irving and others, demonstrating that the intellectual, institutional and popular manifestations of empire, key aspects of colonial affairs in respect of the economy, the environment, race and slavery, as well as global visions rooted in imperialism have to be recognized as developing to a striking degree in the seventeenth and eighteenth centuries.[6] The imperial laboratory was essential to an understanding of the development of so many sciences, including botany, geology, medicine, forestry, microbiology, agronomy, as well as new nineteenth-century disciplines such as geography and anthropology and we are seeing many more welcome studies of these. Moreover, empire penetrated the civic lives of British cities, as I noted earlier, and this has led to studies of Glasgow[7], Liverpool[8], Southampton,[9] the group of Portsmouth, Coventry and Leeds,[10] and, recently, Dundee.[11] Another field which I think is crucial to an understanding of imperialism is the whole question of comparative approaches. British imperial historians have frequently operated in isolation. We need to understand other empires, not only modern European ones, but also those in deeper time and on other continents.[12] In the modern era we also have to understand that empires could be highly cooperative as well as competitive and an important start has been made there too.[13]

Back in my formative years in the 1960s, there were two reports in Britain, those by Hayter and Parry, which proposed the establishment of area study centres to cover Latin America, Asia and Africa. They were important in creating key research centres in each of those regions. But there was perhaps a down side. Such studies, in becoming concentrated, were partly cut off from the mainstream. Imperial history developed in isolation from them. The formation of my ideas had elements of the bottom up as well as of the top down, perspectives from Glasgow, Scotland and the UK, as well as from Africa (and later Canada, South and Southeast Asia and Australasia). But it seems to me that a good deal of imperial history continues to be written from what I call the 'space-station approach', that is an examination of empires in geo-political ways, distant perspectives that often omit the focus on the ground, and hence aspects of the environment, of indigenous peoples and gender. Of course, geo-political history is important, but it should never be pursued in isolation. The great challenge is surely to bring together the area studies approach with that of a wider imperial history. We have moved beyond the era of national histories, the rediscovery of the 'British world', even the bringing together of imperialism and globalization, and need to unite the vision from above with that from below. As I have recently pointed out, notions of a 'ramshackle' British Empire, of one that actually lacked power, need to be very much revised when we look at, for example, the environmental, social and economic history of, say, Malawi, or indeed of those peoples among whom I travelled in the 1970s.[14] Moreover, I remain convinced that the key definition of empire involves the imposition of power of one people over another. When we cleave to that central point, then the history of the United States becomes unquestionably associated with empire, regardless of 1776, and other ideas have to be revised – for example the notion that the First World War marked the beginning of the end of the modern empires. The fact is that the emergence of Dominions' independence simply meant that, from the perspective of First Nations, African, Aboriginal or Maori peoples, the location of power simply moved nearer home, to Ottawa, Pretoria, Salisbury or Nairobi, Canberra or Wellington. We still have many revisions to make to orthodox imperial histories!

In all these ways, my work, however apparently disparate, has been integrated by central themes, recently felicitously described as 'the power of culture and the cultures of power', all surely essential to a full understanding of empire and imperialism.[15] Even my controversial critique of Edward Said (which, as I insisted, did not detract from my admiration for the man, his concept of the organic scholar, or his political positions) was connected with my fascination with museums and art history and my search for genuine cross-cultural influences, some of which emerged from the imperial experience. But there are dangers in all of this. It might be suggested that the excessive foregrounding of personal experience might lead to imbalances in the treatment of the past, that such experiences should be put to one side (if that were possible) in the dispassionate evaluation of evidence. I do not entirely accept this. Lived experience cannot be put to one side. It is better surely to recognize it and expose it. In any case it is precisely those elements of such lived experience that ultimately provide central insights for all scholarship, even that relating to more distant pasts. How we are shaped remains a vital component of our thinking.

Notes

1 The transcriptions of these interviews were deposited in the archives of Zimbabwe and copies are in my possession. The work was published in a number of more or less obscure journals.

2 Of course the great work of Robinson and Gallagher was revolutionizing imperial history in the same period, but in many respects their insights were held in a distinct compartment compared with domestic history.

3 Bernard Porter, *The Absent-Minded Imperialists: What the British Really Thought About Empire* (Oxford: Oxford University Press, 2004).

4 See Andrew S. Thompson, *Writing Imperial Histories* (Manchester: Manchester University Press, 2013) for a critical survey of the significance of the series to date.

5 Keith Jeffery, ed., *An Irish Empire?* (Manchester: Manchester University Press, 1996) was commissioned by me. Later came Kevin Kenny, ed., *Ireland and the British Empire* (Oxford: Oxford University Press, 2004); H. V. Bowen, ed., *Wales and the British Overseas Empire* (Manchester: Manchester University Press, 2011).

6 For example, Kathleen Wilson, *The Sense of the People: Politics, Culture and Imperialism in England, 1715–1785* (Cambridge: Cambridge University Press, 1995); David Armitage, *The Ideological Origins of the British Empire* (Cambridge: Cambridge University Press, 2000); Sarah Irving, *Natural Science and the Origins of the British Empire* (London: Pickering and Chatto, 2008).

7 John M. MacKenzie, '"The Second City of the Empire": Glasgow – Imperial Municipality', in Felix Driver and David Gilbert, eds, *Imperial Cities* (Manchester: Manchester University Press 1999), pp. 215–37.

8 Sheryllynne Haggerty, Anthony Webster and Nicholas J. White, eds, *The Empire in One City? Liverpool's Inconvenient Imperial Past* (Manchester: Manchester University Press, 2008).

9 Miles Taylor, ed., *Southampton: Gateway to the British Empire* (London: I. B. Tauris, 2007).

10 Brad Beavan, *Visions of Empire: Patriotism, Popular Culture and the City* (Manchester, Manchester University Press, 2012).

11 Jim Tomlinson, *Dundee and the Empire: Juteopolis 1890–1939* (Edinburgh: Edinburgh University Press, 2014).

12 John M. MacKenzie, ed., *European Empires and the People* (Manchester: Manchester University Press, 2011); John Darwin, *After Tamerlane: The Global History of Empire* (London: Allen Lane, 2007); Jane Burbank and Frederick Cooper, *Empires in World History* (Princeton: Princeton University Press, 2010); John M. MacKenzie, general editor, Wiley-Blackwell *Encyclopedia of Empire* (forthcoming).

13 A conference on cooperation among modern empires was held in Cologne in January 2013 and its proceedings edited by Volker Barth and Roland Cvetkowski and published as *Imperial Co-operation and Transfer, 1870–1930: Empires and Encounters* (London: Bloomsbury, 2015).

14 In a series of lectures at conferences, including one in Austin, Texas in 2013. For Malawi see John McCracken, *Malawi 1859–1966* (London: James Currey, 2012).

15 Cherry Leonardi, 'The Power of Culture and the Cultures of Power: John MacKenzie and the Study of Imperialism', in Thompson, ed., *Writing Imperial Histories*, pp. 49–73.

4

Empire and Class: The Making of a History Boy

Richard N. Price *b. 1944*

In a very generous review of my book, *Making Empire: Colonial Encounters and the Creation of Imperial Rule in Nineteenth Century Africa* (Cambridge, 2008), that appeared in the *Times Higher Education Supplement*, Joanna Lewis began by asking: 'Whatever happened to Richard Price? . . . When his book on the South African war and the British working class was published in 1972 it was an instant classic – then silence.'[1] Dr Lewis went on to acknowledge that the silence extended only to Africa. In the three-decade hiatus, I had published quite a lot about British social and labour history. It was, perhaps, a flippant comment. But she had highlighted an issue that, by 2008, I had pondered myself. Why had I returned to a focus on empire at a relatively late stage in my career when it had been an interest in empire that had made me want to be an historian in the first place? The answer lies in the way in which 'empire' and 'class' were combined in my consciousness and experience.

I came of age in the post-war Britain of the 1950s. The immediacy of the Second World War hung over my youth. The restraints of economic recovery combined with the nostalgic afterglow of imperial glory. I remember when Wrigley's Spearmint gum made its first appearance in my local sweet shop and when candies themselves came off the rationing. But during my formative years of the 1950s, there were two issues that seemed to dominate civic and political discourse, two themes that were constantly in the news and that shaped the way I thought about the challenges that faced British society at that time. These themes were the politics of class and the politics of empire.

Class and empire stamped themselves upon an impressionable young boy in various ways. Of the two, the issue of the empire was undoubtedly uppermost in my mind during most of the 1950s. I thought more about it and read more about it. And it is natural that this would be so, because 'class' infused the culture in which one lived and its large and trivial manifestations were ingrained in social experience and consciousness. My family were hardly working-class militants. One grandfather was a house painter who worked for a small builder his whole working life. By definition, then, he would not have been a union member. The other was a carpenter who before the war worked in the local railway works, and had played a leading role in the railway strike of 1923. But, three years later, he opposed the general strike. In the 1950s my father was a member of the uniformed working class in a secure, steady job which, if not well paid, allowed an adequate margin of economic security. He was a postman and a member of the union as a condition of the job. He later became a warehouseman for the local council. The particular sense of class place that I absorbed from my parents was decidedly 'respectable', if not genteel. In my home, striving and achievement were prized and the disreputable shunned. It was the aspirational culture of the family combined with the reality of limited resources that brought the reality of class most vividly alive for me. There was a sense that given our socio-economic level, opportunities would have to be worked for and actively solicited – they could not be assumed as part of a birthright. But equally, there was a sense that since 1945 things had changed for the better. There was an awareness of new opportunities for social and educational advancement that had been opened after the war. Juxtaposed to this was the memory of the pre-war depression when the horizons available to the lower class of my parents' youth were more constrained than the opportunities that were proffered by post-war society. My father left school at twelve to work in a garage; my mother left at fourteen to become a shop assistant.

In addition to the personal 'life story' aspect of class, matters of social hierarchy and place were dyed into the milieu of political and civic discourse. The markers of class inherited from Victorian times remained visible. The cartoon character of Andy Capp, created in 1957 for the proletarian newspaper the *Daily Mirror*, for example, was a reinvention of the Victorian Ally Sloper. Like Sloper, he was misogynist and work-shy, addicted to his fags and off-course betting. Andy Capp, of course, was increasingly an anachronism by the mid-1950s. But his cloth cap was still ubiquitous headwear at that moment, especially the further north one went. Similarly, that great Victorian facilitator of mobility, the bicycle, remained the dominant form of working-class transportation – although after 1955 the motor car made major inroads into working-class homes, as did other key items of the consumer economy such as televisions. In any case, the fact of 'class' was impossible to avoid. And the invention of Andy Capp at this particular moment was consistent with a growing theme of political discourse that posited the working class as key obstacles to social and economic modernization. It captured one side of the image of the working man as a truculent impediment to progressive social and economic change that was assiduously fostered from around the mid-1950s. The 1959 Boulting Brothers movie, *I'm all right, Jack*, a vehicle for Peter Sellers' comic genius, projected an even more politicized version of the same *canard*, although it also took aim at the 'old school tie' culture of British management. A growing chorus of concern throughout the 1950s within the political discourse and related commentary stressed how economic modernization was impeded by labour's restrictive practices in industry and its militant flaunting of the power it secured from full employment to get – if necessary, by strike action – what Samuel Gompers had wanted from capitalism for the American working class – that is, 'more'.

The place of empire in my developing consciousness in the 1950s was more extant. My family had only tentative connections with the empire. My paternal grandfather had a brother who emigrated to Canada before the First World War, never to be seen again. There was a distant cousin of my father's mother who went to New Zealand; and a relative of the same grandmother had been unromantically killed serving as a soldier in Kipling's India when a bridge collapsed and his horse fell on top of him, pinning him in the river below. My father had trained Sikhs in transport services during the war, and they had given him a silver dagger as a memento – so I presume that they got on well enough. A good friend of my mother's was an Anglo-Indian who went inevitably by the name of 'Ranji'. And I remember the young teacher in my elementary school who emigrated with her husband to Bulawayo about 1953. None of these filaments of empire amounted to much in my mind. What *did* implant empire seriously into my consciousness was the library, the news from the empire, and school.

Education has always been central to life of the 'respectable' working class. At no time before the 1950s had education served so effectively as an escalator out of one's class place. If the obstacle of the 11-plus exam could be overcome and admission gained to the local grammar school, all sorts of possibilities opened up. Of course, that was not easy. From my elementary class of about 30, only four of us made it over that hurdle – two boys and two girls. But it is a reflection of how effective was that appalling exam of ensuring success, that three off us went on to university and entered the world of the professions. Given this, the library figured very large in my own life. Riding home on my bicycle from school, I would frequently stop by the small wooden building that served as our town library and wander its shelves. The history section was an avenue to the exotic and the different. The books that most grabbed my attention were those about the empire. They were books in the mould of H. E. Marshall's 1908 hagiography, *Our Empire Story*, and I remember them as being predominantly books about the military heroics that built the empire. In any case, the result was that, at an early age, I knew a great deal about Clive in India, Wolfe in Quebec, Kitchener on the Nile and such like. It was also an experience that left me with a secret taste for military history, which I have kept hidden, as if I were reading pornography.

Although I hesitate to call this meandering library activity 'intellectual', it certainly involved a more informed appreciation of empire than my visceral sensations of the class society I was living in. And, like class, empire was impossible to ignore. It was in the news all the time. This was the moment when the future of empire hung in the balance. After the Second World War, there was no clear commitment to decolonization until Macmillan's 'winds of change' speech in Cape Town in 1959, and his concurrent appointment of Iain Macleod as Colonial Secretary put an end to the pretence that Britain could hang on to its empire. Empire constantly intruded into my provincial world. Indeed, the empire was the occasion of a conversation that stoked the first glimmerings of a political awakening.

It was the time of the Mau Mau rebellion in Kenya. My attention had been drawn to a report of the murder of European settlers – probably the infamous Ruck family murder in January 1953. I forget what led me to make a condemnatory remark about their murder to one of my primary school teachers, the wife of an army officer who had served in Kenya – hardly the type one would think would be anti-imperial. But I had touched some sort of nerve, for her response was sharp and reproving: 'Well', she said, 'they [the Africans] never asked us to go there in the first place, you know.' From that moment on, I always read news on the empire in a different, more questioning and reserved, light.

And finally, there was school. The secondary school I attended was a moderately good boys grammar school. Each year graduates went on to university, sometimes even to Oxford or Cambridge. The education I received was distinctly spotty; I thought so at the time, and everything I have learnt subsequently has confirmed that I was right. The big exceptions, however, were history and geography, where the masters and the instruction were first rate. It was a geography teacher who first suggested that I set my sights on university, rather than the teacher training college my parents had held up as the acme of academic expectation. He also pointed out that money would be no problem – that anyone good enough to go to college could get the financing as, indeed, I did. Strangely enough, few boys were interested in history, and so, when I got to the upper school, I had the amazing experience of individual tuition by three separate masters: one for European history, one for British history, and one for empire and Commonwealth history. Commonwealth history was my favourite and, as a result, I spent two years reading books on the histories of India, Australia, Canada, and – in distinctly last place – Africa. This provided a solid – if somewhat conventional – grounding for what was to greet me at university when I entered the University of Sussex to read History in the School of Social Studies.

At that moment, 1962, Sussex was a year old and it was in the full flush of its mission to break the curricular mould of higher education in Britain. There was a sense of optimism, innovation and experiment and, most of all, a sense of being at a special place. A central feature of the curriculum was its attempt to broaden the context of specialization, so that, for example, if your major (and this was the first importation of that American concept into British higher education) was History you read it against a background of social, literary, European or American studies. The idea was that you would learn how to be an historian not by studying history from the beginning of time – one thing after another – but by understanding that 'history' was a product of interactions and interconnections with other spheres of societal experience. There was a first-year course, for example, on 'Napoleon For and Against' that looked at the way historians over time had constructed different interpretations of Napoleon. What this did was push one's thinking in an interdisciplinary direction, and emphasize conceptual approaches over purely narrative modes of thinking. There was another course called 'Contemporary Britain' which brought together sociologists, literary scholars, politics faculty and historians in a multi-disciplinary study of the social issues and problems faced by Britain at that moment. The curriculum encouraged courses that were innovative and unusual, and in my second year I happened to chance upon one of those.

It was a course on 'Imperialism' taught by a newly arrived lecturer by the name of Ranajit Guha. The course appealed to me because of my school readings in the history of the empire. But Guha's course was totally different. Its very title suggested its orientation. Instead of studying the 'Age of Imperialism' or 'European Expansion', as one would have done at any other British university at the time, this course declared its scope to be imperialism as a social, cultural, theoretical and economic formation. The reading list, which, to my regret I have long since lost, opened with V. I. Lenin, J. A. Hobson, Joseph Schumpeter, and the recently published book by Richard Koebner and Helmut Schmidt on *Imperialism: The Political History of Word 1840–1960*. These works and others provided the context within which the historical study of 'imperialism' as a concept was conducted. Nor was the notion of imperialism confined to Britain – although that was its major focus. There were also books on France – Henri Brunschwig, for example – and on the German and Dutch empires.

And then there was Guha himself. An ex-communist who had left the Party after the admissions of Stalin's crimes, a youth leader who had participated in the last stages of the Indian independence struggle, and had been jailed by the British, a somewhat severe ascetic intellectual, who spent one Christmas reading Wittgenstein's *Philosophical Investigations*, Guha conveyed the seriousness and the rigour that were at the heart of the intellectual enterprise. He was the first person I had met for whom the world of the mind was the prism through which the world itself was viewed. And, to cap it all, a man whose Marxism *enabled* and *expanded* his modes of thinking – as epitomized by his course – rather than confined it as one was conventionally taught happened with Marxists. It was Guha who introduced me to those other roomy thinkers, Eric Hobsbawm and E. P. Thompson. On

Guha's recommendation I bought a copy of Hobsbawm's *Labouring Men*, a book that directly inspired my doctoral work and influenced my research agenda for many years after.

Guha's influence was profound, deep and long lasting. But in the short run his imperialism course was important more for what it taught me about how to be an historian than predicting the kind of history I was going to do. It was true that Guha served as principal adviser for my doctoral dissertation, later published as *An Imperial War and the British Working Class, 1899–1902* (1972) – which was the book Joanna Lewis was referring to in her review. But I did not contemplate a career as an imperial historian, nor do I remember Guha urging me to do so. By the end of the 1960s I was firmly committed to British social and labour history and from the start I imagined my dissertation as a study of working-class history. There were many reasons for taking this road. But the main reason had to do with how I understood the key trends in both politics and scholarship that I experienced in Britain at the end of the 1960s.

The prospects of becoming an historian of empire at that moment were not very appealing. Although Ranajit Guha *taught* a different kind of imperial history, there was precious little evidence that anyone was actually doing it. Imperial historiography in the late 1960s seemed to be pretty old fashioned. At least, that was how I experienced it, as an anecdote from those days will illustrate.

As a graduate student, I attended the seminar in Imperial History at the University of London's Institute of Historical Research. It was presided over by Gerald Graham, the Rhodes Professor of Imperial History at King's College. Graham was an avuncular and kindly man, who welcomed fellow Sussex graduate student, John Springhall (who was working on youth and empire) and me into his seminar. But he epitomized the kind of imperial history that people like Springhall and myself were sceptical about. His specialty was maritime history and he wrote books with titles like *The Empire of the North Atlantic* and *The China Station: War and Diplomacy 1830–1860*. He was not hostile to different perspectives – though he did warn me against adopting the 'party line' when he learned of my admiration for the work of Marxists George Rudé and Eric Hobsbawm. But what struck me most about this seminar was how it defined empire entirely as the politics and diplomacy of empire and imperial administration. The other graduate students – all from London – were researching topics that seemed so utterly boring. I remember one in particular, who had been set to work on educational policy in Uganda for her PhD. She was green with envy at the sexy topics that Springhall and I were 'allowed' to work on. Suffice it to say that we learnt little of use from this seminar.

And this was typical. The questions that framed the scholarship of the time seemed to flow from the priorities of empire, making it hard to imagine how the history of empire could be written *outside* of paradigms that were derived from metropolitan perspectives of one kind or another. The biggest bundle of questions revolved around the role and nature of the political economy of empire. Was empire motivated by economic gain? Was there an imperialism of free trade? And what was the relative role of diplomacy, missionary zeal and politics in the motivations for empire? These issues were all gathered up in the big book of the period: Ronald Robinson, Jack Gallagher and Alice Denny's *Africa and the Victorians*: *The Official Mind of Imperialism*, published in 1963. This was a fine piece of scholarship. The book was enormously influential, and it had a long-lasting impact. It attributed the nineteenth-century empire in Africa entirely to key strategic assumptions about defending the Suez Canal and the Cape of Good Hope that were held in the 'official mind' of Victorian statesmen. But it was diplomatic history writ large, with the sub-text of striking a blow against the 'Marxist' economic interpretations of imperialism.[2]

If a British-centred imperial history itself did not seem a very attractive prospect, neither did the other kind of imperial history seem a viable option. Decolonization was not only a political process, it also had scholarly ramifications. If Britain was going to hand back its empire to the Indigenous peoples themselves, then why should it not also hand back their histories? I am not sure that anyone ever expressed it exactly this way, but it was a conclusion that could be fairly drawn from the scholarly trends of the time, and it was a sense that one picked up from Guha. The history of the peoples of the empire belonged to them. This was the moment when area studies were proliferating and local histories were establishing their own 'fields' separate from the embrace of imperial history as part of the establishment of an independent national identity. The decolonization of Indigenous histories was a controversial and, as it turned out, a probably unattainable aim.[3] But in any case, it was in the 1960s that imperial history became more separated from British history than it had previously been. They only began to be put back together again in the mid-1980s when John Mackenzie came up with the quite brilliant conception of the 'Studies in Imperialism' series.[4]

Compared to this tangled mare's nest, the radiant appeal of British social history was irresistible. If, in 1968, the history of the empire needed to be turned over to those who actually lived there, it was equally true that there was much that remained to be uncovered about the history of Britain. It seemed to me that the most important task for British historians was to explore and explain the role of class and class politics in modern British history. This feeling was driven, I think, by two main considerations.

The first was the social change that was unfolding during the sixties, change that was reflected in popular culture as well as in politics. The general direction of progressive politics pointed to the key priority of dismantling the shackles of tradition and custom that in the popular rhetoric had served to hold the country back and that were inseparable from class. The general promise of the Labour Party in both 1964 and 1966 was precisely to begin the task of making 'far-reaching changes in economic and social attitudes which permeate our whole system of society', as Harold Wilson put it to the

Labour Party Conference on 1 October 1963.[5] And although that promise was to fall sorely short, there was a general optimism that this agenda could be fulfilled. The tone of the times was well captured by Anthony Sampson's *Anatomy of Britain*, a magisterial and devastating indictment of the stultifying hold of tradition on the central institutions of the country, first published in 1962. Although Sampson's critique was not extended to the arcane realms of historiography, history writing, too, seemed ripe for revolution.

The place where this seemed to be happening was British social history. And this provided a second reason not to focus on the history of empire. During the 1960s, British social history was the site of exciting and innovative work. I was particularly attuned to this, of course, because the example of Asa Briggs' pioneering work in Victorian social history overshadowed everything at Sussex. But Briggs was only one of a remarkable cohort of historians whose work pointed in the same direction. They ranged from Rodney Hilton in medieval history through Christopher Hill in early modern history to Eric Hobsbawm and Edward Thompson in the eighteenth and nineteenth centuries. For about twenty years – between, I would say, 1960 and 1980 – the kind of history practiced by these, amongst others, was perhaps *the* most influential force in historical study, at least in the Western European and North Atlantic world. It extended even beyond the Euro-world. Hobsbawm's studies of peasant rebellions and political movements were important in Latin American history. And, despite their strongly nationalist tone, even subaltern studies owed a lot to the idea of 'history from below'.

The history of empire suffered by comparison. It was methodologically uninteresting and its close association with British imperialism made it politically dubious. I took the lesson that the central task for the progressive-minded social historian was to uncover histories that mainstream political and economic history had ignored and in the famous phrase of Edward Thompson to 'rescue the poor stockinger, the "utopian" artisan, and even the deluded follower of Joanna Southcott, from the enormous condescension of posterity'.[6] I was excited by these possibilities and of, therefore, contributing to changing the landscape of historical knowledge that Briggs had claimed was the task at hand. It was also important to explain how previously hidden histories had *agency* within the historical process: how they had entered into the dynamic of change over time and had contributed to the total history of British society. This still seems to me to be an important project.

It was that commitment that underpinned my own research agenda until the end of the 1990s. For about twenty-five years, I worked steadily in the area of labour and social history and, after the publication of *An Imperial War and the British Working Class, 1899–1902*, produced *Masters, Unions and Men: Work Control in Building and the Rise of Labour, 1830–1914* (1980) which was a study of worker militancy and its relationship to trade union development in the building industry, and *Labour in British*

Society 1780–1980 (1989), which was an attempt to assess the agency of labour as an estate in modern British history. I also published *British Society 1680–1880: Dynamism, Containment and Change* (1998), which was a general history of Britain that put social agency at the centre of the analysis.

By the later 1990s, however, I felt that I had come to the end of a road. I realized that I had completed the scholarly agenda that had unfolded since the late 1960s. These books said what I had wanted to say about the place of labour in modern British history and the way that social history could lay at the centre of a narrative about society in general. The energies generated by the stimuli of the 1960s had expired; and I feared falling into that familiar academic trap of spending the rest of my career repeating myself in one form or another. A change of focus was in order.

It was then that Ranajit Guha popped back into my life. I had never completely lost touch with him, of course. I had followed the rise of subaltern studies. We had corresponded and had met a couple of times. But two encounters at the end of the 1990s were particularly important as I looked around for a new area of research interest. It was a problem that was familiar to him. He had spent many years ferreting through the archives, debating with the conventional historiographies before settling on the idea of subaltern studies. In one conversation, I was telling him about some digging I had been doing in South African history, and how different the history of empire looked from the frontier than it did from the representation of empire in Britain. 'Yes', he remarked, 'the real question about empire is what it *did* to Britain.' That was all; and we moved off to other things.

But there was a comment that Guha made that struck me. It was: 'Always listen to the young people.' I remembered this as I watched the efflorescence of scholarship that called itself the new imperial history, which began to appear throughout the 1990s. This was especially interesting in contrast to British history, where, by the 1990s, it was my opinion that the capacious possibilities promised by the 'new' social history of the 1960s had closed down. The cultural turn had replaced the social turn. But more properly the cultural turn betokened an *inward turn*. The horizons of British history had narrowed. It no longer grappled with big questions, it offered no lessons as to how to do history differently, it contained no reasons for historians of other countries to read British history. Only the empire gave its history a relevance and a resonance.

And when I turned my attention to empire again, it was like the memory of a first love affair and I was reminded what a fascinating place empire was. In contrast, when I scanned the landscape of British history, it seemed like an affair that had lost its interest or energy. Naturally, I had my own reservations about the biases and assumptions of the much-trumpeted imperial turn. I discussed those in an article 'One Big Thing: Britain and its Empire', in the *Journal of British Studies* in 2006 where I argued that reducing the history of Britain to its imperial lineage was problematic because it directed attention away from other influences on the shaping of British society. But these kinds of differences and debates are essential to scholarly discourse, and the main point was that the direction this new historical fashion was trending seemed to me to promise to re-energize the sagging body of British historiography. Its prime virtue was that it once again placed a big question at the centre of British history: how to understand the significance of Britain's relationship to its empire. This was something that the postmodern, 'cultural' turn of the 1980s and 1990s had singularly failed to do.

My own particular interest in empire, however, lay primarily in the dynamics of the imperial encounter. I was interested in both how Indigenous peoples responded to the imperial presence, and I was interested most of all in how the imperial presence, on the ground, responded to Indigenous peoples. The result was a book – *Making Empire* – that represented both a homecoming and a new beginning. It was a homecoming in the sense that it marked a return to the area of history that first made me want to be an historian. It was a new beginning in the sense that it opened up a whole new field that I continue to explore and research. But it was a beginning that could only have been reached after my apprenticeship as a social and labour historian of modern Britain.

Notes

1 15 January 2009. Joanna Lewis was referring to *An Imperial War and the British Working Class, 1899–1902* (London, 1972).

2 It is important to note that Robinson later published a path-breaking article about the importance of non-European intermediaries to the imperial project. See Ronald Robinson, 'Non European Foundations of European Imperialism: Sketch for a Theory of Collaboration', in Roger Owen and Bob Sutcliffe, eds, *Studies in the Theory of Imperialism* (London: Longman, 1972), pp. 117–41.

3 On the problem of Western and colonial conceptions continuing to shape subaltern history see Dipesh Chakrabarty, *Provincializing Europe: Postcolonial Thought and Historical Difference* (Princeton: Princeton University Press, 2000). Of course, subaltern studies wrote against nationalist elitism of Indian historiography as well as the colonial elitism of the Raj. See Ranajit Guha, 'On Some Aspects of the Historiography of Colonial India', in Ranajit Guha, ed., *Subaltern Studies, I: Writings of South Asian History and Society* (Delhi: Oxford University Press, 1982), p. 1.

4 Published by Manchester University Press and still ongoing.

5 Labour Party, *Annual Conference Report, 1963* (London, 1963), pp. 139–40.

6 In his *Making of the English Working Class* (Harmondsworth: Penguin Books, 1968), p. 13.

5

Inside/Outside: A Non-native Caribbeanist's Journey

Bridget Brereton
b. 1946

I am a child of empire. I was born in Madras (Chennai) in May 1946, and have a scrawny, tattered birth certificate, issued by the Madras City Corporation on cheap wartime paper and indicating my caste as 'European', to prove it.

My father's family had links to the Raj (admittedly rather low-level ones, no ICS members there) going back to Edwardian times. His mother, Susan Cruttwell née Gibb, my much-loved Scottish grandmother, sailed to India to join her older, married sister as part of the fishing fleet around 1908. Her catch was assistant manager of an Assam tea plantation, and their only child, my father (Patrick Cruttwell) was born in Tezpur, Assam, in 1911.

My grandfather's health deteriorated and the family left Assam to return home to Scotland, where he died of TB in 1913. Susan was left alone to bring up her son in her parents' home in Edinburgh. Her older sister, whom I knew as an elderly lady, did much better out of the Raj: her second husband, a tea importer, became very rich; only decades later did I realize he was in fact a classic First World War profiteer. They lived lavishly during the 1920s, but apparently lost most of their loot in the 1929 crash.

These links to India probably influenced my father's decision to go to Burma (Myanmar) in the mid-1930s. He left Cambridge with a degree in English literature in 1933, not the best time to look for a job, and accepted a lecturer post at the University of Rangoon (Yangon). One of his students was Aung San, the nationalist leader and 'Father' of Burmese independence (and, of course, Aung San Suu Kyi's father). By 1941 he was a junior officer in the British/Indian Army and survived the terrible 'walk' out of Burma into India in 1942. He served in the Indian Army as an intelligence officer (he was fluent in Burmese) for the rest of the war, and my older siblings and myself were born in various cities: Mussoorie, Delhi and Madras. Soon after my birth, the family was shipped to Britain and my father resumed civilian life as a lecturer at the new University of Exeter.

Because my mother (a German Jewish refugee from the Nazis) died when I was very young, my sister and I spent our early childhood (1948–55) with our paternal grandmother, a genteel but cash-poor Edinburgh lady. Granny's house, a Victorian semi-detached in a pleasant suburb on the Firth of Forth, was full of Indian relics. The so-called library contained weapons and other bits and pieces from Nagaland, where the people, we were told, had been head-hunters, and other bric-a-brac from the Raj were scattered around the house. And our Aunty Cass, the widow of the war profiteer, lived with us, a different kind of Indian relic. There was also a lot of talk about long-dead relatives who had done well for (and from) the empire, such as Aunt Maud, South Africa's lady golf champion for many years, and her husband, a mining engineer in the Rand. I cannot say any of this made much impression on me. What did make an impression was the set of volumes of *Punch* (which sat next to a leather-bound, multi-volume series of the Waverley novels, a compulsory possession of self-respecting Scottish households in this era). Throughout my childhood I spent countless hours browsing *Punch*, absorbing painlessly a great deal of British social and political history in the process.

In 1955, when I was nine, my sister and I rejoined my father (who had remarried) in Exeter, and I lived there until 1963. At the Maynard School for Girls, an excellent if conventional direct grant grammar school (now of course private and fee-paying), I did my O's and A's. We studied British and (West) European history, and the empire entered into the narrative only very rarely. My 'special subject' for A-levels was medieval English monasticism, not the most useful preparation for a future Caribbeanist. I left the Maynard in 1963 fairly well informed (as school-leavers go) about British history, less so about European, and totally ignorant about anything else.

Looking back, I realize I had virtually no exposure to the post-war immigration from the former empire which was transforming Britain in the 1950s and early 1960s. My childhood Britain was Exeter and Edinburgh; I knew nothing, almost literally, about everything in-between. Exeter was certainly not a multi-racial city when I lived there, and I cannot recall a single non-white girl at the Maynard. There must have been African and Caribbean students at the university, where my father taught, but we lived a long way from the 'new' campus outside the city and rarely went there. It was a big deal when the first Indian restaurant opened in Exeter, around 1961. Birmingham and Leeds were only names to me, and even London was just a place where you changed stations and trains on the Exeter–Edinburgh journey. At the same time, by the early 1960s I had absorbed vaguely 'liberal' ideas, and do recall feeling some righteous indignation about events in southern Africa. But I do not believe I had spoken to a single black person by the time I left school.

My life was transformed in 1963: my father accepted a post as Professor of English at the Mona, Jamaica, campus of the University of the West Indies (UWI). I might have stayed in Britain with my two older siblings who both went to Cambridge; but I was only just 17, and judged to be a dreamy, not to say dopey child, hardly fit for life on my own. Gentle pressure was put on me, and I 'agreed' to go to Jamaica with the family and enrol as a history undergrad at Mona. I have never lived in the UK, other than on fairly brief visits, since.

The Mona campus of UWI opened its doors in 1948, one of several 'colonial' universities set up post-war, most of them originally affiliated to the University of London; UWI gained independent degree-granting powers in 1962, just before I entered. It was the only campus of a university set up to serve all the English-speaking Caribbean territories until 1960, then additional campuses were opened in Trinidad and Barbados, and Guyana established its own, separate university. I did a BA (History) at Mona from 1963 to 1966.

The Federation of the West Indies had been dissolved in 1962, to the lifelong dismay of many of those connected to UWI, but the federal spirit was very much alive when I studied at Mona. Just as an earlier generation of Barbadians, Jamaicans and Trinidadians discovered they were 'West Indian' in London, so did many young people born in the 1940s make the same discovery at Mona. The student body was genuinely pan-Caribbean (that is, they came from all the formerly British territories) and, as a result, quite diverse in terms of ethnicity, class and cultural orientation. The staff were a mix of West Indians, most with degrees from British universities, and 'expats', mostly but not all British. Of course, it was an exciting period for young West Indians, the majority of them of African descent: the US civil rights struggle and Black Power movements, developments in Rhodesia and South Africa, and end of empire events all over the world, shaped student thinking and, for some, activism. Closer to home, political and ethnic strife in Guyana, and the tribulations of new states, either just 'granted' independence (Jamaica, Trinidad and Tobago) or waiting for it (Barbados, Guyana), were followed closely.

The undergraduate history programme which I entered was conventional in its structure, a legacy of course of the years of affiliation to London. We studied European, United States, Latin American history – courses on Africa, India and the Far East were added after I left. There was no course specifically on Britain, but we did a fairly conventional second-year course called

'European Expansion and Imperialism', which concentrated on the British Empire and was the closest we got to African or Indian history.

But the great revelation for me (and for some of my West Indian classmates too) were the courses on Caribbean history. We were taught by some of the outstanding pioneers of Caribbean historiography: Guyanese Elsa Goveia, Jamaican Douglas Hall, St Lucian Roy Augier, Trinidadian Keith Laurence, Barbadian E. Kamau Braithwaite, and others. Goveia taught the compulsory second-year course called 'The History of the West Indies'. I still marvel at how she constructed an all-year (three semester) course from the sparse and hardly satisfactory (for the most part – excluding of course her own books) literature that existed in 1964/5 when she taught me. It is instructive to compare her course reading list, which I still have, with the ones we can draw up for similar courses today: over the last fifty years there has been a genuine explosion in high-quality historical research and publication on the Caribbean. (Needless to say, this does not mean that today's undergrads read more than we did back in 1964/5!)

At Mona I became enthralled with the rich and dark history of the Caribbean, and was infected by the sense that this was still a new and under-researched territory for the student who was relatively free of the baggage carried by older, mostly British, 'imperial' historians. If I had done graduate work at a British university after leaving UWI in 1966, I think I might well have chosen a Caribbean topic. But, as is surely the case for many of us (especially women?), it was a development in another sphere of my life which committed me to a Caribbeanist path.

In 1966, soon after graduating, I married a classmate, Trinidadian Ashton Brereton, and went with him to his country – where I have lived ever since. We soon departed, however, for Canada; we both undertook a one-year (actually nine months!) MA History programme at the University of Toronto. My courses were all on early modern and nineteenth-century European and British history – I must have opted against courses on Canada or the USA. My research essay was on Scottish culture during the Renaissance, which now strikes me as an odd choice, but perhaps it was due to memories of my Edinburgh childhood. At any rate, though none of my MA courses related to the Caribbean or even to the British Empire, it is no bad thing for a Caribbeanist to be solidly grounded in European/British history since 1500; and I got my first full-time teaching post at UWI on the (dubious) premise that I was qualified to teach early modern Europe.

Returning to Trinidad with our MAs in 1968, we began a family and settled down. I was in what used to be called a 'mixed' marriage (Ashton is African-Trinidadian) and we had three 'mixed-race' kids. Such marriages or unions were pretty common in Trinidad even in the 1960s, and persons who describe themselves as 'mixed' to the census-takers constitute between 20 and 25 per cent of the present-day national population. Indeed, the country is famed for the dazzling variety of ethnic mixtures to be found there, arising from the coming together (sometimes coerced, of course) of people of

African, South Asian, Chinese, European and Middle Eastern ancestry. It is hard to imagine a place that would have been more accepting of a family like ours.

I believe my marriage had a direct effect on my work as a historian in at least three ways. First, and most obviously, it brought me to Trinidad and kept me there, leading almost naturally to a teaching and research career at the local campus of UWI, my academic base for well over forty years. Second, it conferred on me a sort of outsider/insider perspective on Trinidad and Caribbean history and society. I was not born, and did not grow up, in the region, so many facets of the society instinctively known to natives remained opaque to me, or had to be painfully and partially understood through reading and conversation. But, as a member by marriage and motherhood of a large, extended Trinidadian family, I was different from the 'bird of passage' scholar who visits to do research or attend a conference but lives and works abroad. And as a UWI graduate twice over (BA and PhD), and as a long-serving staff member, I have the insider perspective of someone trained at the regional university by regional scholars and interacting day by day with colleagues and students rooted in the country and region.

Finally, though I did not think of this at the time, I suspect that my personal and family situation helped to push me towards social history, with a special interest in race relations. I had developed an interest in social history – not the dominant genre yet in the early 1960s, at least not in the English-speaking world – while at Mona, inspired especially by Goveia whose best known book, *Slave Society in the British Leeward Islands*, appeared when I was an undergrad there. My MA courses at Toronto were heavy on social history too. But I believe that my efforts to adjust to life in a multi-racial, postcolonial society, and to form family and professional relationships with people who did not look (or speak!) like me, also led me to the exploration of social and race relations in the history of my adopted country.

The other factor which helped me to pin down my doctoral research, which I began at the St Augustine (Trinidad) campus of UWI in 1969, was a wonderful book by British historian Donald Wood, *Trinidad in Transition: The Years after Slavery* (1968). This social history of Trinidad between 1834 and 1870, with a focus on race relations after the end of slavery, was the sort of thing that I wanted to do. I took up the story where he ended, and quite consciously modelled my thesis on his book. I came to know Donald very well; he was a kind and generous mentor to me, and many other Caribbean historians, helping and advising me until his death. Much later, I co-edited a volume in his honour, *The Colonial Caribbean in Transition* (1999). My thesis, with the dull title 'A Social History of Trinidad, 1870–1900' (1973), was revised and published as *Race Relations in Colonial Trinidad, 1870–1900* in 1979.

The choice for social history represented in part a conscious turning away from the main interests of 'imperial' history as it was in the 1950s and

1960s, at least when applied to the English-speaking West Indies, with its focus on modes of colonial government, and its overall bias towards the doings of Europeans (Dead White Males) in the Caribbean. Social history tends to look inwards, to explore the inner dynamics of a society, while traditional imperial history was generally more interested in policy-making at the metropolitan centre and in comparative colonial governance. There was also, to a lesser extent, a turning away from economic history, which had been the focus of earlier, pioneer historians of the Caribbean, such as Eric Williams and Douglas Hall, who had concentrated on the plantations and trade before and after the abolition of slavery. So while the turn to social history was, of course, part of a wider trend in the discipline in the 1960s and 1970s, for those from the former colonies it also represented a postcolonial rejection of imperial history as it then was. I certainly did not (and do not) consider myself a historian of the British Empire, but as a student of the social evolution of the Caribbean.

Interestingly, the doctoral thesis was researched entirely with locally held sources – and long before the internet, obviously. I did not make the almost obligatory trip to the PRO in London; my supervisors were, I think, keen to show that a decent doctoral thesis could be produced from materials in local or regional archives and libraries. We were still at the start of doctoral research at UWI: I was the first person to get a PhD in the humanities or social sciences at the St Augustine campus. But to revise it for book publication, I did make that trek. In the mid-1970s Kew was still a dream, and I joined other scholars over two summers in the cramped and hot reading room of the section of the PRO housed on Portugal Street, which older empire historians will recall. I added material derived from the Colonial Office correspondence and similar documents for the book.

My academic base remained the St Augustine (Trinidad) campus of UWI, where I remained until retirement, except for the usual sabbaticals (few indeed) and research trips abroad. My research interests and writings were shaped partly by my university teaching, partly by my active involvement in the Association of Caribbean Historians which linked together academics and others based throughout the region and elsewhere, partly by the UWI tradition of historians becoming engaged in public history and helping to improve the way the subject was taught in the secondary schools.

One focus was the development of a national historiography for my adopted country. With a colleague, I designed and taught for many years a final-year undergrad course on the history of Trinidad and Tobago, and I have supervised many research papers and dissertations on aspects of the nation's history. This led me to publish in 1981 (it has been frequently re-issued since) *A History of Modern Trinidad, 1783–1962*, which has become something of a standard text. A general work which synthesized other people's research, as well as my own, and was written in an accessible style without scholarly apparatus, the book was and is much used by advanced secondary school pupils and students in tertiary institutions.

This book, published less than twenty years after national independence (1962), was clearly conceived and written in the 'nation-building' mode. In this it was not very different from its predecessor, Eric Williams' *History of the People of Trinidad and Tobago* (1962) – though less tendentious, less erratic and less powerfully written. I took the narrative up to independence, and ended with this sentence: 'These were the responsibilities and the opportunities that accompanied the possession of power, for Trinidad and Tobago had, at last, taken control of the destinies of their people.' Not a sentence I can imagine writing in more recent times!

My interest in the nation's history has continued, and I have contributed to the production of a respectable national historiography through publications and through supervision of graduate theses. More recently, I have become interested in the evolution of narratives – ethnic, class, regional – about the nation's past, and I have studied how they evolve and change, their mutual contestations, and the roles they perform. This work has taken me a good distance away from the linear kind of national narrative which dominated my 1981 book.

I have always been interested in the social history of the English-speaking Caribbean as a whole, especially after the abolition of slavery there in the 1830s, and more generally throughout the region (Spanish, French and Dutch speaking). In this I was encouraged by the Association of Caribbean Historians, a 'pan-Caribbean' body which has held annual conferences since 1969, and by my involvement in the UNESCO *General History of the Caribbean* (I edited Volume V, *The Caribbean in the Twentieth Century*, and contributed chapters to Volume IV, *The Long Nineteenth Century*, and Volume VI, *Methodology and Historiography of the Caribbean*). Chronologically, I have focused on the hundred years after the abolition of slavery in the British Caribbean (1834–8), a period bounded by emancipation at one end, and the labour protests of the 1930s at the other. In the 1960s and even the 1970s, this was something of a 'dark age' in Caribbean historiography: scholars had concentrated on the slavery era, participating in the 'comparative slave systems of the Americas' debates, or on the period of decolonization which began in the late 1930s or after the Second World War. But this is far from the case today; there has been an explosion of research and publications on this period, especially but not only on the British Caribbean, and I have made a modest contribution to this.

Much, in fact most, of this work has taken the 'new' social history approach, with a turn to cultural history more recently, reflecting trends in the discipline as a whole. I have been interested in, and influenced by, postcolonial theory, cultural studies and postmodernist analysis, but never enthralled, like many from the world of English-speaking academia. And, like other contributors to this volume, I have little sympathy for the dense theoretical excursions and arcane jargon which has made some of this kind of scholarship accessible only to the initiated. This may be partly because I have always been involved in writing for the general reader and for students.

Caribbean historiography has been a continuing interest for me. It is inspiring to contemplate how it has developed over the last fifty years, since Elsa Goveia heroically constructed a course on the region's history, from scanty materials, at UWI in 1964/5. I have written extensively on these developments, especially those relating to the century after emancipation in the British Caribbean.

When I published my first two books, in 1979 and 1981, I had barely been touched by ideas about women and gender in history, both of which are largely missing in those works. But I became involved in teaching course modules in the new field of 'Women's Studies' – new to UWI, at any rate – and then I designed and taught for many years a final-year undergrad course called 'Women and Gender in the History of the Caribbean'. This course tried to combine, not always successfully, the 'women's history' and the 'gender history' approaches. Over the years I have also supervised several graduate research papers and theses on this topic, as it became increasingly popular in the 1990s and beyond. Though I do not consider myself primarily as a gender historian, I have contributed somewhat to research and publications on gender in Caribbean history, a field which, of course, is a conspicuous aspect of the 'new' imperial history overall.

UWI is a public university, mainly funded by regional taxpayers who are mostly, by Western standards, poor. Moreover, until fairly recently, it was the only provider of tertiary education in Trinidad and Tobago (there are now two other public degree-granting institutions and several private ones offering 'franchised' degree programmes). UWI academics are rightly seen as a public resource in the region. As a result, academic staff have always been more directly involved in public service of many different kinds than is common in Western universities (I realize that this is a very broad generalization!).

For me, this has taken three main forms. First, I have been involved in efforts to improve and update the teaching of history in the nation's, and region's, secondary schools. Along with many other UWI colleagues, I have worked with the Caribbean Examinations Council (CXC) in designing, updating and moderating (never marking, thankfully) their syllabuses and examination papers in history at both O and A Levels. The CXC replaced the English examination boards which set and marked the papers of Caribbean school children up to the late 1970s, an important aspect of cultural and educational decolonization. I have been a resource person for the History Teachers' Association of Trinidad and Tobago during its on and off periods of activity. And I have written two school texts, one on a theme or module in the CXC history syllabus at O-Level, one on the history of Trinidad and Tobago for pupils in the first three forms of secondary school. My general history of the nation, first published in 1981, is much used by advanced secondary school kids and university students, though it was not written as a school text. In general, in the Caribbean as elsewhere, producing new school texts and syllabuses is an obvious aspect of decolonization in postcolonial societies.

Second, I have undertaken a few 'public service' projects for the national government or state entities. The most interesting was to chair a committee (2006/7) to consider whether the nation's highest award, the Trinity Cross, should be renamed, and the medal redesigned. Columbus had named Trinidad after the Holy Trinity in 1498, and the cross, of course, is the pre-eminent Christian symbol; the medal itself was a cruciform. It was instituted as the highest award in 1969, when the nation opted out of the British honours system and created its own. At the time there was little reaction, but by the 1990s spokesmen for the important Hindu and Muslim sectors began to object to a name and design which were so obviously Christian. This exercise, which involved public consultations and many written submissions to the committee, highlighted important issues about the nation's heritage and revealed public attitudes to it, as well as wide-spread scepticism among many citizens about the value of secular symbols in a multi-religious postcolonial society. It certainly stimulated my interest in contesting national narratives after the end of formal decolonization. (The committee recommended doing away with the Trinity Cross, and in 2008 the new highest award, the Order of the Republic of Trinidad and Tobago, was awarded for the first time.)

Finally, since 2010 I have written a fortnightly column in the nation's leading daily newspaper about history – I prudently steer clear of present-day politics. I write about historical episodes, interesting but little known personages of the past, or debates and issues in our understanding of the national and regional history. Quite often I review recent books related to that history. I think of it as public education; along with other columns in the three national dailies, I believe it has helped to raise public consciousness about history and heritage in a country not generally noted for this.

I have said that I self-identify as a student of Caribbean social history rather than as a historian of the British Empire. My one foray into what was, unequivocally, empire history was my biography of John Gorrie: *Law, Justice and Empire: The Colonial Career of John Gorrie, 1829–1892* (1997). I first 'met' Gorrie when I was researching late nineteenth-century Trinidad society for my PhD. Reading the lively colonial newspapers, I was amazed at the acres of newsprint devoted to this Scottish chief justice's doings between 1886 and 1892, especially when contrasted with the very limited coverage of his predecessor. This chief justice was a vocal champion of equality before the law, a defender of the 'poor and powerless', in a colonial society just fifty years away from slavery and with indentured Indian immigration in full swing. He was obviously loathed by vested interests and elite groups, and venerated by those who spoke (wrote) on behalf of the ordinary folk. This was a maverick product of the Victorian empire, clearly, and I published an article on his career in Trinidad and Tobago (when Tobago was joined to Trinidad in 1889, Gorrie automatically became chief justice of the combined colony).

But it was obvious from the newspaper coverage in Trinidad that Gorrie had a past: in fact his posting there was his last, as he died in 1892. I thought that his biography might shed some light on the late Victorian empire, and I was encouraged to undertake this project – which took me far away from my core interest in Caribbean social history – by two of his descendants, who gave me access to family papers and helped in many other ways. Gorrie, a Scot from relatively humble origins, qualified as a Scottish advocate (lawyer) in the mid-1850s, was active in radical Edinburgh politics, then moved to London where he worked on Cobden and Bright's newspaper. His interest in colonial affairs was sparked when he went to Jamaica as legal counsel for the victims of the reprisals which followed the Morant Bay Rebellion in 1865. He served as a puisne judge or chief justice in Mauritius, Fiji, the Leeward Islands and Trinidad between 1869 and 1892. In each place, Gorrie created controversy through his outspoken views about equal access to and treatment in the colonial courts, and his vocal engagement with many other aspects of colonial social and political life.

All this, to my advantage, created a huge paper trail, in addition to family documents and his own writings. I read the voluminous Colonial Office records for each of the colonies where he served (now housed in the splendors of Kew), studying his own long and frequent memoranda and letters, endless complaints from people or groups he had insulted or riled, and the minutes of the Colonial Office men as they puzzled over what to do with their troublesome judge. I spent happy days in the Colindale Newspaper Library (now closed) reading the newspapers from Jamaica, Mauritius, Fiji, Antigua, Dominica and St Kitts for the periods of his sojourns there. The outcome was a full-length biography of a man who moved across the empire and who struggled, ultimately unsuccessfully, to use the colonial courts to give practical reality to the doctrine of trusteeship.

I do not think many people read my book, but it had an afterlife: in 2012, John McLaren, who had just published a fine book on 'maverick' jurists in the nineteenth-century empire and had therefore encountered Gorrie, invited me to the first Conference on the Legal Histories of the British Empire in Singapore. I went and presented a paper on Gorrie, which was subsequently published in the book of the same title which emerged from the conference (2014).

Gorrie was a Scot who moved through the Victorian empire and spent his last years serving the (lost) cause of equality and justice in the courts of Trinidad and Tobago. I am a Scot (on my father's side at least) who has lived for nearly fifty years in postcolonial Trinidad and Tobago. It was imperial, or ex-imperial, connections which brought me, first to Jamaica and then to Trinidad, soon after these two Caribbean nations became independent. My whole personal and academic life has been shaped by the postcolonial experience. My academic base has been a regional university set up after the Second World War as an affiliated 'college' of London University, one of several similar institutions established at the end of empire in the decolonizing states. My academic location in a postcolonial university has brought me opportunities, and demands, not usually encountered by historians in

Western academia. My research interests have led me to explore the lives of colonized Caribbean people as they struggled to come out of slavery, indenture and the 'ordeal of free labour'. My life, like those of the people I have tried to study and write about, has been profoundly shaped by empire and its end.

6

With and Against the Grain

Catherine Hall
b. 1946

With hindsight it seems given in the stars that I would become an historian of race and empire. In life the route was rather more rocky.

I was born into a radical nonconformist family in 1946 – the third, and last, child of my father John Barrett, a Baptist minister, and my mother Gladys, nee Hipkin. My father was at that time the minister of a large and flourishing Baptist church in Kettering, a Northamptonshire boot and shoe town in the East Midlands of England. My parents had been there throughout the war, a time when clergymen and their families could play a very significant part in holding together communities riven with fear and anxiety, and they were rooted in that small provincial world. Many of the congregation were deeply devoted to my parents and provided a warm and loving, albeit somewhat narrow, context for us.

Fuller Baptist Church, where my father ministered, was first established in 1696 and was steeped in a particular history. The handsome building that now stands in the centre of the town, with its classic late eighteenth-century dissenting architecture, was named after Andrew Fuller, the minister of the chapel from 1782 and the first secretary of the Baptist Missionary Society (BMS). The idea of missionary work, saving distant 'heathens', had its roots in the evangelical revival of the late eighteenth century, that re-emergence of vital, serious or real Christianity, in contrast with the nominal forms that had come to dominate orthodox religious practice. The Baptists, formed in the crucible of radical Protestantism in the seventeenth century, and surviving as a small dissenting sect in the decades that followed, enjoyed a great revival from the 1780s. Their distinctive belief in the centrality of the individual experience of faith was expressed in their practice of adult baptism. For evangelicals, from the likes of Anglicans such as William Wilberforce to poorer Baptist congregations, the key struggle of the 1790s, in the wake of the French Revolution and English radicalism was for hearts and minds. The nation had become warm in politics, but 'cold in religion'.[1] Heathens at home and abroad must be won for Christ, and an army was needed if this work was to be done. William Carey, a shoemaker and Baptist preacher, inspired others with his belief that Christians must not confine their mission to home but should take it to other parts of the world. 'Our own countrymen have the means of grace', he argued, but the case was widely different for those 'who have no Bible, no written language, . . . no ministers, no good civil government, nor any of those advantages which we have.'[2] Inspired by this appeal a small group of Baptist ministers met in Kettering in 1792 and decided to 'act together in society for the purpose of propagating the gospel among the heathen'.[3] The BMS was the first of the missionary societies established and its initial recruits, including Carey, set up a mission in India. Two decades later men were sent to Jamaica.

Kettering was proud of its missionary history and Fuller Church maintained that tradition, welcoming missionaries on furlough and raising money for the cause. It was particularly proud of its connections with William Knibb, one-time member of the congregation, who was to become a central figure in the struggle for emancipation in Jamaica. Knibb was born in Kettering in 1803. He attended the town's grammar school, and Sunday School at the chapel. In 1816 he was apprenticed, along with his brother Thomas, to J. G. Fuller, the brother of Andrew Fuller, whose business was in Bristol. The two brothers became members of the Broadmead Baptist chapel and Thomas decided in 1822 to become a missionary. In the wake of the revival of anti-slavery sentiment he was sent to Jamaica and established himself as a schoolmaster in Kingston. On his death a year later William chose to take his place and sailed for the island together with his wife Mary. He was deeply shocked by Jamaica, 'the land of sin, disease and death', and soon, despite the political conservatism of the BMS and their instructions to eschew politics and stick exclusively to religious matters, he was heavily engaged in the struggles between the white plantocracy and the enslaved, appalled by the attempts to block access to Christian preaching and teaching. He was ashamed by the conduct of 'the white population' and the atrocities that he daily observed. They 'are worse, far worse, than the victims of their injustice', he wrote.[4] Knibb became a champion of freedom. He was hated by the plantocracy who blamed the Baptist missionaries for what they construed as their incitement to the rebellion that exploded on the island in 1831. Sam Sharpe's rebellion, as it came to be known, was to be a major factor in the imperial government's decision to abolish slavery in 1834. Knibb was celebrated by the emancipated and by his home town. So gratified was Kettering by the connection with Knibb that the arms of the borough depict the figure of a freed man with a broken chain, symbolizing the contribution he had made to the proud moment of abolition. Knibb died in 1845, having established a large network of chapels and schools on the island, including the free village of Kettering on the north coast, the funding for which came substantially from its namesake. He saw himself as the father and pastor of 'his' people, but unlike many of his white brethren he was deeply committed to the establishment of black political rights and envisaged a new Jamaica in which black Britons would play their proper part.[5]

My family left Kettering in 1949 and moved to Leeds for my father had been appointed as the Superintendent of the north-eastern area of the Baptist Union. Leeds, a thriving northern city with its history linked to the industrial revolution and a proud civic presence, was a very different place from the modest, predominantly lower middle-class and working-class town they had left. But the missionary connections were never far away, whether through missionary friends visiting our home, the men and women who featured in the stories we were told of Christian heroism, or the hymns we sang. My father no longer had his 'own' church, but my sister and I were obliged, together with our mother, to attend our local Baptist Church, South Parade, regularly. This was a dispiriting experience for us, both as young children and adolescents. The local minister was no match for my father's powerful preaching, his message of radical nonconformity and equality. The saving grace of those Sunday mornings was the hymns – when we could at least sing our hearts out, loving the tunes, if not fully aware of what we were singing. One of our favourites was 'From Greenland's Icy Mountains'. . .

From Greenland's icy mountains, from India's coral strand;
Where Afric's sunny fountains roll down their golden sand:
From many an ancient river, from many a palmy plain,
They call us to deliver their land from error's chain.

What though the spicy breezes blow soft o'er Ceylon's isle;
Though every prospect pleases, and only man is vile?
In vain with lavish kindness the gifts of God are strown;
The heathen in his blindness bows down to wood and stone.

Shall we, whose souls are lighted with wisdom from on high,
Shall we to those benighted the lamp of life deny?
Salvation! O salvation! The joyful sound proclaim,
Till earth's remotest nation has learned Messiah's Name.

Little did we know that we were singing the words of Reginald Heber, first Bishop of India, who wrote this in 1819, shortly before he left for India where he was to write a journal of his travels, later to be published, which challenged the assumption that white skin was superior to brown.[6] Heber did not doubt, however, that Greenland, India and Africa were places of 'error', unlike Britain, nor that 'we' were called to deliver 'them' from blind worship of wood and stone, nor that 'our' souls were lighted with 'wisdom from on high' and that 'our' task was to rescue the heathen from his foolish ways. Such sentiments were indeed the assumptions of many missionary hymns and tracts. But the missionary movement was founded on the tension between universalism, one family in God, and difference, 'the heathens'. 'There is neither Jew and Greek, there is neither male nor female for ye are all one in Christ Jesus' St Paul had declared, but the contested meanings of that injunction, whether in relation to race, gender or ethnicity, have generated centuries of discord in churches and chapels.

Visiting missionaries, especially from India and China, were only one aspect of my family's connections with empire and the wider world. There were the African students from the university who were entertained to meals and invited for Christmas, the regular collections we made for refugees, the small concerts we held at home to raise money for 'good causes'. Our parents brought us up to recognize 'others' and to have a sense of our privileged place. They were committed Labour voters and we grew up with the daily news on the BBC, a regular diet of newspapers and the weekly *New Statesman*. The house was full of books – all the classics and lots of history, ranging from Macaulay and G. M. Trevelyan to *Our Island Story* and *1066 and All That*. Both parents were the first generation in their families to go into higher education. My father, an illegitimate child, had been adopted into a working-class family, went to work in a chocolate factory when he left elementary school, managed to teach himself shorthand and typing in his spare time, and got a job as a clerk on the railways at Euston. He started to attend Upper Holloway Baptist Church where the inspirational preacher, the Reverend Sydney Morris, became his mentor. He was encouraged to enter the ministry and went to Rawdon College, followed by Mansfield College in Oxford. There he met my mother, the daughter of a family who had been millers in Peterborough for generations, who had won a scholarship to Somerville College in 1927 to study history. She completed a DPhil on the civil war in seventeenth-century England but then married my father in 1932 and gave up any idea of being a professional historian: to be a minister's wife was a full-time vocation. Education was critical to both my parents, opening up possibilities in life, and they worked hard to give those opportunities to their children.

History was always my favourite subject at school – but it was British history that captured my imagination. In truth, I think we studied little else. My mother's love of history meant that our family outings had a strong historical bias – castles, abbeys, battlefields and royal palaces, walking on the walls of York or attending the Mystery Plays, Hadrian's Wall, going down the shaft in Leeds City Museum's reconstructed coal mine, even a holiday in France with a memorable visit to Chartres Cathedral – innumerable different ways of imagining the lives people had led in the past. Then there were the joys of historical novels – Rosemary Sutcliffe, Jean Plaidy and Maurice Druon filled my imagination with Roman soldiers, kings and courts, the 'common people', Roundheads and Cavaliers. A weekly visit to the local library was a vital part of life. My mother admired Oliver Cromwell for his staunch republicanism: I still have the portrait of him which had hung in her room in Oxford, though little did I know then that it was on his watch that Jamaica was conquered in 1655. Margaret Mitchell's *Gone with the Wind* was probably my first engagement with the American South, and the screening of it at our local cinema 'The Lounge' a memorable experience as we swooned over Clark Gable as Rhett Butler and the gorgeous Vivien Leigh as Scarlett O'Hara. (Years later my husband Stuart would enact scenes of it for me – Southern accent intact!) It's hard to know now what I made of the racism – probably not much – despite our household being early supporters of the anti-apartheid movement which was launched in Britain in 1959, shortly before the Sharpeville massacre. There were plenty of other echoes of empire in the 1950s – the 'Mau Mau' uprising in Kenya with the scary press representations of African fighters, never of British brutality, the Pathé news reels at the cinema, providing a particular kind of window on the decolonizing world. I was ten when the Suez crisis hit and have strong memories of my parents' anxiously following the news, soon to be followed by the Soviet invasion of Hungary that October, with its repercussions on the British left. My mother was active in the United Nations Association, then a serious organization with hopes of challenging the binaries of the Cold War and contributing to the development of a more understanding world. Some of her fellow members were in the Communist Party, and were profoundly disturbed by the events in Hungary. Indeed, Leeds had an active New Left group – but at that time I had no idea of this. Then there were the Indian and Chinese restaurants opening in Leeds in the late 1950s, such exciting and different tastes, and the West Indian students arriving to study at Leeds University, making friendships with the girls at our school, Leeds Girls High, just along the road from the university. These were the first intimations of what was to be a transformation of the city's population and culture, as South Asian and West Indian settlement expanded apace.

My father's Christianity was central to his life and I flirted with Young Christians as an adolescent but was soon much more attracted to the radical political aspects of my parents' beliefs. In the Cold War of the late 1950s the shadow of the bomb was all too present and the Campaign for Nuclear Disarmament (CND), 'Ban the Bomb', was formed in 1957. I joined the youth organization, along with the Young Socialists, and vividly remember the Cuban Missile Crisis, the stand-off between the Americans and the Soviet Union in 1962, a moment of real fear. On the Aldermaston march of Easter 1962, the CND march from the Atomic Weapons Research Establishment to Trafalgar Square, I first met my husband-to-be, Stuart Hall, and by the summer of 1963, when my parents had moved to London and I was on my way to university, I was encountering the left politics of the metropolis.

In 1964 Stuart and I got married and I moved with him to Birmingham. Being a mixed-race couple in the city at that time was a challenging experience. A year later we spent some time in Jamaica and, experiencing for the first time a majority black society, I learned something of what it meant to be white, something too of the complex racial hierarchies of the Anglophone Caribbean and the persisting structural inequalities and psychic traumas that were associated with colonialism. 'It is a very charged and difficult moment', wrote James Baldwin, when the white man confronts his own whiteness and 'loses the jewel of his naivete'. Whiteness carries with it authority and power, the legacy of having 'made the modern world, of never being strangers anywhere in the world'.[7] In Jamaica I had to experience myself as white, meeting hostility precisely because of that, being seen as one of 'them', the colonizers who had finally been expelled, being stereotyped by others in just the way that black people were stereotyped by 'us'. But the return to Birmingham meant once again being able to walk the streets, secure at least in my whiteness.

The move to Birmingham had brought the unexpected discovery of the pleasures of medieval history. Rodney Hilton, one of the famed group of Marxist historians who had determined in the post-war period to challenge the Whig orthodoxies of progress and toleration and write histories of England focused on questions of class and revolution, was my inspirational tutor. My decision to do a PhD in medieval history, however, did not work out. By 1968 not only was I heavily involved in student politics but I had my first child – an event which turned my life upside down. The first women's liberation group in Birmingham started meeting the following year. The women's movement gave me a new identity, as a feminist, more able to articulate the inchoate dissatisfactions with left politics, and opening up innumerable questions about women and their forgotten histories. I knew about what was going on in the world and the erstwhile empire – I was in the city when Enoch Powell made his infamous 'Rivers of Blood' speech, went on anti-Vietnam demonstrations, followed the fortunes of the civil rights and the anti-apartheid movements, was horrified by the Birmingham pub bombings of 1974, by Bloody Sunday and the conflicts in Northern Ireland, admired what Michael Manley tried to do in Jamaica and how that project was destroyed – but my political energies went into feminism and feminist history. While Stuart was thinking about a new moment in race politics and had embarked on the collective work that was eventually to become *Policing the Crisis*, I was deeply preoccupied with the women's movement, motherhood, childcare and what kind of history it might now be possible to discover, teach and write.

The pressing questions for me during the 1970s and early 1980s centred on family and class. How might taking gender as a key axis of social structure and historical change alter the established narratives of British domestic history? I was profoundly influenced, like so many of my generation, by E. P. Thompson's *Making of the English Working Class*, published just as I went to university and exemplifying a version of Marxism which critiqued economic determinism and took culture seriously. Yet women were marginal to Thompson's story and gender, unsurprisingly, a category he had not encountered. The task of thinking gender and class *together*, trying to understand how, as we put it, gender was always classed and class always gendered, was the task that Leonore Davidoff and I set ourselves, exploring this issue through case studies of middle-class families in East Anglia and Birmingham. Class as an economic, social and cultural formation was at the heart of our work: the family and the hidden investment of women, we insisted, were central to the development of modern Britain with its capitalist economy, and constructions of masculinity and femininity needed to be understood as not only historically specific, but also fundamental to social, political and economic organization. Like every piece of historical work *Family Fortunes* can only be understood as of its moment. It was inspired by the analytic possibilities that were enabled by the feminist naming of the category of gender and by the engagement with class that was central to the Marxist feminism which had been formative for me and the Weberian sociology that was an important aspect of Leonore's thinking.

In 1987 *Family Fortunes* was finished. I was teaching at the University of East London and heavily involved with the production of the journal *Feminist Review.* The triumph of Thatcherism had meant a very significant move to the right and a long-term crisis for labourism; this was the emergence of neo-liberalism. At the same time Britain was experiencing its own postcolonial moment. While it became clear to the newly independent nations that decolonization had not resulted in total freedom, the impact of the end of empire was being felt in metropolitan society. The presence of settled Afro-Caribbean and South Asian peoples, clearly not going home and insisting that 'we are here because you were there' had profoundly disturbed sections of the white British population. Race politics were volatile, with dangerous eruptions at both the national and the local level. Second generation black Britons were asking whether it was possible to be black and British? Was Englishness, in particular, essentially white? The concept of sisterhood came under fire as black women insisted on the importance of recognizing difference and argued that the white feminist version of sisterhood was exclusive to white women, who only accepted sisters on their own terms. Questions about the imagined unity of women had divided the women's movement for some time – divisions over sexuality, class, race and ethnicity were nothing new. Indeed the last national conference of the women's movement took place in Birmingham in 1978 and broke up in disarray over those issues. But in the early 1980s the critiques of black feminists came home to roost on *Feminist Review.* In 1984 a special issue of the journal, *Many Voices, One Chant: Black Feminist Perspectives*, was produced by a group of black feminists. They were insistent that this should not be a token exercise and that there was an 'ongoing need for white women to take note of and act upon Black feminist critiques of the content and form of contemporary British feminism'.[8] A white Eurocentric Western feminism had attempted to establish itself as the only legitimate feminism, they maintained; this feminism did not speak to the experiences of black women and there was little recognition of the ways in which the gains of white women were made at the expense of black women. British feminist history was far from immune to this criticism. White women historians suffered amnesia and ignored the lives of black women, they argued, effectively reproducing a form of imperial history.[9]

This was a biting political and intellectual critique. But it took a more personal confrontation to force upon me the need to not just think differently, but be different. The guest editors of *Many Voices, One Chant: Black Feminist Perspectives* had hoped that their issue would open up *Feminist Review* to a proper recognition of racist practices as 'ordinary', simply a part of commonsense British culture.[10] Far from this happening, however, three of the group of black women who had agreed to join the editorial collective left, frustrated by the lack of will to tackle the issues they had individually and collectively raised, about the everyday ways we behaved, about whose voices counted, about which names we referred to, about what work we knew. Their most pressing question was: who is 'we'? Their intervention inspired a sustained confrontation with the working practices of the journal and the ways in which they continued to reflect raced assumptions. This was a thorny and difficult set of conversations over a long period of time. Putting 'our house' in order meant leaving old forms of feminism behind.[11] This engagement made me re-think the work I was doing, and re-think what it meant to be white and English. It was the direct nature of the political challenge to us as women who saw ourselves as progressive, anti-racist, feminist, that complemented the psychic work of dislodging the common sense assumptions which had underpinned both the forms of Christian humanism that I had grown up with and the forms of white feminism that had been in some respects so enabling – forging in that process, on my part, a new urgency to unpick aspects of the history of Britain and empire. This meant working both with and against the grain – not abandoning past understandings but reordering them, aware of the dangers of amnesia and denial, the English 'blind eye'.

Civilising Subjects was the book which came out of that, an exploration of the long and unequal connection between England and Jamaica and of the ways in which the identity of colonizer was one of the constitutive outsides of Englishness. The project mirrored my own troubled encounters with myself as English. The initial question came from a visit to Jamaica in 1988. Meandering along the north coast road of the island from Ocho Rios to Falmouth we came to the small village of Kettering, with its Baptist church. Why, I wondered, was this place called Kettering? And why did the Baptist church have pride of place? These were questions which took me on a long journey, tying up some of the threads of my own life while exploring the lives of others. I started with Kettering, with William Knibb and the Baptist Missionary Society, investigating the mission to Jamaica and the tensions and contradictions at the heart of the project of 'civilizing subjects'. 'We' would save 'them' and in the process make ourselves; men who were 'nobodies' in England could become 'somebodies' in Jamaica, on account of the influence they had won over large numbers of enslaved men and women whose hopes and aspirations for freedom they were able to speak to, and thought they could articulate. Those missionaries aspired to make new black Christian subjects, men and women in their own image, who would live familial, domesticated and industrious lives under the watchful eyes of their pastors. Missionary families were to serve as a model of how to live, the men would take on the public roles, the women be supportive wives and mothers. But this was never an uncomplicated endeavour – some of the missionaries, like Knibb, were open to the radical possibilities of freedom, able to change themselves and believe in a society that would be more egalitarian, dominated by black voters. Others remained locked in the assumption that they knew best. Something of the contradictory elements within missionary endeavours is captured in the adoption by Marcus Garvey's United Negro Improvement Association, the aim of which was to unite all negro peoples across the world and establish their own country and government, with the missionary hymn 'From Greenland's Icy Mountains' as its anthem. It was to be sung at the beginning and end of every meeting, evoking the unity of black people.

If Kettering England and Kettering Jamaica were two of the places which provided the geographical framework for this piece of work, the third was Birmingham: this was a history which spanned metropole and colony and was embedded in a notion of the grammar of difference, whether organized by class, gender, race or ethnicity. I was drawing on many other critics of colonialism, from the classic formulations of Edward Said to Ann Laura Stoler and Frederick Cooper and the 'new imperial histories' that began to appear from the early 1990s. The method of the case study was one I had learned from the work on *Family Fortunes*, and the preoccupation with gender and family remained central to the new work. But race, ethnicity and questions of national identity were now key concepts, again reflecting the political moment from which this work came, with the ending of the Cold War, the break-up of the former Soviet Union, and the re-emergence of religious and nationalist forms of belonging. Birmingham in the early nineteenth century, I discovered, a Midland town built on the metal industries, was proud of its reputation as a hotbed of reform and anti-slavery action. It represented itself as having provided the leadership for the campaign against apprenticeship, the system of unpaid labour by the so-called freed slaves, which was part of the package won by the slave-owners in 1833. Yet by the time of the rebellion at Morant Bay in Jamaica in 1865, and the passionate public debate which followed it as to the rights and wrongs of Governor Eyre's actions in suppressing that rebellion, Birmingham men and women scarcely figured as 'friends of the negro'. What had happened to those anti-slavery enthusiasts and that missionary public which had so vigorously supported the idea of a humanitarian empire? In tracking the shifts in opinion in Birmingham between the 1820s and the 1860s I began to fill out a history that had been forgotten. By the 1950s when the city became a place of settlement for large numbers of West Indians, collective memories of an earlier time when Brummies were familiar with Jamaica had been completely erased.

Whiteness and Englishness had become my objects of study. The meanings of civilization and freedom, who were the civilized and who were those to be civilized, and whose definitions of freedom ruled, when and where? But in focusing on those who regarded themselves as most sympathetic to oppressed peoples and were often critical of official imperial policies, I had left untouched 'the establishment', the 'ruling class' and its institutions. Where did they fit in the forgotten story of the racing of Englishness? My attention turned to Macaulay, most English of English historians. Whig historians were not interested in empire was the conventional view – but was that really true? This time my interest in history was at the heart of my exploration – what part had this historian played in establishing a narrative of England that seemed to have nothing to do with race? Once again family played a crucial part – this time in exploring the psychic dynamics of Macaulay's family, his complex and ambivalent relationship with his father, his passionate love for two of his sisters, his utter despair when each of them married and he felt himself to be abandoned, his retreat into reading and writing as the only ways to save his sanity, his conviction that it was better to live with the dead than the living. Writing history became his way of keeping troubled and troubling issues at bay. His assumptions about what it meant to be English, the rule of law, the values of language and literature, a particular notion of civilization, underpinned his understanding of others, whether Irish, Indian or African peoples, the working classes, or indeed women. His grammar of difference structured his story both of nation and empire, one built on inequalities, assumed as common sense.

Toni Morrison's *Playing in the Dark* has been one of my lodestars. It was not just inspiring, it spoke very directly to me about my discipline, history, and the ways that it might be possible to re-think how British historians have encoded and evaded the issue of race. Morrison addressed how, as a black woman writer, she has had to struggle with and through a 'language that can powerfully evoke and enforce hidden signs of racial superiority, cultural hegemony, and dismissive "othering" of people and language'. Until very recently, she argued, American fiction had positioned its readers as white. She wanted to investigate, 'what that assumption has meant to the literary imagination'. 'How do embedded assumptions of racial language work', she asked, in a literary enterprise that likes to think of itself as humanistic?[12] Empire, I came to think, was central to definitions of Englishness. Race might not have been lived *inside*, in the way it was in the US where slavery was endemic, but it was lived *outside*, through empire, and that *outside* was constitutive of the *inside*. It is trying to understand that *outside/inside* that continues to haunt me.[13]

Notes

1 Reverend F. A. Cox, *History of the Baptist Missionary Society from 1792–1842*, 2 vols (London: T. Ward and Co., 1842), I, p. 2.

2 William Carey, *An Enquiry into the Obligations of Christians to use Means for the Conversion of the Heathens* (Leicester, 1792), p. 13.

3 Cox, *History*, I, p. 2.

4 John Howard Hinton, *Memoir of William Knibb, Missionary in Jamaica* (London: Houlston and Stoneman, 1847), pp. 48–9.

5 For more on Knibb and Kettering see Catherine Hall, *Civilising Subjects: Metropole and Colony in the English Imagination, 1830–1867* (Cambridge: Cambridge University Press, 2002).

6 Reginald Heber, 'From Greenland's Icy Mountains'.

7 James Baldwin, 'Stranger in the Village', 1st edn 1953, reprinted in *Notes of a Native Son* (Harmondsworth: Penguin, 1995), pp. 151–65.

8 *Feminist Review* 17 (Autumn 1984), editorial.

9 See, for example, Valerie Amos and Pratibha Parmar, 'Challenging Imperial Feminism', ibid, 3–19; Hazel V. Carby, 'White Women Listen! Black Feminism and the Boundaries of Sisterhood', in Centre for Contemporary Cultural Studies, *The Empire Strikes Back: Race and Racism in 70s Britain* (Routledge: London, 1982), p. 223.

10 Gail Lewis, 'Racialising Culture is Ordinary', in E. B. Silva and T. Bennett, eds, *Contemporary Culture and Everyday Life* (Durham: Sociology Press, 2004), pp. 111–29.

11 Editorial, *Feminist Review* 40 (2005), p. 2.

12 Toni Morrison, *Playing in the Dark: Whiteness and the Literary Imagination* (Cambridge, MA: Harvard University Press, 1992), pp. xii–xiv.

13 Most recently in the Legacies of British Slave-ownership project – see www.ucl.ac.uk/lbs – and Catherine Hall, Nicholas Draper, Keith McClelland, Katie Donington and Rachel Lang, *Legacies of British Slave-ownership: Colonial Slavery and the Formation of Victorian Britain* (Cambridge: Cambridge University Press, 2014).

7

In and Out of Empire: Old Labels and New Histories

Marilyn Lake b. 1949

I have not really thought of myself as an imperial historian. The label does not quite fit. In fact it was imperial condescension towards colonials and my own anti-imperialism that initially made me into a historian of the nation. I later re-turned (as it were) to the history of empire from work in Australian, labour and feminist history and on transnational movements for gender and racial equality that often began in Australia. Our work is always located geographically, historically, subjectively. Everyone writes from a standpoint or point of view. As the *Athenaeum* reviewer noted of Charles Pearson's *magnum opus*, *National Life and Character: A Forecast*, in 1893: 'His view in not purely or mainly European . . . The reader can indeed discern that Mr Pearson's point of view is not London or Paris, but Melbourne. He regards the march of affairs from the Australian point of view, and next to Australia what he seems to see most clearly is the growth of Chinese power.'[1]

For the last thirty years or so – with breaks in Stockholm and Harvard, Sydney and the Australian National University – Melbourne has also provided my point of view on the march of affairs. And more than a century after Pearson wrote, one of the things Australians again see most clearly is the growth of Chinese power. China has long been Australia's top trading partner. Its market for minerals has been crucially important in sustaining our standard of living. Then in 2009, China became our biggest source of migrants, pushing the United Kingdom into third place after India. It is now commonplace to speak of our region as the 'Asian Pacific' and to note that, felicitously, we live in the 'Asian Century'. China has become a major holiday destination, while hundreds of thousands of Australians live and work in that large and diverse country.

This changing present has, not surprisingly, transformed our understanding of the past, as we have looked anew at the long history of Australian/Chinese relations dating back to the 1850s, when 20 per cent of new arrivals came from China and Melbourne became one of the world's leading Chinatowns along with San Francisco. My own recent work has focused on the political dynamics of encounters between the British and Qing empires, Greater Britain and Greater China, in the nineteenth-century Australian colonies, encounters that gave rise, amongst other things, to early claims for 'common human rights' on the part of Chinese-Australians as well as the 'White Australia Policy' as an expression of self-government, that sought to restrict Chinese immigration. In the course of such conflicts around the Pacific, national sovereignty came to be defined globally in terms of border control, as Adam McKeown has noted.[2]

My interest in Chinese/Australian history is also personal: my husband's first cousins trace their family tree back to Chinese who migrated to Victoria in the 1860s; three of our small grandchildren are part-Chinese, their other grandfather a Chinese/Malaysian Colombo Plan student who came to study in Australia in the 1950s. The Asian family connection goes further. My niece and nephew – my brother's children – are half-Japanese. He met his Japanese wife while on a diplomatic posting in Tokyo. Before then he had enjoyed that most imperial of educational awards, a Rhodes Scholarship that took him to Oxford in the late 1960s. Empire offered an escape route from the confines of home, but in training as a Japanese linguist he consciously turned his back on England and Europe.

In some ways, empire offered me an escape of sorts too, but in my case, from the confines of Australian history with its relentlessly masculinist narratives about exploration, the gold rushes, nationalism, strikes and war. I found myself following the journeys of earlier generations of feminists, whose post-suffrage activism and search for international solidarity had taken them to conferences in the United Kingdom, the United States and Europe. For feminists in London in the 1920s and 1930s, especially those campaigning for Aboriginal rights, empire was a political resource. But Australian feminists were also active in the Pan-Pacific congresses that began in Honolulu in 1928; and in Shanghai, where Eleanor Hinder used her Australian training to secure improved working conditions for women and girls working in local factories. Empire opened up a pathway into internationalism both for earlier feminists and recent scholars. Then working at Harvard in 2001 and 2002 brought more clearly into view the transnational ties between Australia and the United States, especially during the Progressive era. Imperial, international and transnational histories all in some ways transcended the nation; but in other ways they brought its distinctive history more vividly into view. Distance can sometimes lend a clarity of vision.

The empire whose legacies framed my childhood is clearer to me now than it was then. My brother, sister and I grew up in a small fishing village and farming community called Kettering located on the D'Entrecasteaux Channel in Tasmania, the southern island-state of Australia. Tasmania was named after the Dutch explorer, Abel Tasman. The Channel was named after the French explorer, Admiral Bruni D'Entrecasteaux, whose pretty birthplace in Provence celebrates its famous citizen son in monuments and plaques. Some historians have speculated counter-factually on how differently Tasmanian history would have unfolded had the island been colonized by the French.[3] All around us place names suggested the existence of larger worlds, but not local Indigenous ones. The original Kettering in Northamptonshire, England – dating from the tenth century – lies about 80 miles north of London. Later I heard that there was another Kettering in the United States and yet a fourth in Jamaica – such different sites of empire joined by a common name remind us of our linked, if very different imperial histories.

My first school was Kettering state school, which housed six grades and two teachers in one room warmed by an open fire, from whose hob hot cocoa was dispensed to ward off the chill of the southern latitudes. After a year, I graduated, aged six to the new modern 'Area School' in the neighbouring town of Woodbridge. My siblings and I attended excellent state schools taught by first rate teachers and we felt sorry, if we ever thought about it, for those few children who were sent to starchy private schools with lower educational standards and who rarely progressed to university. Labour governments dominated Tasmanian politics for decades and the educational system was, as a result, well funded and progressive in character. The modern idea was equal opportunity for all. This was my sense of the world in which I grew up, but I felt compelled to check the record. My memory served me well. 'Tasmania had a long-established egalitarian tradition', wrote the historian of comprehensive education in Australia. 'The first new-style comprehensive opened at Taroona in 1957 and within a further three years Tasmania had abolished its selective academic and technical high schools.' I enroled at Taroona High School in 1961 aged twelve. One of my teachers was Henry Reynolds, who many years later would join me in co-authoring *Drawing the Global Colour Line: White Men's Countries and the International Challenge of Racial Equality*. As I mentioned, we had excellent teachers.

Though intensely proud of being twentieth-century moderns, we young Tasmanians knew that we also belonged to an older aristocratic British world, whose Tudor and Stuart history I learnt in my final year at Hobart High School, whose anthem 'God Save the Queen' we sang in public places and whose current monarch visited us from time to time, because she was, much to my adult indignation, our monarch too. I later became a speaker in the republican cause, but we lost the referendum in 1999 because of bitter division over the method to be used to elect our first President. Should she be appointed by parliament or elected by the people?

The British world also left its legacy in the convict ruins at Port Arthur, Tasmania's most famous tourist attraction and an object lesson in British tyranny and cruelty. The beautiful sandstone neo-Gothic church, set amidst manicured lawns at the entrance to this historic site was just a shell, because the last convicts had tried to burn it down. So the story went. Interestingly, when I went to visit the French equivalent on Ile des Pins in New Caledonia a couple of years ago, the site was almost impossible to find. Guided by an old survey map we walked many kilometres down an unmarked dirt road through bush full of wild pigs and roosters to find this once imposing convict establishment. The gaol had held the Communards of 1871, among hundreds of other prisoners, and was not closed until 1922. Now strangled by tropical vegetation, these convict ruins seem to be an embarrassment best forgotten by the fiercely loyal French residents, who still govern this colonial outpost, despite a long and persistent independence movement waged by the Kanaks. The abandoned convict site of New Caledonia presents a stark contrast to well publicized Port Arthur, one of Australia's best known symbols of British oppression.

Growing up in the former colony of Tasmania we did our fair share of forgetting too. Much closer to my family's farm than the famous convict ruins were traces of a settlement called 'Black Station' at nearby Oyster Cove. We swam there in the summer months, but I always assumed its name derived from the colour of the mudflats – we preferred to swim at Conningham with its gleaming white beach, which seemed more modern as well as more beautiful – but it took longer to get there and my father was always tired after a long day's work. Only much later did I become aware of the role of 'Black Station' as a reserve for 'the last Tasmanians', the Aborigines who had, so it seemed then, entirely disappeared.

History now tells us that in 1847, forty-seven Tasmanian Aborigines had been transferred from incarceration at Wybalenna on Flinders Island to this former convict settlement at Oyster Cove, where they pined away until the 1870s, when it was closed and the last survivor, Truganini, was moved to Hobart. We learnt no Aboriginal history at school and nothing of Indigenous–settler relations. One day, though, my sister and I found an old partly burnt boomerang in the local bush and took it to school for 'show and tell', but the teacher kept it and I have no idea what happened to it.

In the 1970s, descendants of local Aboriginal people began to point out to their fellow Tasmanians and Australian academics that they still existed. In 1977, the archaeologist Rhys Jones provoked a storm of protest among mixed descent Aborigines with his film *The Last Tasmanian*, which suggested that Aborigines had completely died out with the death of Truganini. Despite the offence it caused, the film nevertheless brought home to a world audience the brutality with which the original inhabitants had been exterminated by British colonists.

In the 1980s Aboriginal memory and academic history merged in demands for acknowledgement of the violence of Indigenous–settler relations. In

1981, historian Lyndall Ryan published *Aboriginal Tasmanians* and the Tasmanian government proclaimed the Oyster Cove Station, just a short distance from my family home, an 'historic site'. In 1995, the land was transferred to the Tasmanian Aboriginal people, who commemorate their historical association with this site in the annual Putalina cultural festival. Historical scholarship continues to debate whether the experience of empire in Tasmania was genocidal.

I did not know anything of local nineteenth-century history, but I did know that my forebears had migrated from England in the early decades. Importantly, too, I knew that they were not convicts, but proud free settlers. It was the convict stain, not Aboriginal dispossession that most troubled settlers' memory, and they sought to erase the shame by changing the name of Van Diemen's Land to Tasmania in 1855. Not long afterwards, however, the novelist Marcus Clarke brought the convict past to life again, in his sensational bestseller about cannibalism, *For the Term of His Natural Life*. On the other hand, Tasmanian nationalists such as Attorney General and Supreme Court judge Andrew Inglis Clark saw in this imperial history a provocation, a legacy to be overcome, an argument for building a New World free from the tyranny and degradation of the old.

Earlier generations of my family had arrived in Van Diemen's Land from northern England to take up land and eventually came to farm a considerable amount of southern Tasmania, in South Arm, the Huon and Channel district, where I grew up. I later learnt that the man employed full-time by my grandfather to manage the orchards and livestock was of Aboriginal descent. My mum was his wife's best friend and I often looked after the younger children. Our two families grew up together. One day I heard that one of the girls, my god-child as it happened, by then at high school, had identified as Aboriginal and liked, as she put it, to 'go walkabout'. Our colonial past of which I had been utterly ignorant was suddenly giving new meaning to our daily lives, even as it also demanded a rewriting of Australian history.

The history I studied at the University of Tasmania was a mix of Australian, American, Asian and European – but not British or imperial. Our Australian history lecturer was a charismatic, radical nationalist called Malcolm McRae, who died too young. He was a passionate republican and a labour man. I studied American history, which I loved, with a leading intellectual historian, Michael Roe, who published *The Quest for Authority in Eastern Australia 1835–51* in 1965 and gave me a lasting interest in the history of ideas. My lecturer in European history was a young social historian, Kay Daniels, just back from studying with Asa Briggs in England. Trained as a British historian, she would become one of Australia's most influential feminist historians.

A friend of Liz Reid, the women's adviser to radical Prime Minister, Gough Whitlam, Kay Daniels was appointed to head up the national women's history research project in International Women's Year in 1975. Along with many other young women historians, I enjoyed my first paid employment researching the archives with a view to identifying records that might inform a new women's history. The subsequent reference work, *Women's History in Australia: A Guide to Records*, proved invaluable as a stimulus to women's history across Australia. In the introductory essay, Daniels also offered an insightful critique of the assumptions and procedures of traditional (male) history. 'We have not thought', she wrote, 'that women's invisibility in historical writing is because they have in some way "fallen through" its "cracks and crevices" but that historical writing has been deficient in the examination of that fabric and has consequently left unrevealed the basic processes and relationships of society and the integral role of women in them.'[4]

Daniels introduced us to the 'new social history', insisting we read E. P. Thompson's *Making of the English Working Class* and think about how to write 'History from Below', but a history in which women were integral to historical processes and relationships. She also introduced me to the work of Michel Foucault and his book *Discipline and Punish*, which provided a valuable conceptual frame in which to understand the lives of soldier settlers, the subject of my PhD thesis at Monash University. The rich state-based archive, including inspectors' reports and vast numbers of letters written by settlers and their wives, documenting the experiences of work and home, budgets and purchases, family life and political activities, were a wonderful resource for writing a thesis about state surveillance that brought together social, cultural and political history. I became especially interested in documenting shifting political discourses, in identifying what people were able to say and the language available to them to say it.

The soldier settlement scheme also alerted me to the post-war resurgence of the British Empire, which sought to lock Australians back into the imperial embrace even as they were exhorted to take pride in the landing at Gallipoli as the birthplace of the nation. I became conscious of the language of 'whiteness' and the heightened expectations of life in 'a white man's country'. When one of the settlers protested against his demeaning living conditions – his abject poverty and indebtedness – he wrote angrily about being forced to live 'in a bag humpy in a white man's country'. He was an Englishman in an imperial settlement scheme. The British government had asked the Australian government to accept British ex-servicemen for settlement on the land alongside Australians. Sir Henry Rider Haggard had toured Australia during the war, signalling, as I wrote in the book based on my thesis, *The Limits of Hope*, a 'British intention to reinvigorate the empire strategy' at a time when the British Empire was in decline.[5]

Another aspect of the history of soldier settlement that interested me was the vocal political protest of wives, 'the mobilization of women' as I titled chapter seven, who were forced to do excessive outdoors work, treated as 'slaves' by husbands, who had failed, according to their partners, in their manly duty as breadwinners. Women often invoked the language of separate spheres to refuse exhausting workloads. I was interested in the gendering of political language, the invocations of manhood and womanhood, femininity and masculinity that shaped political expression, including discourses on labour, national character, socialism and feminism. It was the mid-80s and feminist history across the world was being transformed by the analytical possibilities of the concept of gender, by discussions of the gendered nature of citizenship, politics, nation and empire. At the same time my own awareness of the deep significance of gender – for the present as well as the past – was heightened by the birth of my two daughters, Kath and Jess, in 1977 and 1981. The implications of the 'double load' for women with children were the focus of a commemorative volume I co-edited at that time that we called *Double Time: Women in Victoria, 150 Years*, published in 1985. Little children kept me close to home.

As my girls grew up, international travel became easier, happily for me, just as feminist history became increasingly transnational and comparative in approach. The first wave of women's history generated by women's liberation had been decidedly national in focus – think of the work of Sheila Rowbotham in the United Kingdom, Mary Ryan, Alice Kessler Harris and Linda Kerber in the United States and Anne Summers and Miriam Dixson in Australia – but from the late 1980s and early 1990s, just as gender as a category of analysis was transforming the history discipline, so feminist history became more international in orientation. Scholars organized symposia at Bellagio, Bielefeld and Berlin on the gendered nature of national identities, nation states, citizenship and empire. Catherine Hall and Judy Walkowitz jointly convened a conference on 'Gender, Nationalisms and National Identities' at the Rockefeller Centre, Bellagio in 1992, which I attended, along with Ann Curthoys and Dipesh Chakrabarty from Australia and other historians and literary scholars from across the world. It was a transformative intellectual event, bringing together analyses of nation, race, gender and empire.

But at the same time, the interventions of Indigenous and Black women were unsettling our confident generalizations as we were insistently asked: which women? As Australian Aboriginal activist and lawyer, Pat O'Shane, had written in 1976, when she looked at the women's liberation movement, she saw not feminist activists, but 'white women'. The women's movement should, she wrote, 'examine whether or not their aims as white women are necessarily those of black women'.[6] A particular provocation occurred in Australia with the publication of Anne Summers' best-selling *Damned Whores and God's Police* about the impact of sexist stereotypes in Australian history, an account she sub-titled *The Colonization of Women in Australia*, begging the question as to which women had been colonized and by whom.[7]

In the light of challenges by Aboriginal women writers, such as O'Shane, Bobby Sykes, Larissa Behrendt and Jackie Huggins, and later Aileen Moreton-Robinson, how could the category 'women' continue to be treated as undifferentiated and how could 'gender' continue to be thought of as the primary relationship of power?[8] In 1994, Pat Grimshaw, Ann McGrath,

Marian Quartly and I published a new feminist history of Australia called *Creating a Nation,* in which Ann McGrath built on her extensive research in Aboriginal women's history to put the historical agency of Aboriginal women – and their experience of colonization – front and centre. In the introduction we wrote about the feminist idea of women's historical agency:

> In agency there is also responsibility. As the beneficiaries of the dispossession of Aboriginal peoples, European women, along with men, were complicit in an imperialist, civilizing project that saw the near destruction of Australia's indigenous peoples and their languages and cultures. Aboriginal women's memories of white brutality focus on the domestic violence and confinement perpetrated by the mistress in the home, as well as the exploitation and sexual violence that so often characterized their encounters with white men on the frontier.[9]

Feminist history had been productively troubled by the politics of representation in the context of the ever present history of colonialism.

Although the empire was thus brought into focus, subsequent political struggles for Aboriginal rights were fought out mainly in the national domain and the focus was on national history. What was the real character of Australian history? In 1993, I published my first paper on the 'politics of whiteness' in relation to feminism ('Colonised and Colonising: The White Australian Feminist Subject') for the British journal *Women's History Review*. In a subsequent contribution to an international collection of essays on the 'politics of recognition', arising from a series of workshops at Stockholm University in the late 1990s, I suggested that the white women's movement and the Indigenous women's movement might be understood as recognition struggles in dialogue. Both shared a sense of the importance of history, they both invoked history to make their case for recognition, but their interpretations of Australian history differed dramatically.[10]

In the light of Indigenous women's challenges and new international feminist scholarship on imperialism, much of it inspired by Antoinette Burton's influential work on British feminism and Indian women, new research focused on the complex role of imperial feminists.[11] In the political relations of empire, feminism was clearly 'complicit' (a favourite word of the 1990s) with imperialism, even as empire was used by feminists at organizations, such as the British Commonwealth League in London, as a political resource in international campaigns for Aboriginal rights.[12] In a series of essays on what I called 'frontier feminism', I suggested that Australian women's feminism was shaped in distinctive ways by settler colonialism as a politics that sought to 'protect' Aboriginal – and other vulnerable – women from the rampant masculinity unleashed by the conditions of colonial life. In 1995, I spoke on 'Frontier Feminism and the Marauding White Man' to the International Federation for Research in Women's History Conference (a key international network for feminist history) in Montreal, which was later published in two separate collections on gender and imperialism (one edited by Clare Midgley, the other by Napur Chauduri and Ruth Pearson).[13] In 1999, I published the first full-length history of feminism in Australia, called *Getting Equal,* in which feminists' ambivalent relationships to nation and empire were major themes. Postcolonial critique had shaped a new Australian women's history, with work by Pat Grimshaw, Ann Curthoys, Jackie Huggins, Ann McGrath, Fiona Paisley and Angela Woollacott all making major contributions.

While the whiteness of women as agents of imperialism had been well established by the 1990s, white manhood had largely escaped historical scrutiny. At the beginning of the new century, I returned to read a major Australian imperial text from the last century, Charles Pearson's work of prophecy, *National Life and Character: A Forecast*, published by Macmillan in 1893. At Harvard in 2001 to take up the Chair in Australian Studies, I read Theodore Roosevelt's long review of Pearson's book in the *Sewanee Review*, a dusty volume held in the stacks of the Widener Library. Reading Roosevelt in America offered me a new perspective on the transnational sense of 'fellow feeling' that bound self-styled 'white men' together in imperial solidarity. At a seminar in the Harvard history department on the gendered, racialized figure of the 'white man', one chap said he could see how the 'white man' was a racialized figure, but could not see the gender. In the later book on the subject, documenting the anxiety of the white man confronting a postcolonial world, *Drawing the Global Colour Line: White Men's Countries and the International Challenge of Racial Equality*, co-authored with my former history teacher, Henry Reynolds, the gendered nature of political discourse across empire was a key theme. And not just for 'white men'. When subjugated, colonized or other non-white men, such as W. E. B. DuBois and Lajpat Rai, demanded their rights, they often demanded recognition of their manhood.

When we first planned this book, Henry and I had intended to begin at the Versailles Peace Conference, in 1919, when the Australian Prime Minister, W. M. Hughes, was vociferous in his opposition to the bid by the Japanese representatives to have a racial equality clause written into the Covenant of the League of Nations. Then we thought that we should begin with the publication of Pearson's book in 1893 and its impact in alerting the world to the rise of the 'coloured races'. But then I realized that Pearson's book was itself written in response to what he called 'changing world forces' and most important among these was the modern mobility of the Chinese, the force of 'Greater China'. We decided to underline the historical agency of the Chinese in the modern world by opening the book with the arrival in Melbourne of a leading young merchant, Lowe Kong Meng, who would play a major role in the commercial and political affairs of the colony of Victoria.

Closer research confirmed that Pearson and his parliamentary colleagues were deeply influenced by the political interventions and writings of Chinese Australian activists in the 1870s and 1880s, including their demands for 'cosmopolitan sympathy' and recognition of their 'common human rights'.[14] I found that Pearson's most famous prophecy ('The day will come . . .') echoed a passage written by Cheok Hong Cheong warning of the coming power of China, which became the basis of Pearson's 'forecast', read in Asia, the UK, North America, Southern Africa, as well as in Australasia. British imperial policy was clearly an important context and provocation for these events; but it was the clash of empires, the conflict between British and Chinese imperial subjects, that were the key dynamics in this history. As other Australian historians had already begun to insist, it was not good enough to cast Chinese Australians simply as the passive victims of local racism. They were a large, dynamic and internationally connected community whose role in the making of nation – and empire – was complex and multi-faceted.

Indeed their role in the making of the Australian working class, whose leaders demanded state intervention – 'state socialism' – to secure decent conditions, a legal minimum wage and shorter hours can only be understood in the broader context of labour and empire, a response to the historical memory of the British Empire's exploitation of slave, then 'coolie' indentured Chinese and Indian labour – in Southeast Asia, the Caribbean, Fiji, Mauritius and Australia. In the local context of Chinese competition in the furniture industry in Melbourne – on the part of Chinese capitalists, as well as workers – it was the historical memory of imperial indentured labour that shaped the determination of radical political leaders in the British colony of Victoria to introduce the first compulsory adult male minimum wage in the world, in 1896. Labour and empire provide the crucial framework for understanding these developments that looked both back and forwards, anticipating the international regulation of labour at the International Labour Organization from 1919.

Even so, the principle of the minimum wage – now under siege in Australia by conservative so-called 'neo-liberals' – needs to be defended at the national level in campaigns that invoke national traditions and values. When I wrote a newspaper op-ed recently defending the idea of a legal minimum wage, I did not choose the headline, but nor did I object when a sub-editor entitled it, 'Minimum wage is more than a safety net, it's a symbol of Australian values'. This was history written specifically for a broad national audience about an important national – as well as international – issue. I noted with interest that the economics editor of Melbourne's *Age* newspaper had followed my lead with a story on attacks on the minimum wage prefaced with the observation: 'There's nothing more Australian than the minimum wage.'[15]

Although cognizant that empire – and the clash of empires – provided the crucial context for understanding feminist and labour history and relatedly the history of Australian race relations – my political commitments to Aboriginal rights, equal opportunity, multiculturalism, environmental conservation and action on climate change – keep me writing national history for a local audience because, like it or not, it is in the national domain that political activism, often grounded in contests over national narratives – sometimes dubbed 'the history wars' – is most effective.

At a recent conference on 'Labor and Empire' at Santa Barbara, Paul Kramer, historian of US imperialism, was heard to lament that the participants' historical project was not linked to, or enlivened by, a grass roots political movement. His comment begged the question about the apparent lack of relationship between the writing of US imperial history and Native American history, which is clearly animated by grass roots activism; and between academic history and movements for political and economic justice on the part of Mexicans, Filipinos, Hawaiians and Puerto Ricans.

National history remains a powerful discursive resource in current political struggles. Even so, my historical scholarship continues to be shaped by ever-expanding conceptual frameworks – imperial, regional, global – reflecting larger historiographical and theoretical shifts in the broader discipline. How and why they happen I'm not sure, but I now see empire as providing an essential analytical framework for understanding our interconnected past (not least, the 1896 innovation of the minimum wage). But not just the British Empire, for it is clear that Australia was shaped in diverse encounters – some cordial others deadly – between different empires and peoples in the Asia Pacific region.

There is a new vibrancy in Australian history as our country is re-imagined within these frameworks. No longer conceived as an isolated outpost at the edge of the British imperial world, Australasia is now seen as the site of multiple surprising, unexpected and transformative encounters between Aborigines, Afghans, British, Chinese, Japanese, Pacific Islanders, Australasians and Americans. These intersections are the focus of much new work by younger historians, who no longer define themselves in terms of the old labels. As one young interlocutor, who works on relations between Sydney and Shanghai in the 1920s and 1930s, said to me recently, never had there been a more exciting time to be doing history. Is it national, imperial, regional or global? Younger people's work is all of these and more. This is the new history.

Notes

My deep thanks to Antoinette Burton and Dane Kennedy for their valuable comment on, and conversation about, earlier versions of this chapter.

1 Quoted in Marilyn Lake and Henry Reynolds, *Drawing the Global Colour Line: White Men's Countries and the International Challenge of Racial Equality* (Cambridge: Cambridge University Press, 2008), pp. 91–2; on the politics of location see Antoinette Burton 'Introduction: Imperial Optics',

The Empire in Question: Reading, Writing, and Teaching British Imperialism (Durham, NC: Duke University Press, 2011).

2 Adam McKeown, *Melancholy Order: Asian Migration and the Globalization of Borders* (New York: Columbia University Press, 2008).

3 See Jim Davidson, 'What if Tasmania had become French?', in Stuart Macintyre and Sean Scalmer, eds, *What If? Australian History as it Might Have Been* (Melbourne University Press, 2006).

4 Kay Daniels, 'Introduction' in Kay Daniels, Mary Murnane and Anne Picot, eds, *Women in Australia: An Annotated Guide to Records* (Australian Government Publishing Service, Canberra, 1977), p. vii.

5 Marilyn Lake, *The Limits of Hope: Soldier Settlement in Victoria 1915–38* (Oxford University Press, Melbourne, 1987), pp. 31, 154.

6 Pat O'Shane, 'Is There any Relevance in the Women's Movement for Aboriginal Women?', *Refractory Girl*, 12 (September 1976): 31–4.

7 Anne Summers, *Damned Whores and God's Police: The Colonization of Women in Australia* (Melbourne: Penguin, 1975).

8 See, for example, Jackie Huggins, 'A Contemporary View of Aboriginal Women's Relationship to the White Women's Movement', in Norma Grieve and Ailsa Burns, eds, *Australian Women: Contemporary Feminist Thought* (Melbourne: Oxford University Press, 1994), and Aileen Moreton-Robinson, *Talkin' Up to the White Woman: Indigenous Women and Feminism* (St Lucia: University of Queensland Press, 2000).

9 Patricia Grimshaw, Marilyn Lake, Ann McGrath and Marian Quartly, *Creating a Nation 1788–1990* (Melbourne: Penguin, 1994), p. 1.

10 Marilyn Lake, 'Woman, Black, Indigenous: Recognition Struggles in Dialogue', in Barbara Hobson, ed., *Recognition Struggles and Social Movements: Contested Identities, Agency and Power* (Cambridge: Cambridge University Press, 2003), pp. 145–60.

11 Antoinette Burton, *Burdens of History: British Feminists, Indian Women, and Imperial Culture, 1865–1915* (Chapel Hill: University of North Carolina Press, 1994).

12 Fiona Paisley, *Loving Protection? Australian Feminism and Aboriginal Women's Rights 1919–39* (Melbourne: Melbourne University Press, 2000).

13 Marilyn Lake, 'Frontier Feminism and the Marauding White Man', in Clare Midgeley, ed., *Gender and Imperialism* (Manchester: Manchester University Press, 1998), pp. 123–36; Marilyn Lake, 'Frontier Feminism and the Marauding White Man', in Napur Chauduri and Ruth Pierson, eds, *Empire, Nation, Colony* (Bloomington, IN: Indiana University Press, 1998), pp. 94–105.

14 Marilyn Lake, 'Chinese Colonists Assert Their "Common Human Rights": Cosmopolitanism as Subject and Method of History', *Journal of World History*, 21, 3 (September 2010): 375–92.

15 Peter Martin, 'Hard won Australian right under attack', *Age* (25 January 2015), p. 31.

8

An Education in Empire

Dane Kennedy
b. 1951

In September 1977 I boarded a flight from San Francisco to London to begin my dissertation research. This was only the second time I had been on an aeroplane and the first time I had travelled to another country. Having grown up in California, everything east of the Mississippi River was terra incognita to me. I was a naïf, utterly unfamiliar with the wider world. Yet here I was, about to venture abroad to study white settlers in Kenya and Zimbabwe (or Rhodesia, as it was then known). Why? What drew me to a subject so foreign to my own upbringing? What made me a historian of the British imperial experience?

My education in empire began long before I flew to London. The adventure stories I read as a youth stirred an early interest in exotic places and peoples. The ethnic tensions that roiled the small town where I grew up provided a point of reference for comprehending the social conflicts in the colonial world. And the anti-war protests that loomed so large over my education at the University of California at Berkeley shaped the moral preoccupations and political perspective I brought to bear when I turned to imperial history. Though none of these events and experiences had anything to do with the British Empire per se, it seems apparent to me now that they aroused my curiosity about empire and informed the ways I made sense of it. Even so, prior to boarding that transcontinental flight, the British Empire remained an abstraction to me, meaningful mainly by way of analogy. It was the year I spent doing dissertation research in Britain, where I seemed to encounter the remnants of its imperial past almost everywhere I turned, and above all in Rhodesia, where I found myself observing a colonial society in its death throes, that made that empire a visceral reality for me and gave my engagement with its history a personal dimension.

I can trace my initial interest in this subject to the tales of adventure I read as a kid. The juvenile literature produced for British youths, especially boys, was of course steeped in a sense of imperial pride and racial superiority. Much the same was true in the US, where it usually involved tales about cowboys and Indians. I acquired a taste for a more exotic version of such juvenilia when my father introduced me around the age of ten to Edgar Rice Burroughs' Tarzan novels. For those of you unfamiliar with the story of Tarzan, he is the child of an English aristocratic couple who are shipwrecked on the coast of Africa, where they soon die, leaving their infant son to be raised by apes. Tarzan's innate superiority as a white man of noble birth eventually leads him to establish his dominance over apes and Africans. I now cringe at my youthful enthusiasm for this racist imperial fable, but it opened my eyes to an exotic world of difference, a world I would investigate more seriously and systematically in the future. It is tempting in this context to interpret my recent work on exploration, notably *The Last Blank Spaces: Exploring Africa and Australia*, as a belated attempt to historicize and de-romanticize a subject I was initially drawn to as a racialized fantasy.

Another adolescent avenue into empire came from Rudyard Kipling's 'Gunga Din', which I memorized for a class recitation. I was so taken with the poem that I took to reciting it as a party trick (which may explain why I did not get invited to many parties) and reading more of Kipling's poems and stories about British India. Although patronizing in its praise of the eponymous Indian water-bearer for his service to British imperial troops, the poem's central moral message – 'you're a better a man than I am, Gunga Din' – provided a healthy antidote to the crude racism and social Darwinism of the Tarzan novels.

The Cuban Missile Crisis occurred around the time I discovered Burroughs and Kipling, and soon after my family moved to Visalia, a small town several hundred miles north of Los Angeles in California's Central Valley, where my parents thought we were less likely to be incinerated in a nuclear war. Though deceptively safe and quiet, Visalia was hardly insulated from the upheavals that began tearing the United States apart in the 1960s. Social conflicts were readily apparent at my high school, where simmering ethnic tensions occasionally exploded in gang fights between 'Mexican' and 'Okie' students – most of the former from poor families that had come from Mexico to work as field labourers in the surrounding farms, most of the latter from poor families that had fled the 'dust bowl' in Oklahoma and surrounding states to seek out the same farm work a generation earlier. Going to school in this place at this time was an education in the manifold ways social and economic marginalization fuelled ethnic and racial resentments, and it provided an early introduction to a theme that would prove relevant to my subsequent studies of colonial societies.

Coming of age in Visalia also offered an education in political mobilization by oppressed peoples. We were at the epicentre of the United Farm Workers Union's struggle to improve wages and working conditions for California's migrant farm labourers. The union was then at its height, and its imaginative campaign for workers' rights involved strikes, marches and boycotts. The inspirational leader of the union, Cesar Chavez, helped instil a sense of solidarity and pride in the Latinos who made up most of the migrant workers. The rejection of the label 'Mexican' in favour of 'Chicano/a' symbolized this shift of sentiment. There were obvious similarities between the labour movement led by Chavez and the contemporaneous African-American civil rights movement under the leadership of Martin Luther King. Both Chavez and King looked to the great Indian nationalist leader, Mohandas Gandhi, for moral inspiration and strategies of resistance; Chavez even emulated Gandhi by going on a hunger strike.

America's military interventions overseas also began to intrude into my political consciousness and sharpen my moral conscience during these years. My family avidly watched the evening news on television, which brought viewers unprecedented visual access to violent conflicts at home and abroad. I remember my shock at an event caught on camera during the US invasion of the Dominican Republic in 1965–6: an American soldier shot a Dominican man, as I recall, for refusing his order to pick up trash in the street. Around the same time, shocking images from the Vietnam War started to appear on American television screens. We saw American soldiers setting fire to Vietnamese villages in order to 'save' them, Vietnamese children fleeing from combat zones with their skin burned off by napalm, and many other obscenities. It became increasingly hard to deny that America's military involvement in Vietnam was unjust and immoral. The war politicized my parents. They campaigned for Eugene McCarthy, the anti-war senator from Wisconsin who challenged President Johnson, and became active in the California Democratic Council (CDC), the constituency-led organization that dominated Democratic politics in the state. They took me to a CDC convention in Los Angeles, where I heard Martin Luther King Jr. give a fiery speech against the Vietnam War just months before his assassination. My parents have remained politically active ever since, campaigning for other candidates, running for office themselves, serving as city council and school board members, and more. I found it impossible, needless to say, to avoid politics.

In the fall of 1969, I matriculated at the University of California Berkeley. By this time, Berkeley already had a reputation as the most politically engaged campus in the country, and it did not disappoint. Protests against the Vietnam War roiled the university during my undergraduate years. There were sit-ins and mass marches, violent clashes with truncheon-wielding, tear-gas-deploying police, and, in the aftermath of the US invasion of Cambodia in May 1970, a student strike that shut down the university. We condemned the United States as an imperialist aggressor in Vietnam and proclaimed our opposition to the draft, agonizing about what we would do when our student deferments ran out. We sang Country Joe's anti-war anthem, 'I Feel Like I'm Fixin' To Die', and marched to chants of 'Ho Ho Ho Chi Minh, the NLF is going to win'. We expressed outrage at the imperial state's oppressive actions at home, especially after police murdered two black activists in Chicago and National Guard troops killed four students during anti-war protests at Kent State University. Some concluded that violent oppression by the state had to be met with liberationist violence by the people: the Weather Underground and the Black Panthers (an organization founded and headquartered in nearby Oakland) serving as their self-proclaimed vanguard. Franz Fanon enjoyed a posthumous revival among New Left radicals as an intellectual proponent for such action. I still own the paperback copy of Fanon's *The Wretched of the Earth* I bought then: its cover announces that it is 'the handbook for the black revolution that is changing the shape of the world'. So it seemed.

These were exhilarating, if deeply troubled times. In an effort to make sense of the disorienting events that swirled around me – and perhaps in part to escape them – I was drawn to history and, more particularly, to British imperial history, which gave me a comparative context for making sense of American imperialism. At the time, the British Empire had largely disappeared from the history curriculum in American universities, but Tom Metcalf taught a course on the subject at Berkeley (though I did not realize until reading his essay in this volume that he had only recently introduced it). Tom's course strengthened my interest in Britain's imperial past and scrubbed away any residues of the romance of empire that I may have acquired from Kipling and Burroughs. Reinforced by my revulsion at the carnage in Vietnam, it gave me a far more critical perspective on the imperial subjugation of one people by another.

Still, I did not expect to become a historian of the British Empire. I applied to graduate school mainly because it allowed me to delay any decision about my future – and I stayed at Berkeley because I could not imagine a better place to be, not least because Marty, the woman I would marry a year later, was there. I gravitated to British history because my foreign language skills were too poor to pursue most other options. Sheldon Rothblatt, whose work on the social history of Oxbridge I admired, became my supervisor: although he had little interest in imperial history, he supported my forays in the field. Tom Metcalf also became an important mentor, and I spent far more time with his Indian history graduate students than my counterparts in British history. If my faculty advisers had been more conscientious, they might have warned me away from a field for which there was so little demand. Then again, the collapse in the academic job market at this time meant that there was little demand for newly minted historians of any sort, so they probably figured it did not make much difference what I studied. This gave me the freedom to choose a dissertation topic – Kenya and Southern Rhodesia's white settler populations – that the faculty I worked with knew little about. Once again, my interest was influenced in part by contemporary events: Rhodesia's renegade white regime was much in the news as a problem for the international community. Who were these settlers? Where did they come from? Why did they treat the Africans the way they did? These were crudely simple questions, unleavened by any theoretical yeast, but they got me going.

And so I set off on my overseas adventure. London was a revelation. It was so grand, so enthralling, so disorienting that for the first month or so I was in a state of hyper-consciousness, my senses pitched to a level of awareness that I had never experienced before. Everything seemed steeped in history, and the empire seemed an integral ingredient of that history. I found a flat on the evocatively named Sumatra Road. I began my research at the Royal Commonwealth Society on Northumberland Avenue, just off Trafalgar Square, and every morning I passed the busts of Cecil Rhodes, Alfred Milner and other imperial icons as I ascended the staircase to the library. The library itself was a cosily dishevelled place, filled with archival riches that only its long-serving librarian, the courtly Donald Simpson, could find. (It has since closed and the collection been transferred to Cambridge University Library.) Periodically, its sleepy quiet was broken by the arrival of an ex-colonial official, who invariably spoke in the booming voice that such men acquired to give orders to the natives. On lunch breaks I would wander through an underground warren (now gone as well) between the Waterloo and Embankment stations, where rare coin dealers put out bins of old coins from the colonies, and then up the Strand past South Africa House and Australia House or along the Thames embankment past the permanently docked HMS *President* and the Egyptian obelisk known as Cleopatra's Needle, one of the city's many imperial trophies.

Once a week I attended the imperial history seminar that Peter Marshall and Andrew Porter directed at the Institute for Historical Research. Here I listened to imperial historians speak about their research and met other graduate students working on imperial topics, reassuring me that in Britain at least my subject was alive and well. Occasionally I attended Shula Marks' Southern African history seminar at the Institute for Commonwealth Studies, where the no-holds-barred debates exposed deep ideological fissures and demonstrated how much was at stake in alternative interpretations of that region's history. I once witnessed a seminar speaker being reduced to tears by a barrage of criticism. I became increasingly aware of the highly contested nature of the subject I had so blithely chosen to study.

In March 1978 I flew to Rhodesia, where the pariah white regime of Ian Smith was crumbling under the military onslaught from the Zimbabwe African National Union (ZANU) and the Zimbabwe African Peoples Union (ZAPU) and diplomatic pressure from the United States, Britain and even South Africa. Thirteen years earlier, Smith's newly elected Rhodesian Front government had unilaterally declared independence from Britain (using the American Declaration of Independence as its model) in what would prove a futile effort to forestall black majority rule. Although it ceased to be a colony, Rhodesia remained very much a colonial society, intent on maintaining the power and privileges of its white minority population. Its strategic position began to unravel after 1975 with the collapse of Portuguese colonial rule in neighbouring Mozambique. When I arrived in Salisbury (now Harare), Ian Smith was negotiating the so-called Internal Settlement, a power-sharing agreement with three pliable African leaders in a last-ditch effort to prevent the regime's collapse.

I had moral reservations about entering a country that the international community had justifiably condemned and ostracized, but I saw no way I could write my dissertation without consulting the Rhodesian archives. And, of course, I was curious to see the place I had spent so much time studying. Rhodesian authorities probably permitted me entry because they needed the foreign currency, even what little a poor graduate student would spend, and because they figured that my interest in white settlers made me politically safe. (Later, it would make me politically suspect at African Studies Association meetings.) For all the reading I had done on Rhodesian history, I was utterly unprepared for what I observed and experienced when I entered that troubled land. The time I spent there was relatively brief, but it had a profound impact on how I came to understand colonialism and colonial societies.

Recently, I rediscovered a diary I kept while I was in Rhodesia. Up to this point, I have relied on my own dodgy memory to tell the story of my education in empire, but the diary allows me to recount my Rhodesian experience with greater accuracy. What first struck me as I disembarked from the aeroplane (to piped music of 'Green, green grass of home') was the colonial attire of the white men I saw at the airport: they wore 'white or khaki shirts and knee-length pants, with high white socks and white shoes'. My second impression was of the sumptuousness of Alexandra Park, the Salisbury suburb where I was staying. The houses were large, handsome bungalow-style dwellings, surrounded by spacious, beautifully landscaped gardens graced with shimmering swimming pools. It was as if I had been transported to one of California's tonier suburbs. The similarities extended to the white residents' reliance on cars: only gardeners and other household staff – all Africans here, mainly Latinos in California – ventured out along the streets on foot. A key difference, however, is that Rhodesian whites' sense of racial solidarity was so strong and deeply ingrained that they repeatedly stopped to ask if I wanted a ride as I walked to and from the archives.

My Rhodesian-born landlady, a widow who housed student boarders, was a liberal by the standards of the ruling regime, which she despised. A gracious hostess, she invited me to a variety of social events and introduced me to many of her friends. All were white and most were self-professed liberals. One was a lecturer in English at the University of Rhodesia who heatedly objected to my use of the term 'settler' because it implied that whites had less right to be there than Africans. Another was the only liberal member of the city council, an elderly gentleman who believed that blacks who were wealthy enough to purchase homes in expensive whites-only suburbs should be permitted to do so. He cautioned, however, that most Africans 'were not trained to accept responsibility', and hence it was not realistic to abolish residential segregation across the board. A young man who worked for the Internal Affairs Department managed 'protected villages' in the Zambezi valley, whose residents had been forcibly removed from their homes to keep them from aiding the guerillas. He saw 'his role as a progressive, liberal one', but his main task, he told me, was 'to wean the villagers from their dependence on government aid' by getting them to grow crops despite their new conditions of incarceration. As I wrote in my diary, I had begun 'to understand why [Ian] Smith and the [Rhodesian] Front had so completely overwhelmed the Rhodesian "liberals" – their position was so incredibly hollow'.

I also spent a good deal of time with two of my fellow boarders, both South African students studying geophysics at the university, and an English graduate student from the School of Oriental and African Studies (SOAS) whom I met in the archives. One of the South Africans was an Afrikaner, the other an Indonesian-born 'Dutchman' whose family had immigrated to South Africa. The latter's complexion hinted at a mixed-race heritage, but he was an unabashed racist and defender of apartheid, as was his countryman. The SOAS student had been doing dissertation research in Rhodesia for the past five months, and the place clearly had gotten into his head. A chain-smoker with nicotine-stained teeth, he talked incessantly 'about the guerrilla war, about land mines, attacks, makes of machine guns, patrol tactics, on and on'. He admired the Selous Scouts, Rhodesia's notorious special forces unit, and claimed that Rhodesia was winning the war against the rebels. It would not have surprised me if he had subsequently chucked the dissertation and joined the Rhodesian military.

The four of us went out on several pub crawls that revealed to me some of the tensions and contradictions that plagued Rhodesian society. One evening we were entering a hotel when a large white man who was exiting suddenly sucker-punched the black doorman who opened the door for him. Such unprovoked white-on-black attacks were distressingly common, several patrons of the hotel bar told me. Later, after the white bars had closed for the night, two Africans from the university who knew the SOAS student took us to a black bar in a district known as 'sin mile'. We were the only whites present and, not surprisingly, most of the customers gave us hostile glares. Prostitutes, however, propositioned us, and one of them mistook me for a frequent customer whose nickname, my African interlocutor explained with amusement, was 'the penis of the dry wheat'. Another pub crawl ended in a seedy Chinese bar and restaurant filled with elderly alcoholic white men, some young white people who sported vaguely counter-cultural fashions, and a number of interracial couples, the most memorable being a 'wealthy-looking white man, attired in tuxedo and goatee' and his black companion. 'Everyone seemed very drunk,' I noted in my diary, and 'no one seemed very happy.' Ann Laura Stoler has referred in an oft-quoted phrase to the 'tense and tender ties' that inform race relations in societies shaped by colonialism.[1] From what I observed of Rhodesian society, relations between whites and blacks were clearly tense, but rarely tender.

This point was brought home to me with particular force when a woman I met in the archives invited me to join her and her husband on a Sunday outing. At last I had an opportunity to meet members of the Rhodesian Front's core constituency. The husband, a Royal Air Force veteran who managed a fertilizer plant, was 'a Colonel Blimp in his 50s, a small man with a large nose, a bushy mustache, thinning grey hair, and a military swagger of a walk'. Aptly named Dickie, he and his wife, Beryl, who wrote scripts for radio shows, lived on the edge of town in a modest home. They took me on a drive to Bindura, a farming community some 60 miles north of Salisbury. Both of them brought loaded pistols. Once we entered the countryside, we saw few vehicles apart from armoured military trucks with heavy-calibre machine guns mounted over the cabs. At one point we made a wrong turn and drove with increasing unease down a road that passed a cluster of mud-and-wattle dwellings and dwindled to a dirt track: we soon made a hasty retreat.

Our destination was a hotel near Bindura, a gathering place for the surrounding white farming community. It was Easter Sunday, and more than a hundred people were there to celebrate the holiday. They were drinking on the veranda, lounging by the pool, and eating a hearty midday meal in the dining room. For the children there was an Easter egg hunt. In keeping with the holiday's Christian spirit, a poster announced that the theme of the hunt was 'Catch a Ter[rorist] – Dead or Alive'.

Once we had made it safely back to my hosts' home that evening, Dickie and Beryl lectured me at length about the problems confronting Rhodesia. In their view, the only discontented Africans were the ones educated by the missionaries, 'who should have been shot when they tried to enter the country'. Weak-willed and unmoored from traditional values, they had been turned by communist agitators into revolutionary terrorists. Americans like me did not understand that Rhodesia was an essential bulwark of the Free World, bravely defending its values. Americans also failed to appreciate that Africans were 'stupid, incompetent, and corrupt . . . incapable of governing themselves'. The majority of them were 'satisfied with white rule', grateful for the 'stability and progress' it provided. I do not recall if their evidence included working telephones, a trope that Luise White has identified as a key feature of the Rhodesian rationale for resisting black majority rule, but their rhetoric was certainly consistent with her analysis.[2] Working plumbing, it seemed, was another matter. In the midst of their harangue, an African servant entered the room to report that a water pipe had burst in his quarters. Beryl told him that 'the Boss' (i.e. Dickie, who was sitting just a few feet away) would look into it in the morning.

Finally, there was an incident towards the end of my stay that served as a reminder that the Rhodesian crisis was intertwined with the imperial trauma that had torn my own country apart. I was attending a public lecture when a man about my age came up and introduced himself as a fellow American, a veteran of the Vietnam War who was attending the University of Rhodesia.

He invited me to join himself and other Americans who gathered every Saturday at the Salisbury home of Robin Moore for burgers and beer. Moore was the author of *The Green Berets*, a bestselling novel about the military heroics of this US special forces unit in Vietnam. (It was made into a movie starring John Wayne.) I knew that Moore had recently moved to Rhodesia, denouncing the Carter administration's sanctions against the white regime and declaring himself America's unofficial ambassador to the country. I had also heard rumours that a number of US Vietnam veterans had come to Rhodesia to fight for the renegade regime, and that some of them had enrolled in the university to collect GI benefits. Had I been an intrepid investigative journalist, I might have leapt at this opportunity to hang out with Robin Moore and his mercenary buddies, but the prospect sent shivers down my spine. I declined the invitation.[3]

What I witnessed in Rhodesia were the death throes of a late colonial society. This was 'the last of the British wars of decolonization', as Andrew Thompson has noted.[4] It seems evident to me now that what I saw there did much to shape my subsequent views on colonial encounters and imperial projects. I originally envisioned a dissertation that compared the social composition of Rhodesia's and Kenya's settler populations (colloquially known to contemporaries as 'the sergeants' mess and the officers' mess'), anticipating that I would find evidence of stark differences in their policies and practices. Increasingly, however, I became convinced that the social origins of the two settler communities mattered less than the political and economic circumstances they faced in colonial Africa. Above all, it was their need to subjugate and exploit the African population and their accompanying anxiety about the sustainability of that strategy that did most to shape the character of these colonies. This shift of orientation gave my first book, *Islands of White: Settler Society and Culture in Kenya and Southern Rhodesia, 1890–1939*, a schizophrenic character: I focused in its first half on the distinct social origins of the two settler communities, but turned in the second half to their shared cultural anxieties about the colonial project. I revisited the latter theme in the context of colonial India with a clearer sense of purpose in *The Magic Mountains: Hill Stations and the British Raj*, which argued that the British sought refuge from their colonial subjects in the highland enclaves they called hill stations. More recently I have had cause to reflect once again on my Rhodesian experiences in the context of a short book I am finishing on decolonization.

My education in empire certainly did not end in Rhodesia in 1978. It continued in more ways than I can recount here, though a few experiences deserve note. Further research trips to Britain and other ex-colonies gave me a sharper appreciation of empire's afterlife. In particular, I witnessed some of the ethnic tensions and political instability that continue to plague many postcolonial societies, being present in Kenya during an attempted coup against President Daniel arap Moi and in India when Rajiv Gandhi was assassinated by Tamil Tigers. Meanwhile, my intellectual understanding of empire was both challenged and enriched by postcolonial studies and the new imperial history, which came to prominence after I got my degree. Like many historians of empire, I was perplexed by postcolonial studies' use of theory and put off by its jargon, but I also was drawn to its cultural and epistemological lines of inquiry. In 1996 I published a somewhat polemical essay about the implications of postcolonial studies for imperial history that tried to strike a balance between my objections to its methods and my appreciation for its aims.[5] The new imperial history I found more accessible and appealing, though perhaps not entirely as new as it claimed to be. In *Britain and Empire 1880–1945*, I drew on several generations of scholarship to survey the connections between Britain and its empire. Still, my intellectual debts to the new imperial history and postcolonial studies were amply evident in my next book, *The Highly Civilized Man: Richard Burton and the Victorian World*, where I made a 'belated attempt to practice what I [had] preached' in my initial essay on postcolonial studies and imperial history.[6]

Finally, the US invasions of Afghanistan and Iraq in the aftermath of 9/11 brought the empire back home to me. Being present in Washington, DC during the attacks on the World Trade Center and the Pentagon, I shared the emotions of that traumatic day, but I watched with growing dismay as those emotions were manipulated for political purposes. It became increasingly difficult to deny that the United States had launched imperial campaigns in two past graveyards of empires, places our British partners knew all too well. These events caused me to think more systematically than I had since the Vietnam War about the relationship between my interest in the British Empire and my complicity in America's empire. In recent years I have sought in several essays to address these issues, and their evident inescapability stand at the heart of the reflections I have offered here.

Notes

1 Ann Laura Stoler, 'Tense and Tender Ties: The Politics of Comparison in North American History and (Post)Colonial Studies', *The Journal of American History*, 88, 3 (December 2001): 829–65.

2 Luise White, 'The Utopia of Working Phones: Rhodesian Independence and the Place of Race in Decolonization', in Michael Gordin, Helen Tilley and Gyan Prakash, eds, *Utopia/Distopia: Historical Conditions of Possibility* (Princeton: Princeton University Press), pp. 94–116.

3 Moore's role as an agent of American mercenaries in Rhodesia is discussed by White, pp. 107–8.

4 Andrew Thompson, 'Afterward: The Imprint of the Empire', in Andrew Thompson, ed., *Britain's Experience of Empire in the Twentieth Century* (Oxford: Oxford University Press, 2012), p. 332.

5 Dane Kennedy, 'Imperial History and Post-Colonial Theory', *Journal of Imperial and Commonwealth History*, 24, 3 (September 1996): 345–63. I recently published further reflections on the subject in Graham Huggins, ed., *The Oxford Handbook of Postcolonial Studies* (Oxford: Oxford University Press, 2013), pp. 467–88.

6 Dane Kennedy, *The Highly Civilized Man: Richard Burton and the Victorian World* (Cambridge, MA: Harvard University Press, 2007), pp. 343.

9

A Child of Decolonization

Philippa Levine
b. 1957

One spring afternoon in 1966, our teacher announced that our usual roster of lessons that day – English grammar exercises, arithmetical problems, great heroes of history, penmanship – were suspended. We were escorted, in our customary double-file, to the school hall, as were all the other classes, where we were directed to sit cross-legged on the floor. There was an air of excitement in the room, for the huge floor-to-ceiling windows on either side of the small stage had been covered with blackout cloth and a projector at the back of the room stood ready to roll a film. I do not recall any introductory remarks, though in retrospect it seems likely that the headmistress, the redoubtable Miss Sharland, or someone almost as senior, might have prefaced this screening with some explanation, but if that was so, I do not remember it. I do, though, remember the film we saw, not least because even at the time and at the relatively accepting age of 9, it struck me as rather odd. It told of a far-away place that had recently changed its name from Tanganyika to Tanzania, where great progress towards economic security and political stability was occurring thanks to a long association with Britain and a colonial past. Agriculture was undergoing thorough modernization; industry was expanding; diseases were being fast eradicated; and hunger was soon to be a thing of the past.

I have no idea why I have always retained a memory of this curious little episode and I have equally little idea why such a film was regarded as suitable for a primary school in a lower middle-class suburb in north-west London. It was by no means my first encounter with Britain's colonial presence, but it clearly made an impression and when, decades later, I began to read about the merging of Tanganyika and Zanzibar as the new nation of Tanzania, the memory of this film – which I am guessing was a state-sponsored pro-development narrative – came flooding back. I wonder now whether the adults who opted to interrupt our daily routines to show this film marvelled only a few years later at the changes wrought in the vicinity of the school by the Africanization policies that precipitated migration from Tanzania as well as from Kenya and Uganda. My primary school, Wembley Manor, was in a neighbourhood whose demographic would, a few years hence, be radically altered by the coerced flight of South Asians from those former colonies; by the time I left for university a decade later, the samosa and the sari were as ubiquitous as the sausages and ham sandwiches of an earlier era. Though it would be a while before I understood the policies that had helped usher in this ejection of long-standing communities from East Africa, the changes on the ground were palpable.

Yet 1966, looking back, was by no means the first moment of my colonial encounter as a London kid growing up quite literally alongside decolonization. We had only moved to Wembley that year; it was a memorable move which took place only a few weeks before the epic World Cup in which England played – and beat – West Germany, an occasion for some considerable degree of patriotic boastfulness. Our new flat – on what would become the infamous Chalkhill Estate – was a few minutes walk from Wembley Stadium. On match day, when 98,000 people crowded into the stadium, standing on the lawn in front of our block of flats we could hear the fans cheering and chanting. Everything shook slightly when the crowd roared for England. It was an intense moment of mass patriotism in an era in which Britain's status and power were rapidly declining.

The move was memorable in other ways too. We had lived since I was two in the north-east London suburb of Stoke Newington, then a working-class neighbourhood with no pretensions or aspirations. The school my brothers and I attended, Northwold, was an early London School Board institution with separate entrances for girls and boys, narrow dark staircases where we were constantly enjoined to be quiet, and concrete playgrounds with no grass. Wembley Manor's spacious and modern one-storey building with attached playing fields underlined the class differences which separated the two schools, but so too did the family lives of each of these schools' pupils. It was a fairly regular occurrence at Northwold that we would bid farewell to a classmate whose family was emigrating, mostly to Australia but sometimes to New Zealand or Canada. For working-class Londoners the promise of a better life, of economic security and the potential for home ownership must have been enormously tempting. Few of the kids at Northwold hailed from families who owned property (including my own family). Hackney, or at least our segment in Stoke Newington, was a land of tenancies, private as well as public. The mostly Edwardian and late Victorian houses up and down the streets on which we lived and walked to school, were almost all divided into rental flats.

It was in the flats opposite our purpose-built council block that my Jamaican friends lived. I was the only kid in Benthal Court – an all-white block when we lived there – who was allowed to play with the Jamaican girls across the street. Pamela, Marian and Leslie, the other little girls in Benthal Court, were strictly forbidden from associating with them and for a while they shunned me for crossing that line. The number of Caribbean kids in the neighbourhood, I think, must have been quite small at the time; a photograph I have of my infant school class, which must date from around 1964, perhaps even a little earlier, sports only one black child in our class of thirty-plus kids. Such diversity as there was at Northwold in the early 1960s was limited to a smattering of London Irish kids, distinguished for us only by accent and religion. Jewish kids such as myself mostly blended in as did the Irish children. The common currency, although we hardly knew it at the time, was class.

This I learned fast and hard when we transferred from our council flat in Stoke Newington to a newly-built one in Wembley. At my new school I was bewildered and alienated at first by rigid social niceties and well-policed gender norms unknown in Hackney. Diversity at Wembley Manor was religion. The area had a well-established Jewish population and the Jewish kids who opted for kosher food could leave the school grounds at lunchtime to take lunch in the cafeteria at the local synagogue close by. Though the South Asian expulsions from Africa would radically alter Wembley in the years to come, in 1966 it seemed even to my nine-year-old eyes a securely white and highly conformist environment, perfect for the message of the film relating Tanzania's move from dark to light. I do not recall a single family emigrating to the settler colonies when I was at Wembley Manor and no kids were prevented from befriending black children for the simple reason that there were none yet living in the community.

This, of course, would change radically only a few years later when this corner of north-west London became home to large numbers of South Asians forced out of East Africa by Africanization policies which were themselves a direct consequence of colonial rule. Yet curiously my first awareness of these policies, which would herald such changes in the British demographic, political and cultural landscape, came not from witnessing this influx of desperate South Asians but by the arrival in my school class, around 1970, of a white child born to Welsh parents working in Kenya. In the face of the political upheavals in newly decolonized East Africa, the Jones family had chosen to move back to the UK, settling in London. Their three children attended my comprehensive school, their parents finding work nearby. At school we were intrigued by the idea of a white African, the likes of which we were wholly unaware existed. Still ignorant of the reason for both colonial white and South Asian migration from newly independent African states, we found the notion of a white African wondrous and deeply odd. What my barely teenage self did not register at the time was the sea change Cathy's presence marked in how the empire was packaged for us in those years. Both my primary schools – Northwold in north-east London and Wembley Manor in the north-west suburbs – were in their different ways steeped in the Empire. Northwold, opened in 1903, was a product of the years when anxious politicians sought to inculcate colonial pride in an ever more visible and increasingly enfranchised working class. Mothers and children were seen as key to the survival and burnishment of Empire as much as were the adventurers, soldiers and statesmen who still peopled our history textbooks. Imperial motherhood arrived on the scene at much the same moment that schools like mine were popping up in working-class districts in urban Britain.[1] At Wembley Manor, the brickwork might not have been steeped in the Empire the way it was at Northwold, but that 1966 film screening certainly suggests that the invocation of imperial pride was paramount, as did the Great Lives lessons that formed a regular part of our curriculum, and in which classes we learned of the exploits of David Livingstone and Cecil Rhodes alongside Edith Cavell and Florence Nightingale, imbibing gender norms alongside imperial patriotism.

By the time I had moved to my secondary school in the late 1960s, however, the flag-waving epitomised by the creation in 1902 of Empire Day, had turned inward as the Empire got smaller and smaller. Now we heard more about the Commonwealth than about Britain's Empire. It was with this allegedly more collaborative arena that our future, we were told, lay; we would be the generation that enjoyed the benefits of a mutually profitable and peaceful co-existence between Britain and at least some of its former colonies. We were the children of decolonization, and at the heart of the metropolis we were also witness to its many manifestations.

It must have been around the same time that Cathy's family returned from Kenya that I had my first personal brush with racist violence. One of my neighbourhood friends, whose parents were post-war Polish émigrés, had friends among north-west London's South Asian community who were active in the Indian Workers' Association, a British organization dating initially from the 1930s but revived in the late 1950s by Punjabi immigration. As a special treat my friend and I were taken one evening to a gala event at the Southall branch attended by the actress Nargis. (I still have a photo of her, regal and beautiful, flanked by two gawky pre-teen girls who really had no idea who she was.) Returning home through the streets of Alperton, our car was forced to a halt by a fight between two rival gangs of skinheads. While some rolled and wrestled with one another in the path of the car, others were slamming their boots through the windows of cars parked on the street. Gaggles of skinhead girls shrieked aggressive encouragement from the margins of the scene. It was terrifying. Our driver was the Indian friend of Yvonne's parents and the racism for which skinhead gangs were known, with their boasts of 'Paki-bashing', was not lost on anyone in the car that night. We could barely breathe as we waited to see if they would notice us and turn their collective anger our way. At some point, they rolled to one side and our driver hit the pedal and sped away. We could hear the police sirens moving towards the melée as we left the scene unharmed physically but profoundly shaken, not just by the encounter with such raw violence but by the underlying and unspoken racist threat the episode so vividly represented. The current romanticization and indeed depoliticization of skinheads as all style masks the ugliness of a movement fuelled principally by a racist intent grounded in Britain's long-standing class inequalities as well as its colonial past, the two intimately and complicatedly bound.[2] As a white kid living in an increasingly racially diverse neighbourhood, my schoolmates and I chose, if not always consciously, between different performances of Britishness available to us. For those out of sympathy with mainstream conformity, the skinhead option was one route while anti-apartheid activism (the precursor to the anti-racism movement of the late 1970s) was another, its opposite. Both emerged out of Britain's long imperial past. I remember the regular and frequent vigils outside the South African Embassy in London, and the calls for Barclays Bank to divest from South Africa, as much as I remember the skinhead fight that night in Alperton.

One other episode stands out in my mind from these early and unprocessed encounters with Britain's colonial history. By 1968 the visually horrifying images of starving children caught in the Biafran War had become a mainstay of the British press, and in every house in the land fussy children were being told by exasperated parents that the food they refused to eat would be happily consumed by a grateful child in Biafra. Indeed the 'starving Biafran' was one of the catch-words of my generation: everyone knew it, so pervasive was the visual emplotment of the new humanitarian of the press. Once again, though, as a youngster I saw no connection between the plight of those faraway children and Britain's prior involvement in the region. The image of emaciated peoples of colour was not new, even if the Biafran example was at the far end of the spectrum. We knew about famines, about crop failures and the hunger they sparked, and somehow we also knew that these things were associated with places that were 'backward' and 'undeveloped'. That was the message of the film we had watched in 1966: that 'we' would be instrumental in preventing such tragedies in a bright (neo-colonial) future.

We knew, too, of the Irish famine, another product, as we were given it, of a nation too backward and impoverished to cope without 'our' help. The presence of an Irish working class in Britain's big cities confirmed both the good sense of British involvement and a picture of the Irish as somehow backward in development. They were, in a language used even by my left-of-centre parents, 'navvies', a term I now see as akin to 'coolie' but which was in common use in England (though perhaps not everywhere in Britain) in the 1960s and beyond. I would be well into my teens before I knew much of Irish culture; in my child's world, tattooed Irishmen worked on building sites as unskilled labourers while the women tended large broods of children, an unchanging and eternal verity.

By the time I was in my mid-teens, however, Irish activism had re-emerged as a serious threat in cities around Britain. The ruins left by IRA bombs became a common sight and we carefully looked for unattended packages on trains and tube platforms, in post boxes and on the streets. It was, I think, the first time I made a concrete connection between Britain's imperial past and its troubled present, the first time I began to formulate an anti-imperial agenda for myself. Yet as an undergraduate I nonetheless made a conscious decision to avoid imperial history, a field at that time indelibly associated with stuffiness, misplaced patriotism and and a kind of conservative smugness with which I wanted no truck. What was really astounding, looking back, was that though I was choosing to specialize in modern British history, I was allowed to get away with ignoring the Empire and indeed with constructing a degree that consisted in large part of English history. In the curriculum subscribed for us, I read widely, for sure, and both in an older canonical literature and in up-to-the-minute work, but the Empire might just as well have not existed. It did not figure in the monographs and articles assigned, nor in the weekly supervisions that characterized my undergraduate education. I did not question this lacuna in the slightest; I could see no particular connection between what was happening at 'home' and what was afoot in the colonies, even as the IRA worked, in bloody fashion, to force Britons to confront the consequences of colonial rule.

Yet, here I am, a historian who now insists on the close connection across and between colonies, as well as between colonies and the locus of imperial rule. How did that happen? As I have intimated, many of the episodes I have described thus far only began to coalesce for me as linked and as signalling the persistence of empire in post-war Britain much later in life when I became caught up in the history of imperialism. Even in the late 1970s when I had chosen the paths of anti-racist activity and feminism, I was blind to the lingering effects of colonial rule in Britain. I would certainly have identified as an anti-imperialist but the material ways in which the world in which I lived was shaped by the British Empire were not yet all that obvious to me.

It took the toll of Thatcherism to wake me from my stupor. Those grim years of rising unemployment and unrest coupled with the enriching of a class of young white urbanites bent on material accumulation were accompanied by a strident patriotism at its most vivid, of course, during the 1982 Falklands War. I was far from alone in watching with horror the evocation of a British greatness exemplified by the glory years of imperial rule, notwithstanding the fact that the government had recently downsized its defence of the very islands now to be gallantly rescued from the clutches of a cruel dictator. Empire was back alongside the allegedly 'Victorian values' the Thatcher government espoused even as they embarked on a brutally modernizing onslaught on banking and finance, albeit couched in the language of Victorian liberalism.

Three years later, there being little prospect of employment for a humanities scholar in the Thatcher years, I made my way rather nervously to Australia where a generous multi-year postdoctoral fellowship awaited me. Still trapped in the unexamined prejudices of my post-war English upbringing, I assumed that I would be stepping back into a world that would resemble nothing so much as provincial England in the 1950s. Indeed a senior scholar with whom I had worked and who had visited Australia came back saying exactly that. I envisioned boorish sexism alongside prissy Anglicanism, provincial cultural outlooks and minimal sophistication. But it was a well-paid job, there was nothing else on offer and I told myself I would return before too long.

It was thus that my unconsciously imperial and imperious self arrived in Adelaide in 1985 to find an intellectual, feminist and artistic milieu which quickly forced me to rethink my stand. This was not the narrow-minded sub-England we had been brought up to think it was. This was not a land peopled by those who could not 'make it' in Britain, as was sometimes hinted at in metropolitan discourse. I met plenty of migrants, and not just from Britain, and most proclaimed quite fairly that their standard of living was far higher than that which they had left behind. Many had brought with them, of course, ideas already imbibed elsewhere about racial hierarchies which allowed them to ignore or justify some of the rampant inequalities in Australian society – the almost total marginalization of Indigenous Australians as well as a growing anti-Asian sentiment aimed in this region at East Asian populations rather than, as in Britain, South Asians.

But when I arrived in the 1980s, Aboriginal as well as feminist activism was beginning to have an effect in the political arena as well as in daily life, and understandings of the Australian contemporary situation were powerfully grounded in the country's colonial past. One of the phrases I would hear over and over in the two years I spent living and working there was 'cultural cringe', indicating a persistent sense that metropolitan culture – meaning European/British – was innately superior to anything produced locally. Such cringe extended from music and literature to cheese-making, from painting to poetry. Change was in the air, but was hard-won and slow. Radio stations were, by the time I arrived, required to broadcast a minimum percentage of Australian performing or composing artists in their repertoire, but Christmas cards still often sported scenes of snow and cosy winter fires rather than the Australian reality of sunshine and summer fruits.

British history was still a standard feature of the school curriculum though no longer instead of more local histories. In universities, literature departments were shifting towards new work beyond the canon and beyond a Eurocentric focus. Australian history, Australian writers and artists (though as yet few Aboriginals among them) were beginning to form the focus of much scholarly work. These were interesting times to be in Australia and there were some remarkable institutional and political changes that would have been impossible in the Britain I had left behind. Both at the state and federal level, for example, offices of women's affairs staffed by activist feminists were carving out new political paths. No such positions existed or were envisioned in Britain where, despite having a woman prime minister, the system of gender privilege had barely been touched. It was impossible not to be impressed by the gains made by Australian women in so many arenas.

Persistent and structural racism prevented Aboriginal women from sharing many of these gains and the stain of prejudice was everywhere apparent: in the invisibility of Aboriginal peoples in the populous cities, in their absence from decision-making and in their cultural marginality. Australia was throwing off only elements of its colonial past, and they were largely those which enriched the lives of its now-dominant settler culture. That is not to downplay how many Australians were sensitive to such inequities, but merely to note the immense power of a colonially-inflected racism of extraordinary tenacity.

As a white British woman, however, I gained an immense amount, losing along the way those absurd imperial prejudices that elevated me by accident of birth over a clumsy provincial population. It was here, 'down under', where I learned that historical studies could move productively beyond the empirical, where I read the work of feminist theorists such as Liz Grosz and Genevieve Lloyd, then barely known in Britain but whose ideas would force me to push my own intellectual limits. Australia was where the critiques of colonialism I had dutifully read, without much real interest, came to life in the works of some of the best minds I had ever encountered. There was a sharp, critically-minded freshness to the work of my colleagues which made the English intellectual scene I had left behind seem stale, dowdy and stuck in a self-repeating rut. It was an exhilarating loss for me of long-formed prejudices shaped, as I quickly realized, by a narrative of empire that could not put aside deep-seated assumptions of superiority and centrality.

It would still be some years before my own work turned to questions of empire, not least because I was under contract for a couple of books conceived before I arrived in Australia, and which were wholly English in their vision. Australia showed me, however, what my English upbringing could never achieve, that Britain was not the centre of a political and cultural universe. It had achieved a profound degree of economic and political power globally though, in reality, for a fairly short span of time, but its power was evanescent, fitful and always open to challenge. I had learned, too, that the challenges to that power could facilitate tremendously exciting ideas and research in myriad arenas.

Australia, then, was an intellectual watershed for me. It sharpened my historical skills in a more theoretical vein. It challenged the colonial stereotypes of my upbringing. It showed me a feminist activism at work in governance. I still, though, could not envisage a scholarship focused on empire; indeed the option never occurred to me. It would take a move to the United States to precipitate that and it was the product of a curious mix of opportunities and the AIDS crisis of the late 1980s which opened that door.

Shortly after arriving in the United States I became involved, alongside my historical work, in public policy. Asked to assess how far the gender-neutral statute governing prostitution in the state was, in practice, punishing women more than men, it was impossible not to get embroiled in the emerging politics of AIDS, which verged at the time on the hysterical. Although associated mainly (and erroneously) at the time with gay men, public health officials worried also about transmission among drug users and in commercial sex exchanges. In the American context, these conversations invariably turned, however well-intentioned the strategy, on race. Everywhere I looked I found not only the gender bias I had been asked to test (and it was quite palpable) but, closely tied to it, deep racial bias – in arrest rates, assumption of culpability, attribution of 'dangerous' behaviours and likelihood of suspicion. I was, of course, witnessing the poison at the heart of American social life and as a historian, I could trace its roots not only in slavery but in a colonial past that made racialized enslavement possible and justifiable.

I could trace not only a tenacious and powerful racism rooted in colonialism and slavery but anxiety about non-normative sexualities and sexually transmissible diseases. One of the reasons I was asked to undertake this work was because I was at the time writing on feminist activism in Britain that had gelled around the Contagious Diseases Acts passed in the 1860s. Fears around what were known at the time as venereal diseases prompted draconian legislation that targeted women sex workers servicing a military clientele, while ignoring those who sought out their services. The double standard that so irked activist women at the time was also, of course, one which spoke to the key role of sexual norms in shaping social conformity: active sexuality belonged in the male realm alone. Thus men seeking paid sex were scratching a healthy itch, but the entrepreneurial women providing them with the necessary services violated the tightly governed parameters of female behaviour. In the late twentieth century, the identification of AIDS as either a gay plague or a foreign import originating in non-Western arenas played on startlingly similar fears. It was women, as well as men, selling sex; it was immigrant communities; it was gay men who threatened the socio-sexual fabric. The more I witnessed these reactions in the late 1980s, the more I looked to the links between race, gender and class in earlier eras to understand them, and the more the persistent spectre of imperialism struck me as a central explanatory feature. Finishing the domestic projects I had begun in Australia, I knew that my future work could no longer afford to treat the Empire as a separate and hermetically-sealed phenomenon. The colonial sphere was no longer the province of besuited men making decisions at the centre, but a melange of resistance, complicity and experimentation complicated by perceived racial and sexual difference.

These realizations could hardly have come at a more opportune moment for this was an exciting time in the academy. Postcolonial and feminist theory were finding one another, albeit not always harmoniously. Queer theory, energized by the AIDS crisis, was pushing the boundaries of what was possible. Attention to empires was moving from a dominantly diplomatic mode to more comprehensive and expansive considerations, a change sometimes dubbed the 'new imperial history'.

I often wonder what kind of scholarship I would have produced had I stayed in my native Britain rather than moving first to Australia and then to the United States. The rich work on empires that has since emerged in the UK (and is well represented in this volume) would doubtless have pushed me to think seriously about such a shift in emphasis. I suspect, though, that my rethinking might have come at a later moment and that understanding the links between race, sex and and empire which have, since the 1990s, been so central to my work, might have taken longer for me to see. The immediacy of the challenges posed by new environments and by scholars already steeped in critiques of empire, and in racial and gender politics, was exactly what I needed as I found my feet as a newly-minted scholar committed to social justice. Staying put, even in the hostile Thatcherite environment which had been responsible for my leaving the country in the first place, would have brought its own challenges, and I deeply admire those in my generation who stuck it out against all odds. For me, however, the traces of empire threaded through my childhood moulded me in ways I came to recognize only after leaving Britain. Although a child of decolonization, the effects and impacts of Britain's colonial past remained opaque to me even as the sensibilities shaped by empire took root. Australia offered me the legacy of a determined and unabashed feminism and the beginnings of a consciousness about imperial hierarchies. The United States, where racial tensions continue to scar the landscape painfully (riots in Ferguson, Missouri, are headline news as I write) but where the politics of sexuality – depite the best efforts of evangelical Christianity – has pointed the way for more than thirty years now, honed my understanding of the critical connections between gender, race and sexuality. Britain trained me as a historian, and trained me well if narrowly, but it took my leaving to appreciate just how much the politics of empire, and perhaps most powerfully of decolonization, had shaped me in every way imaginable.

Notes

1 Anna Davin, 'Imperialism and Motherhood', *History Workshop*, 6 (1978): 9–65.

2 Derek Ridgers, *Skinheads 1979–1984* (London: Omnibus Press, 2014) and articles in, for example, *The Guardian* ('Skinheads: a photogenic, extremist corner of British youth culture', 19 August 2014: http://www.theguardian.com/artanddesign/2014/aug/19/skinheads-derek-ridgers-portraits-street-photography-70s-80s-youth-culture) and *The Telegraph* ('Being a skinhead was about sharing a sense of style', 20 August 2014: http://www.telegraph.co.uk/men/fashion-and-style/11034834/Being-a-skinhead-was-about-sharing-a-sense-of-style.html).

10

From South Asian Studies to Global History:

Searching for Asian Perspectives

Shigeru Akita
b. 1958

The trajectory of my academic career reflects the changing position of Asia in the global economy during my lifetime. Contemporary India is now officially recognized as one of the most dynamic BRIC countries and attracts heavy investments around the world. China, in turn, has become the largest economy in the world, according to the International Monetary Fund (IMF). Meanwhile, Japan, Korea, and other East and Southeast Asian countries are important contributors to the world economy as well. When I was a student at the Hiroshima University, these developments were scarcely discernible anywhere apart from Japan. The key question at that time was why so much of Asia remained economically underdeveloped, and the answer seemed tied to European, and especially British, imperial domination of the region before the Second World War. In the decades since then, my understanding of Asia's role in the global economy has changed. I have adopted a broader historical perspective that reaches back into the early modern era, prior to European domination, and acquired a more nuanced appreciation of the relationship between British imperial and local Asian economic interactions. While imperial hegemony remains an important factor in understanding the historical roots of globalization, Britain and Europe loom less large in my historical analysis, just as they loom less large in the contemporary global economy. We can identify the shifting relationships among several regions, particularly the formation and development of an

Asia-Pacific economy, as contributors to the development of the global economy. This reinterpretation of world or global history seeks to be relevant for the twenty-first century.

I studied at Hiroshima University for eight years (1977–85) as an undergraduate, MA and PhD student. Hiroshima University has a long tradition in British (domestic) history, especially in early modern political thought and state finance. However, I was originally attracted to the history of the British Empire as a result of my interest in the historical origins of Indian 'poverty' in the 1960s and 1970s, often referred to as the North–South Divide.

In my fourth year as an undergraduate, I had the chance to listen to a lecture by the prominent economic historian, Akihiko Yoshioka. Yoshioka was a famous economic historian at Tohoku University, where he specialized in British history, publishing several books on British capitalism. Among his books, there was a small one for Japanese general readers, entitled *Indo to Igirisu* [*India and the United Kingdom*] (Tokyo: Iwanami-publishers, 1975), which dealt with the economic history of British colonial rule in India in the nineteenth and twentieth centuries. He analysed the historical origins of Indian poverty as rooted in colonial underdevelopment, focusing on the colonial mechanism of the 'drain of wealth' from India to the UK. His study of British India seemed to me a pioneering work of so-called 'dependency theory', or metropolitan-peripheral analyses of the capitalist world economy. Yoshioka's intensive lecture on British imperialism in the early twentieth century encouraged me to study the British Empire and the Raj on a bilateral Indo-British basis. I was not satisfied with the metropolitan analysis of modern 'British' capitalism and economic development.

While I was studying for my MA in 1981, Immanuel Wallerstein's provocative book, *The Modern World-System I*, was translated into Japanese, introducing me to world-systems analysis.[1] Soon Wallerstein's criticism of European-centred studies of capitalistic development provoked a controversial debate with Patrick O'Brien about the contribution of the periphery in *Economic History Review*.[2] I was sympathetic to the arguments of Wallerstein about the economic significance of the periphery, and the stimulating debate between Wallerstein and O'Brien gave me a great stimulus to locate my research on British India within the wider context of the world-system framework.

As for the studies of the British Empire, the famous debate on 'the imperialism of free trade', provoked by J. Gallagher and R. Robinson in 1953, still continued to resonate in the late 1970s in Japan, where free-trade principles were considered crucial to Japan's economic 'miracle' from the 1960s on. Kenzo Moori, a prominent economic historian at the University of Tokyo, published a book on the imperialism of free trade in 1978, introducing major debates in the Anglo/American world to Japanese historians, which led to the controversies between Yoshioka and Moori on the peculiar features of British imperialism.[3] Even though these Japanese debates on nineteenth-century British imperialism were heated and intense, the basic framework of their argument was still limited to the 'British' nation-state or national economy. Colonies and dependencies were treated as appendages of metropolitan society and economy, while formal and informal methods of rule were seen as interchangeable and complimentary to each other. I was strongly influenced by the works of Japanese economic historians in these debates on British imperialism. However, at this stage, my approach was completely dependent on the European-centred framework and the extension of (British) national history, only introducing and partly modifying the excellent works of Anglo-American scholars.

After getting a job at Osaka University of Foreign Studies (OUFS) in 1985, I became more familiar with the research being carried out in Asian area studies, especially on South Asian studies. I became more attentive to the active and important roles played by local Asian agents and Indigenous peoples in their interactions with metropolitan imperial powers.

The OUFS was a small college, concentrating on foreign language education and area studies. I was attached to the English Department as an assistant lecturer, teaching British history and culture. Fortunately for my research activities, I soon became a member of a research group on Asia-Pacific Studies, organized by Osamu Akagi. This small group consisted of specialists in Asian and American area studies who knew every detail of local/regional customs and cultures and had strong personal networks with their own research regions. They usually used local and vernacular languages as well as English for their field-work and contemporary analyses. I was greatly impressed by their energetic and deep understanding of Asian local societies and their affection for the regions they studies. Fortunately for my research on British India, I learned a lot from the work of my colleagues in the Department of Hindi/Urdu languages, especially Sho Kuwajima, who is a specialist in Indian contemporary history and international relations.[4] He kindly introduced me to several prominent Indian historians of British colonialism and its impact on Indian local society. Through joint research with these Asian area specialists on the Second World War,[5] I was able to broaden my perspectives, paying more attention to Asian local peoples as active and autonomous actors, even under colonial rule.

In addition to these encounters with Asian area studies, I learned a lot from excellent works about Asian economic history and British urban social history in the 1980s. When I moved to Osaka, I became a member of a small research forum. This forum had been organized and chaired by a prominent economic historian, Sakae Tsunoyama at Wakayama University, and it held bi-monthly research meetings on British urban social history in Kyoto. The forum paid keen attention to the transformation of urban social and economic life in the United Kingdom from the eighteenth century onwards, through the expansion of overseas trade and increased imports of various primary products (tea, sugar and tobacco) and Asian manufactured goods (cotton textiles and porcelain). These imported goods drastically transformed the material life of the British people, and their pattern of consumption was 'globalized', to a great extent, by British overseas expansion and the formation of a world economy. Tsunoyama and his colleague, Minoru Kawakita, edited four books in the 1980s and 1990s about British socio-economic or urban social life in the nineteenth century.[6] In addition, Tsunoyama wrote a bestselling book about the world history of tea drinking, and Kawakita published a popular book on the history of sugar. Both scholars successfully presented the simultaneous development of the mass-consumption society in Great Britain and the underdevelopment of the non-European world, especially the West Indies and British India, by utilizing the key concept of 'world capitalism' or the modern world-system.[7] I was strongly influenced by their ideas and methodology for connecting local (British) history with the global development of the world economy.

From the mid-1980s, a new trend in 'global/world history' studies appeared in Japan, partly due to the slackening and then the demise of the Cold War regime, but mostly to new developments in Asian economic history in the 1980s, which were responding to the implications of the 'East Asian miracle' or the resurgence of the East Asian economy. The distinctive features of these newly emerging studies were the challenges to Eurocentric structures and paradigms by Asian economic historians. It is worth mentioning here the works of three distinguished Japanese scholars, Takeshi Hamashita, Heita Kawakatsu and Kaoru Sugihara, who share a common critical viewpoint towards Eurocentric or Western-oriented historiography.

Hamashita insisted on the importance of the development of a Chinese-centred world-system and its resilient tributary trade system. He also emphasized the active roles of Asian merchants' networks in the promotion of intra-Asian trade in the early-modern period.[8] Kawakatsu pointed to the two different paths of development followed by the West European and Japanese cotton textile industries, and revealed the coexistence of coarse Asian cotton goods with fine cottons from Manchester.[9] While the arguments of Hamashita and Kawakatsu were oriented towards the identification of the indigenous roots of the Asian regional economies, they were unable to incorporate global linkages or the development of a capitalist world economy.

In contrast to these two scholars, Kaoru Sugihara revealed that the formation and development of intra-Asian trade from the late nineteenth century to the early 1940s was related to global economic developments. Using multi-national archives of trade statistics, Sugihara observed that industrialization in Japan and British India was not only generated through the 'cotton-centred' linkage, but promoted by the rise in income as a result of the growth of exports of primary products to the West. He calls this the 'final demand linkage effect'.[10] Both sets of connections contributed greatly to the promotion of industrialization-based trade under the umbrella of the 'Pax Britannica'. In this context, Sugihara's work clearly linked imperial and international history in Asia and gave me insight into the importance of Asian trading networks and their unique importance within the world economy. The new developments in Asian economic history confirmed the usefulness of 'relational history', which I learned from the excellent works by and intimate discussions with Tsunoyama and Kawakita in Osaka and Kyoto.

In 1994–5, I was able to obtain a one year research grant from the Japanese Education Ministry to go to London for intensive research. This was my first long overseas stay using public funds. (I had lacked experience of overseas study in my student days and had been teaching at OUFS for almost ten years.) Owing to the appreciation of the Japanese yen against the US dollar and the pound sterling from the late 1980s, especially after the Plaza Accord of 1985, it became easier for Japanese scholars to make long overseas research trips after they had teaching positions. I decided to attach myself to the Japan Research Centre (JRC) at the University of London's School of Oriental and African Studies (SOAS) and asked its director, Kaoru Sugihara, to arrange my appointment. Fortunately, I obtained the status of visiting research fellow of JRC and was able to attend seminars on Japan and East Asia. Once settled in London, I also spent time at the Institute of Historical Research (IHR), University of London, where I had opportunities to meet and talk with many prominent British imperial historians.

The IHR is a unique research institute for historical studies. Many seminars are held on weekday evenings from 5.00 pm, and there is a comfortable common room for members. Fortunately, through the kind introduction of my Japanese colleague, I met Steven R. B. Smith, the Academic Secretary, and Patrick O'Brien, the Director of IHR. Smith warmly encouraged me to attend several evening seminars, such as those devoted to British Imperial History, Victorian and Edwardian Society, Social and Economic History, the Long Eighteenth Century and so on, in order to become familiar with the British style of academic discussion. In particular, I became a regular member of the British Imperial History seminar, organized by Peter Marshall, Andrew Porter and Glyn Williams. This seminar focused on political and diplomatic history topics rather than cultural or postcolonial discourse analyses. The organizer, Marshall, warmly welcomed me and after almost one year of regular attendance, I was offered the chance to present my research at the seminar, which became the turning point of my research career.

Before starting my overseas research in London, my research was concerned with the overseas dispatch of Indian armies in the late nineteenth century and its implications for Indian society and finance in the context of the transformation of the British-centred imperial order. However, when I was asked to present a paper at the imperial history seminar, Marshall asked me to speak about the relationship between the British informal empire and East Asia, especially in connection with Meiji Japan. Marshall's suggestion was based on a study I had begun to make comparing South Asia (British India) and East Asia (Japan and China) in the context of inter-imperial relationships. I had just finished writing a short English essay for contribution to an edited volume by Ray Dumett of Purdue University, and I gave that essay to Marshall after my arrival in London.[11]

Before coming to London, I had attended a round-table session on 'gentlemanly capitalism' at the American History Association (AHA) conference in San Francisco in 1993. Here I was greatly influenced by the 'gentlemanly capitalism' paradigm developed by two prominent imperial historians, A. G. Hopkins and Peter Cain. I first met Tony Hopkins in 1992, when he came to Osaka as our guest speaker. In Japan, some of my colleagues and I had organized a research group, entitled the Japanese Society for the Study of British Imperial and Commonwealth History (JASBICH) in November 1989, for the purpose of enlarging our perspectives and establishing closer scholarly networks with British historians. With strong support from my friend, Yukio Takeuchi of Nihon University, who had strong personal connections with Peter Marshall and Tony Hopkins, we had started to invite prominent British scholars to Japan for academic discussions. Hopkins was the second guest speaker at JASBICH and as general secretary of our Society, I had arranged his seminar in Osaka and a short visit to Kyoto, the old capital of Japan. When I guided Hopkins to Kyoto for sightseeing, instead of seeing the sights we talked almost non-stop about my research on British India and the Japanese historiography of British imperial history. He strongly encouraged me to do comparative studies of modern empires and expressed appreciation for my research. That was the first time I had intensively discussed my studies with a prominent British scholar. It gave me the self-confidence and motivation to engage in academic collaboration. The AHA roundtable widened my interests still further, and Marshall's offer of a seminar at IHR brought me another opportunity to conduct intensive comparative research on empires.

Having decided to accept Marshall's proposal, I asked for advice from Kaoru Sugihara, and he suggested that I examine some rarely used documents on the economic conditions of Japan and China at the turn of the century, the *British Consular Reports on Japan and China*. Consular reports are neglected records for economic historians. They contain a wide array of fragmentary first-hand information on economic affairs as reported by British consuls and consul generals to the Board of Trade, and it is difficult to analyse this detailed data and locate it in a wider context. But I sought to place the gentlemanly capitalism paradigm in an Asian perspective, examining 'intra-Asian trade' and the complementary relationship that developed between British financial interests and Asian industrialization, by using British consular reports and some related economic magazines such as *The Economist* and *The Banker's Magazine*, all of which were located on the basement floor of the London School of Economics and Political Sciences (LSE) library.

In order to connect Asian or Japanese historiography with that in the West, one can here point to a mutual connection or interdependence of economic interests between a hegemonic Great Britain and the peripheral East Asian countries. We can detect several kinds of 'complementarity' from the turn of the twentieth century. For example, complementarity evolved between rapid Japanese industrialization and increased British exports of capital goods.[12] The decline of British cotton goods exports to Japan was traded off against the growth of Japanese demand for capital goods, especially for British-made cotton textile machinery. Around the same time, the Japanese government issued five Russo-Japanese War loans of 1904–5 on the London and New York stock exchanges, using the international networks of merchant banks. During the period 1900–13, Japan's large capital imports accounted for over 20 per cent of total foreign government loan issues in London.[13] This close Anglo-Japanese financial relationship and Japanese dependence on the City of London is another aspect of Anglo-Japanese complementarity in economic relations.

This complementarity between British financial power and East Asian economic development remained an important element in Anglo-Japanese economic interaction until the late 1930s. In the 1930s, after the restoration of China's tariff autonomy, a similar relationship arose between Chinese industrialization and British financial interests. With regard to the economic interaction between the United Kingdom and East Asia, a new interpretation of the international order of Asia can be offered.[14] In the 1930s, the Chinese currency reform of 1935 was the central focus of economic interaction. After the success of the currency reform, the new Chinese dollar was stabilized against sterling and the US dollar, and was linked in a *de facto* fashion with sterling. The stabilization of currency promoted the development of Chinese industrial production and the export of consumer goods under the protectionist policies of the Nationalist Government.[15] Thus the rise of economic nationalism in China was achieved by taking advantage of the international order of Asia and the financial influence of Great Britain. In British India, economic development, also centred on cotton goods, was helped by the rise of tariff protection after the acquisition of 'fiscal autonomy' in 1921. As long as British financial interests were protected by the high fixed exchange rate of the Indian rupee at 1s. 6d., the Government of India allowed Indian industries to grow and export their products to Asian countries.[16] Dependency theory failed to make sense of these cases of colonial industrialization.

We can clearly understand these unique developments by reference to the Cain–Hopkins thesis, which held that core British economic interests had shifted from manufacturing to finance and services, the main economic basis of gentlemanly capitalism. This kind of complementarity, which in effect encouraged industrialization in East Asia, represents a special relationship, especially in the non-European world. It implies not rivalry or competition but cooperation or alignment as long as individual national interests are in concert with each other. The coexistence between British economic interests and East Asian industrialization added to the hegemonic power of Great Britain, and strengthened the status of the City of London as an international centre of high-finance.[17] The similar type of economic complementarity might be recognized between the 'Pax Americana' and the 'East Asian miracle' from the 1970s to the present, with the formation of interdependence between the financial and services interests of Wall Street and the rapid industrialization of East and Southeast Asian countries in the late twentieth and early twenty-first centuries.

My first long overseas stay in London became very fruitful and successful in broadening my perspectives and making intimate collaborating networks with British scholars, thanks to the friendly support and encouragement of many friends, especially John Mercer and regular members of the imperial history seminar at IHR. After returning to Osaka in September 1994, I was inspired to organize a cross-boundary joint research network in Osaka, with cooperation from other Asian economic historians and international relations (IR) specialists. Fortunately, I was nominated as one of the leaders of a huge joint-research project on contemporary South Asia, organized by Nobuko Nagasaki, and I was able to explore the transformation of contemporary India and its relationship to the modern world-system from longer historical points of view and perspectives.[18]

I had a second opportunity to conduct overseas research in London, financially supported by the Japanese Foreign Ministry, in 2000–1. This time, I was attached to the department of economic history at the London School of Economics as a visiting professor. My host was Patrick O'Brien, who had returned to LSE as Centenary Professor of Global History after his official retirement from IHR. O'Brien started his new initiative by creating a 'global economic history' course at LSE. I was influenced not only by the academic challenge posed by him and his Global Economic History Network (GEHN) project,[19] but by the contemporary transformation of the world economy, notably the resurgence of East Asia from the late 1990s. I have sought to highlight the Asian impetus to globalization in the context of global history.

British imperial history in the 'long nineteenth century' can be seen as a bridge to global history.[20] The orthodox interpretations of the modern world-system have been challenged by the emergence of new studies about the modern world economy that focus on Asia, and by recent developments in Asian economic history in Japan, as well as in the Anglo-American academic world.[21] The main focus of reconsideration and the front line of new research are concerned with the early modern world (the 'long eighteenth century') and the resurgence of the contemporary East Asian economy or the 'East Asian miracle'.

The modern world-system was sustained and stabilized by the presence of hegemonic states. Thus, the rise and fall of hegemonic states and the transformation or shift in hegemony become important subjects to explore in the field of global history. I started to evaluate the role played by Great Britain in the capitalist world-economy and its implications for economic development (especially industrialization) in the 'long nineteenth century'. As I mentioned before, I reconsidered the international order of East Asia in the first half of the twentieth century, which was partly shaped by Britain's influence but which maintained a relatively unique autonomous status in a capitalist world-economy.[22]

In October 2003, after my return from London, I obtained a new professorship at the Graduate School of Letters, Osaka University. From this date, my interest greatly shifted to global history and I started a new series of seminars and workshops on global history with my colleagues at the department of world history.[23] In our department, we have tried to integrate the excellent work in area studies, especially those on Asian studies, with which we are more familiar and where we have the comparative advantage of multi-archival researches in indigenous Asian languages. In order to examine the interactions or connections between the regional factors revealed through area studies and global history, we have adopted a stimulating field of research on 'maritime history', and organized several workshops with specialists in Asian, Japanese and European maritime history. My closest colleague, Shiro Momoki, and his group have revealed the densely developed trade networks of Chinese, Indian and local merchants in Asian waters from the tenth century to the early modern period, especially from the time of the Ming dynasty in China in the latter half of the fourteenth century. European powers encountered these Asian trading networks and utilized them for their own long-distance trade between Europe and Asia in the 'long sixteenth century'. They also made huge profits from their entry into the intra-Asian trade network, with the collaboration of Asian merchants and the acquiescence of political authorities in Asia. By fully utilizing local Asian historical documents as well as European sources, Momoki and his group published an introductory book in 2008, which is the first comprehensive book on Asian maritime history in the world.[24]

Meanwhile, my research group, led by Tsukasa Mizushima of the University of Tokyo and George Souza of the University of Texas at San Antonio, is evaluating the 'long eighteenth century' from the perspectives of Asian port cities and their hinterlands. This group uses the new concept of 'commodity chains'[25] to reveal wider economic linkages and connections in Asia, and has tried to differentiate Asian patterns of commodity chains in the early modern period from modern European/American ones.[26] By using the framework of 'maritime history' and exploring connections or linkages, we can integrate a trans-regional or intra-regional perspective into studies of global history.

Through these academic collaborations, my department of world history is now acting as one of the leading centres of global/world history studies in Japan as well as in Asia, with the official recognition of Osaka University. In May 2009, a new network for the study of global/world history in Asia, the Asian Association of World Historians (AAWH) was formed in Osaka and more than 200 scholars and school teachers attended its inaugural congress there to discuss world/global history studies and world history education.[27] The AAWH launched a new academic e-journal, entitled *Asian Review of World Histories* in January 2013.[28] We are continuing to collaborate further with other international and transnational academic networks for the creation of a truly non-Eurocentric global history from Asian perspectives.

My interest in British imperial history has been shaped by my search for Asian perspectives on its economic consequences. In the course of my career, I have followed a line of inquiry that began by interpreting the British imperial impact in the context of dependency theory and Asian area studies, shifted towards an examination of the 'Pax Britannica' as a system that facilitated Asian economic development, and led me in recent years to a broader understanding of the place of Asia in the process of globalization. I realize in retrospect that my intellectual trajectory has mirrored in certain respects the broader shifts that have taken place in Asia's relationship with the West and its place in the global economy.

Notes

1 Immanuel Wallerstein (Minoru Kawakita trs.), *Kindai-Sekai Sisutemu I* (Tokyo: Iwanami-publisher, 1981).

2 Patrick O'Brien, 'European Economic Development: The Contribution of the Periphery', *Economic History Review*, 2nd series, XXXV-1 (1982); Immanuel Wallerstein, 'European Economic Development: A Comment on O'Brien', *Economic History Review*, 2nd series, XXXVI-4 (1983).

3 Kenzo Moori, *Jiyuboueki-Teikokushugi* [*The Imperialism of Free Trade*] (Tokyo: Tokyo University Press, 1978).

4 Sho Kuwajima, *The Mutiny in Singapore: War, Anti-War and the War for India's Independence* (Ahmedabad: Rainbow Publishers, 2006).

5 The Association of Asian Studies, ed., *The Chronology of Asia in the 1940s* (Osaka University of Foreign Studies, 1995).

6 Sakae Tsunoyama, ed., *Seikatsu no Sekaishi 10: Sangyo-Kakumei to Minshu* [*The World History of Everyday Life 10: The Industrial Revolution and the People*] (Tokyo: Kawadeshobō-shinsha, 1975); Sakae Tsunoyama and Minoru Kawakita, eds, *Rojiura no Daieiteikoku* [*The British Empire Seen from a Rear-lane*] (Tokyo: Heibon-sha, 1982); Minoru Kawakita, ed., *'Hi-rōudō-jikan' no Seikatsu-shi: Eikouhu Raifustairu no Tanjyo* [*History of Everyday Life during Non-working Hours: The Birth of the British Life-style*] (Tokyo: Ribroport, 1987); Minoru Kawakita and Akihiro Sashi, eds, *Shūen karano Manazashi* [*A Look from the Periphery*] (Tokyo: Yamakawa-shuppan, 2000).

7 Sakae Tsunoyama, *Cha no Sekaishi* [*World History of Tea*] (Tokyo: Chuo-Koronsha, 1980); Minoru Kawakita, *Satò no Sekaishi* [*World History of Sugar*]

(Tokyo: Iwanami-shoten, 1996). These books were translated into Korean and Chinese.

8 Takeshi Hamashita, *Kindai Chugoku no Kokusaiteki Keiki: Choko Boeki Shisutemu to Kindai Ajia* [*International Factors Affecting Modern China: The Tributary Trade System and Modern Asia*] (Tokyo: Tokyo University Press, 1990); Takeshi Hamashita, *China, East Asia and the Global Economy: Regional and Historical Perspectives*, ed. Linda Grove and Mark Selden (Abingdon: Routledge, 2008).

9 Heita Kawakatsu, 'International Competition in Cotton Goods in the Late Nineteenth Century: Britain versus East Asia', in W. Fisher, R. M. McInnis and J. Schneider, eds, *The Emergence of a World Economy, 1500–1914, Beitraege zur Wirtschafts- und Sozialgeschichte*, Band 33-2 (Wiesbaden, 1986); A. J. H. Latham and Heita Kawakatsu, eds, *Japanese Industrialization and the Asian Economy* (London and New York, 1994).

10 Kaoru Sugihara, *Ajia-kan Boeki no Keisei to Kozo* [*Patterns and Development of Intra-Asian Trade*] (Kyoto: Mineruva-shobo, 1996), chapter 1.

11 Shigeru Akita, 'British Informal Empire in East Asia, 1880–1939: A Japanese Perspective', in Raymond E. Dumett, ed., *Gentlemanly Capitalism and British Imperialism: The New Debate on Empire* (London: Longman, 1999), chapter 6.

12 Shigeru Akita, '"Gentlemanly Capitalism", Intra-Asian Trade and Japanese Industrialization at the Turn of the Last Century', *Japan Forum*, 8, 1 (1996), pp. 51–65.

13 Toshio Suzuki, *Japanese Government Loan Issues on the London Capital Market 1870–1913* (London: Athlone Press, 1994), pp. 1–3, 83–4.

14 See also, Shigeru Akita and Naoto Kagotani, eds, *1930 nendai no Ajia Kokusai Chitujo* [*International Order of Asia in the 1930s*] (Hiroshima: Keisui-sha, 2001).

15 Toru Kubo, *Senkan-ki Chugoku Jiritsu eno Mosaku: Kanzei-Tsuka seisaku to Keizai Hatten* [*China's Quest for Sovereignty in the Inter-war Period: Tariff Policy and Economic Development*] (Tokyo: Tokyo University Press, 1999).

16 B. R. Tomlinson, *The Political Economy of the Raj 1914–1947: The Economics of Decolonization in India* (London, 1979); B. R. Tomlinson, *The New Cambridge History of India*, III-3, *The Economy of Modern India, 1860–1970* (Cambridge, 1993), chapters 3 and 4.

17 Shigeru Akita, *Igirisu-Teikoku to Ajia Kokusai Chitujo* [*The British Empire and International Order of Asia*] (Nagoya: Nagoya University Press, 2003).

18 Shigeru Akita and Tsukasa Mizushima, eds, *Sekai-Shisutemu to Network* [*Networks and the World System*], Vol. 6 of *Contemporary South Asia* (Tokyo: University of Tokyo Press, 2003).

19 Global Economic History Network (GEHN) at LSE research project – http://www.lse.ac.uk/economicHistory/Research/GEHN/Home.aspx (accessed 8 July 2015).

20 Shigeru Akita, 'Introduction: From Imperial History to Global History', in Shigeru, Akita ed., *Gentlemanly Capitalism, Imperialism and Global History* (Basingstoke: Palgrave Macmillan, 2002).

21 R. Bin Wong, *China Transformed: Historical Change and the Limits of European Experience* (Ithaca: Cornell University Press, 1997); Takeshi Hamashita, *Choukou Shisutemu to Kindai-Ajia* [*Tributary System and Modern Asia*] (Tokyo: Iwanami-shoten, 1997); A. G. Frank, *Re-Orient: Global Economy in the Asian Age* (Berkeley and London: University of California Press, 1998); Kenneth Pomeranz, *The Great Divergence: China, Europe, and the Making of the Modern World Economy* (Princeton: Princeton University Press, 2000).

22 Shigeru Akita and Nick White, eds, *International Order of Asia in the 1930s and 1950s* (London: Ashgate, 2010).

23 Global History Online at Graduate School of Letters, Osaka University – http://www.globalhistoryonline.com/ (accessed 8 July 2015).

24 Shiro Momoki, Kayoko Fujita, Shinji Yamauchi and Takeshi Hasuda, eds, *Kaiiki-Ajiashi Kenkyū Nyūmon* [*Introduction to Research on Maritime Asian History*] (Tokyo: Iwanami-shoten, 2008).

25 As for the concept of 'commodity chains', see Steven Topik, Carlos Marichal and Zephyr Frank, eds, *From Silver to Cocaine: Latin American Commodity Chains and the Building of the World Economy, 1500–2000* (Durham, NC: Duke University Press, 2006).

26 Tsukasa Mizushima, George Souza and Dennis Flynn, eds, *Place, Space, and Time: Asian Hinterlands and Political Economic Development in the Long Eighteenth Century* (Leiden: Brill, 2014).

27 See *The Proceedings of The First Congress of The Asian Association of World Historians: World History Studies and World History Education, 29–31 May 2009, Osaka University/Nakanoshima Center*, CD-ROM (Osaka, March 2010) – http://www.theaawh.org/ (site temporarily closed).

28 *Asian Review of World Histories* (The Official Journal of AAWH) – http://www.thearwh.org/5_journal1.htm (accessed 8 July 2015).

11

Crooked Lines and Zigzags:[1]

From the Neo-colonial to the Colonial

Mrinalini Sinha
b. 1960

If there are obstacles, the shortest line between two points may be the crooked line.

BERTOLT BRECHT

I began my graduate training in India – that erstwhile 'Jewel in the Crown' – at a time when interest in the study of imperialism was more likely to be provoked by US imperialism in Southeast Asia and Latin America than by the history of the British Empire. My generation of middle-class graduates in India – a second generation of the 'daughters of independence' as it were – considered ourselves sufficiently removed from the history of the British Empire that had once produced such cherished imperial slogans as 'The sun never sets on the British Empire' and 'Britannia rules the waves'. In fact, we considered ourselves equally removed from our parents' generation who had come up with the irreverent nationalist send-ups of these slogans: 'The sun never sets on the British Empire because even God wouldn't trust an Englishman in the dark' and 'Britannia waives the rules'. I considered myself heir to a different struggle against imperialism. The latter was most memorably epitomized in the renaming of the street address for the American Consulate in Calcutta (now Kolkata) to Ho Chi Minh Sarani (street) and in the chants that rang out in the streets of that city: '*Amar Nam, Tomar Nam, Vietnam, Vietnam*' (My name, your name, Vietnam, Vietnam). Yet, since I was born too late, this was only my inheritance; it was never really *my* struggle.

There were other inheritances, to be sure, from the days of the Raj, but these I had chosen wilfully to neglect. Growing up in a family with parents who were of my parents' age, and with an extended family of grandparents and uncles and aunts, there was never any shortage of 'Plain Tales from the Raj'. I suspect that at some point I must have asked my parents the Indian equivalent of the Euro-American question, 'What did you do in the War, Daddy?': 'What did you do in the freedom struggle (as the anti-colonial nationalist movement in India was called), Daddy and Mummy?' Yet I would probably have found the answers to those questions wholly unsatisfactory as a child. On my father's side of the family, with which in true north Indian patrilineal and patrilocal tradition we identified most strongly, there was a family tradition of having served the Raj loyally in the Indian Police. My father, breaking from that tradition, to be sure, joined the British Indian Army towards the last years of the Second World War, when independence was on the near horizon. This strong tradition of colonial service was complicated by the fact that my family over the years had also contracted marriages into families with strong ties to the Indian National Congress, long after that organization had ceased to be Her Majesty's Loyal Opposition. My great grandfather, who was the first Indian (the term 'native' had by then been banned in official parlance to be replaced by 'Indian') appointed to the rank of an Inspector General of Police in colonial India, is reported to have created quite a stir in Bihar by inviting his British subordinates and superiors to the wedding of his son into a family with strong Congress credentials. My grandfather, who had followed his father into the police, carried out his line of duty on one occasion by arresting the Congress leader and future president of India, Rajendra Prasad; at the same time, his cousin was a veteran of the 'underground' along with the Congress Socialist leader Jayaprakash Narayan ('JP') during the Quit India Movement (1942). Likewise, my mother was a staunch *khadi*-wearing Gandhian when she married my army-officer father who would soon be leaving for Southeast Asia to fight under the flag of an already-tottering British Empire. These ironic twists and turns were hardly the kind of neat black-and-white stories likely to appeal to my childhood mind.

Even the more obvious stirringly patriotic stories, which I heard from that side of my family with a long history of involvement with the Congress and with anti-colonial politics, were too full of complications to allow for the kind of comforting narratives that I had probably desired at the time. The fascination with 'England', and all things 'English', especially in the days of the Congress before M. K. Gandhi, would have struck this still-hopelessly-naive daughter of independence as inexplicable. There was an old poignant family story, for example, that was the subject of much laughter in my family, but it used to make me inexplicably both angry and ashamed. An ancestor, a scion of a family with a solid Congress background, returned from London sometime in the early 1900s – one of the then very few, if not the only, 'England-returned' (as they were called) persons in his small town in Bihar – to attend the wedding of a young woman in his family. News of his arrival spread quickly throughout the town; and the groom's family, also old Congress stalwarts, not to be outdone by the bride's family at the wedding, sent spies to gather intelligence from them about the latest in London sartorial fashion. One of these spies – a *nai* (barber) – spotted this ancestor one morning as he was drinking his bed-tea in a 'dressing gown' (housecoat or robe) worn over his pajamas; he promptly reported this prized bit of intelligence to the groom's family. As a consequence, on the day of the wedding, all the men in the groom's family, including the groom, arrived at the wedding banquet wearing newly tailored dressing gowns made for the occasion over their otherwise perfectly appropriate wedding clothes! I only wish now that I had stopped to pay more attention to these stories that could have told me so much more about the *habitus* of the *mofussil* (small town) in colonial India than what I would later learn only, incompletely, from books.

As a child, instead, I tried to live vicariously through my sister, ten years my senior, and to identify with the causes that had inspired her generation. The heady days of radical student politics in the late 1960s in India, during the period that she was studying at the university, has since been fictionalized in Dilip Simeon's book *Revolution Highway*.[2] I suffered from an acute case of generation envy. One of my earliest childhood memories of 'political awakening' – allowing for the unreliability of its retrospective construction – is of my sister, back home from Delhi University, sobbing as she sat glued to the radio that was broadcasting the news of the assassination of Robert F. Kennedy. I do not think I knew then of either Martin Luther King, Jr or of Robert Kennedy, but I could sense at that moment that somehow the assassinations of both these men from some far away exotic land had changed the horizons of hope even for us in India. My other memories from those days are of learning to sing, courtesy of my sister, 'The Internationale' as well as 'We shall overcome' in several different Indian languages. Sometime during this period I seem to recall also being exposed to the stirring Chilean homage to the late Salvador Allende, 'El Pueblo Unido Jamás Será Vencido'. All this is by way of saying that it was the struggles against what was then called *neo-colonialism*, especially of the US variety, rather than the history of the British Raj, that shaped the contours of my earliest political horizon, however childish or second-hand.

I began to slowly acquire some political chops at a time that I now recognize was the fag end of that ambitious 'Third World project', whose rise and fall has been charted in Vijay Prashad's *The Darker Nations*.[3] Belonging broadly to the tradition that Ramchandra Guha has called 'Nehruvian

Indians', marked by their espousal of an avowedly inclusive patriotism that was not confined to any particular language, religion, gender, caste, class, or region, I was easily swept up in the hemispheric romance of the politics of the 'Third World'.[4] This was reinforced during my graduate work at Jawaharlal Nehru University (JNU) in New Delhi, where I encountered the works of the Latin American *dependendistas* and of the world-systems scholars. The names of Andre Gunder Frank, Samir Amin and Immanuel Wallerstein rolled easily off my tongue. At the time, ideas such as the 'development of underdevelopment' and 'core-semi-periphery-periphery' spoke directly to the kind of expansive mental map that I was creating for myself. I may not have had a revolution of my own to champion, but I was certainly very eager to dream one up. What remains most with me from this moment is the commitment to conceive of the impact of imperialism and colonialism on *both* the metropolitan and colonized societies and to insist, correspondingly, on the interconnected, or what I learned to call the 'uneven and combined development', of different parts of the world.

The autodidactic nature of my study in JNU – where I was ostensibly getting a Masters in International Politics, but in reality had my eye on preparing to take the coveted Indian Civil Services' examinations – made for an undisciplined and idiosyncratic training. The library canteen, the famous JNU *dhabas* (tea-stalls) and the late night *chais* (tea) on the sprawling JNU lawns – rather than in the class-room – was where I did most of my learning. These conversations, in typical JNU fashion, included current students, my peers, as well as several 'perpetual students' for whom JNU had long become a home of sorts. This multi-generational bubble, where I was always trying desperately to punch way above my weight, provided me with a crash-course on some of the writings of classical Marxism as well as on more contemporary Marxist debates. Through slow accretion, I was trying to build up a vocabulary to articulate an understanding of contemporary imperialism and anti-imperialism. The most telling memory from that time, however, is the feeling that I had once again of being belated: of having missed, as the veterans in the group reminded us, the heady days of JNU in the 1970s, epitomized by the legendary study circle led by the student-activist, Jairus Banaji, that had so energized the political and intellectual life of the campus. Reading Banaji's essays from that period, his important interventions in the 'transition' debate on modes of production, was exhilarating, but it was not quite the same as having myself been part of that intellectually generative moment or having witnessed its making first-hand.[5] One upshot of my time in JNU, however, was the decision to seek more systematic graduate training for which I decided to proceed to the United States, the veritable belly of the beast from which hostilities against the Nicaraguan government were being funded.

The sense of belatedness – of having come at the tail end of the post-independence 'baby boomers' generation in India with whom my own political imagination was so closely tied – began to lessen only subsequently during my graduate training in the US. Yet my fascination with that broad generation of India's 'midnight's children', I like to think, was formative for me in important ways. The most crucial thing I learned from that experience, perhaps, was to pay attention to the specificities of particular historical conjunctures: theirs as well as mine. This was brought home to me at the start of my graduate career in the US when I had the opportunity to attend the famous Marxism and Interpretation of Cultures seminar at the University of Illinois at Urbana-Champaign (1983). Here I had the privilege of sitting in on classes taught by the likes of Stuart Hall, Frederic Jameson and Gayatri Chakaravorty Spivak. The conference had the very palpable feeling of excitement and anticipation as a prelude to an intellectual break-through of sorts: new ways of talking about the past as well as of theorizing our present.[6] The most liberating experience for me personally, perhaps, was in absorbing the implications of Hall's rigorous insistence to think in conjunctural terms: that is, in terms of a mode of critical analysis that was informed by, and articulated as a response to, a particular moment. This way of thinking would set me eventually on the path of reflecting on my own historical moment rather than being stuck in a borrowed moment – and on what it meant for me to be coming of intellectual age in the years just past what Hall had characterized as the 'The Great Moving Right Show' of the Thatcher–Reagan decade; and, equally relevant in my case, in the wake of the post-Emergency years in India. To take conjunctural analysis fully on board would entail the renunciation of certain premature resorts to familiar patterns of structure.

None of this, of course, was immediately transparent to me. Most of my graduate work, after all, came broadly under the rubric of 'The Expansion of Europe', which already, by then, had a decidedly dinosaur-ish ring to it. Most history graduate students I knew at the time were in clearly nationally defined fields of study. I recognized, and perhaps embraced, the risk of being out of step. I had the good fortune to work under a historian of Britain, Bernard Semmel, who had also written extensively on imperialism. His interest in the theories of imperialism also made him somewhat unusual at the time for a scholar of Britain and of Britain's Empire. He put me through my paces with readings not just from Robinson and Gallagher – the twin deities then of British imperial history – but from Adam Smith through to J. A. Hobson, Joseph Schumpeter, and the various Marxist writers leading up to Lenin and beyond, as well as several 'Third World' theorists. He re-kindled in me an interest in the British–Indian connection, but, most of all, he made me fall in love with doing history. As the author of such works as the 1960 *Imperialism and Social Reform: English Social-Imperial Thought, 1895–1914* and the 1969 *Democracy versus Empire: The Jamaica Riots of 1865 and the Governor Eyre Controversy,* moreover, he had no truck for the rigid delimiting of domestic British history from imperial history.[7] There could have been no one better, or more rigorous, from whom to learn how to deepen and sophisticate my thinking about imperialism and colonialism.

At the same time, I remained in practice a bit of an autodidact, a tinkerer who zigged and zagged from the archives of imperialism to its 'Theory' and back again; and who habitually browsed in several supposedly distinct subfields. Such eclecticism, however, was now better grounded by the range of approaches from Liberal to Marxist that I had absorbed from Semmel.

By choice and by necessity, my graduate school training also included a healthy dose of readings in Latin American, African, US and European history. Here I encountered timely critiques and debates about the 'dependency school' and 'world-systems' approaches as well as examples of some excellent new social histories, among which I found the efflorescence of feminist historiography across several different fields the most invigorating. My decision to work on a doctoral project that would combine British history and Indian history, and to take the colonial Indian past as the site from which to interrogate British Empire history, a decidedly metropolitan-heavy field, was less cutting-edge and more a throw-back to the by-now outmoded field of British imperial history. If still unfashionable, however, I had begun to write back and forth across several histories – British and Indian, but also gender history and political history – that were too often understood as separate and compartmentalized. I wanted to think in unfamiliar ways about what in fact belonged to the 'political' sphere in colonial India.

My years as a graduate student in the US had put the insidious persistence of the British imperial legacy squarely on my political and intellectual agenda. These years had coincided with an unexpected – and largely uncriticized – burst of what various scholars have since diagnosed as 'British Raj nostalgia': the Oscar-winning film *Gandhi*; the extravagant TV production of *Jewel in the Crown*; the numerous less significant films such as *A Passage to India*; *Heat and Dust*; *Far Pavilions*; and the hugely popular *Indiana Jones and the Temple of Doom*. The ways in which the 'Raj nostalgia' of the Reagan–Thatcher decades subtended not only demagogic appeals to a bygone era, but also the aggressive flexing of imperial muscle in the Falklands and Grenada were too obvious to miss. The Israeli invasion of southern Lebanon, drawing renewed attention to the continuing occupation of Palestine, was only further evidence that we were not living with a 'dying colonialism'. The layering of new imperial ventures through a return of well-worn colonial themes, only barely updated and made to seem innocuous, suggested a certain ominous continuity that was in need of more analysis.

At around the same time, moreover, the legacy of the Raj was re-entering public debate in India in a somewhat different way. The 1980s in India, which had begun inauspiciously with a violent separatist movement in the Punjab; the government's blundering military operation on the holiest of the Sikh shrines, the Golden Temple of Amritsar; the horrific anti-Sikh pogrom in Delhi following the assassination of prime minister Indira Gandhi and the unimaginable industrial disaster of the Union Carbide gas leak in Bhopal, would end, as we would subsequently learn, with the closing of the curtains on an era. Indeed, as Aditya Nigam puts it, the conjuncture of 1989–92 marked a 'discursive break' in India, which was characterized by three developments: the upper-caste backlash against 'reservations', or affirmative action, surrounding the implementation of the Mandal Commission's recommendations in 1990; the neo-liberal structural adjustment programme started by the International Monetary Fund in 1991; and the anti-minorities politics of the Hindu Right that resulted in the demolition of the Babri masjid (mosque) in 1992.[8] We would have had no way, of course, to foresee these events just about to come, nor to diagnose the impending demise of the zeitgeist with which many of us urban middle-class Indians had grown up; but the feeling was, nevertheless, around in the 1980s that the times were seriously out of joint.

The slow unravelling of the modernist nationalist consensus in India – Nehru's National Philosophy of India, as one scholar put it – was already several years old at the time I was beginning graduate work in the US. The foundations of this nationalist consensus lay in the official nationalist movement that had brought an end to colonial rule in India, even though, as some scholars were beginning to inform us, the movement itself had remained trapped by the legacies of colonialism in important ways. The challenges to this consensus, indeed, were coming from many different political quarters. The aftermath of Prime Minister Indira Gandhi's authoritarian 21-month period of 'Emergency' rule in 1975–7, for example, had provided the impetus for the appearance of a vigorous civil-liberties movement in India as well as for the renewal of a variety of 'new social movements' – the women's movement, *dalit* ('untouchable') and anti-caste movements, the environmental movement, the farmers' movement, and so on – that acquired new prominence by the 1980s. Collectively these developments represented new approaches to the state and to social change, and, in effect, posed a challenge to, as well as engaged in a dialogue with, the hitherto dominant Marxist perspectives on liberation. At the other end of the spectrum, however, there were new challenges emerging from the political mobilization of, and coalescence around, various essentialized identities and practices in an effort to liberate a supposedly more authentic 'Indianness' from one that had allegedly been contaminated by British colonialism. This included the grotesque glorification of such practices as *sati* (or the immolation of widows at their husband's funeral pyres) by fringe groups, as in the case of the widow-immolation of Roop Kanwar in 1987; the growing popularity of a chauvinistic Hinduism fostered in the name of a supposedly more genuine Indian *qua* Hindu culture; and the debates over minority religions and women's rights that emerged around the case of the Muslim woman Shah Bano's search for justice in the 1980s. Thinking of these contexts in India and the US together required a reappraisal of the legacy of colonial rule and an effort to account for the continuing popular circulation of the British Empire. These new questions and contexts exposed my earlier models for the study of imperialism and colonialism as inadequate to such a task.

This was the context in which I, and many in my generation of students of imperialism, was discovering Edward Said's work.[9] The constituency for his work had been created out of a recognition of the inadequacy of, among other things, certain 'economistic' models for the critique of imperialism; of the limits of many of the dominant forms of opposition to colonialism and imperialism; and of the growing recognition of the nexus between knowledge and power – which Said called *Orientalism* – for understanding not only the continuing pattern of unequal exchange between the so-called West and the Rest, but also for the ways in which the spectral legacies of colonialism and imperialism were still alive in both. The opening provided by Said's work produced a flood of what has been called 'new imperial histories' of the British Empire. These histories differed from traditional imperial history in their vastly altered subject-matter as well as in their expanded unit of analysis. Through my intellectual encounter with Said's work, I found an opening to my own experiments with writing about power on several scales simultaneously.

To the more traditional concerns of the imperial historian with imperial administration, with the political and economic causes and effects of imperialism, or with the relation of different classes to imperialism, were added whole new areas of study: imperial culture; gender relations; sexual identities; racial formations; and even the history and development of entire academic disciplines, including that of history itself. Here the crucial point was that such innovative subject-matter – say the articulation of gender relations with colonial policy – was now seen as no less integral to the dynamics of imperialism and colonialism than its administrative and economic operation. In addition, these histories also provided an expanded unit of analysis for the study of imperialism: Indian and British, Algerian and French, American and Native American histories were now seen as crucially interdependent. This is what Said in *Culture and Imperialism* called 'overlapping territories' and 'intertwined histories'.[10] It entails, as he insisted, keeping in mind two ideas that were in many ways antithetical: the fact of the imperial divide, on the one hand, and the notion of shared though differently inflected experiences, on the other. To be sure, neither of these points originated with Said; nor did his work always provide the openings for the lines of inquiry that others drew from it; and not all of the new work on empire that had begun to roll off the presses was done under the imprimatur of his scholarship. Yet he managed to capture a moment in ways that would enable the wholesale revival of a field of study that had for long been declared moribund. Attention to the micro-physics of 'capillary power', notwithstanding, the 'arterial' scale of imperial power came into renewed focus.

Several new 'historiographical turns' in the 1980s, moreover, reopened a vigorous debate in Indian historiography about the nature of colonial rule and colonialism in India. These parallel 'turns', each in its own way, began to revise some of the hitherto dominant nationalist and Marxist preoccupations of Indian historiography and contributed in placing colonial India at the centre of wider intellectual currents. The emergence of the innovative Subaltern Studies Collective in 1982 was an important landmark that both revitalized a tradition of 'history from below' and, especially in its subsequent trajectory, accorded the knowledge/power relationship (the production and dissemination of colonial knowledge) a central place in its interrogation of colonialism. The latter, one of the primary ways in which Said's influence came to be figured in national Indian historiography, provided a greatly expanded terrain for exploring the legacies of colonialism. At the same time, a 'revisionist historiography' of the early decades of colonial rule in India, the 'early modern school', through insightful interrogations of the nexus between trade and political power and of state formation, was revising understandings of the transition to colonial rule in India – raising, in effect, important questions about the relation between the pre-colonial and the colonial. Finally, the burst of women's activism in the late 1970s and 1980s in India provided the stimulus for the emergence of a vibrant new feminist historiography that took on the task of dismantling supposedly gender-neutral methodologies with the result of reversing many of the stock narratives of colonialism and nationalism in the historiography of colonial India. The interrogation of the colonial and nationalist past by feminist scholars took its cue, in part, from the questions that had arisen in the present. Granting that some of the historiographical interventions of the 1980s remain controversial today, there is no denying the fact that they occasioned a richer and far more vigorous debate about the colonial past in India than had existed for a long time before then.[11] For me, this opportunity resonated with my attempt to bridge the spheres of the social and the political.

The political and historiographical moment of the 1980s was formative for my intellectual engagement with the history of colonial India and of the British Empire. The engagement for me took the form of articulating some divergent theoretical frameworks into the analytics of what I have called an 'imperial social formation': a global grid of intimately linked but different and unequal societies. It offers, as such, a more pointed acknowledgement of imperial power relations than the sometimes banal or simply impossible invocation of the 'global'. My approach to the past, which relies on a heavy use of the archives, consists most broadly of subjecting received paradigms to intense contextualization and historicization in order to pay attention to their moments of shift, of realignments and of rupture. I have explored the colonial Indian past, from the perspective of an imperial social formation, at specific historical conjunctures: the late nineteenth century as well as the post-First World War period of the 1920s and 1930s. A situated engagement with the present provides the backdrop for the questions that I have brought to the exploration of these particular moments in the past. Through all this, I have retained a willingness to tinker, to play the *bricoleur*.

My emphasis in this account on the formative years of my intellectual development, on the 1980s, is intended neither to sanctify it as an 'originary' moment that carries more privilege than it can bear nor to give the patently erroneous impression of a consistency in either the methods or the concerns of my work ever since. My point, in fact, is quite different. It is to share the hard-earned lesson of a zigzagging intellectual trajectory that was enabled by, and has attempted to remain true to, a mode of conjunctural thinking: a way of doing history that is shaped by, and is designed as a response to, very particular moments. The point is not about the ebb and flow of the latest academic trends or fashions, but precisely about paying attention to how, in Said's terms, the *worldly* circumstances of the historical moment impinge upon our scholarship. It may be useful to recall now that some of the dust has settled on the heated partisan responses provoked by Said's work that his influence is too often misrepresented by his followers – whether in studies of colonial India or of the British Empire – by associating it primarily with a 'culturalist' trend. His most enduring legacy was his constant exhortation that scholarship be ever attentive to its own 'worldliness'.

I write this essay at a time when I am acutely aware of the challenges that our own contemporary moment poses for critical reflection. We are living, as is frequently noted, in seemingly apocalyptic times. We are living with the prolonged aftermath of the 2008 world financial crisis; with the collapse of the worldwide people's movements of 2011, which nevertheless gave us the resonant slogan of the 1 per cent; and with the catastrophic aftermath of the US invasion of Iraq that is evident everywhere in the wider region. We are, of course, living with the growing fear of the effects of anthropogenic climate-change on our planet. The list could go on: we are living with the continuing conflict in Darfur; with the escalation of Israeli aggression in occupied Palestine; the Russian military intervention in Ukraine; with the struggle within Muslim communities over Islam; with the ascendancy of Hindu nationalists in India; and with the drift to populist right-wing movements elsewhere; and so on. Yet, as has been obvious for sometime, our previous languages of emancipation, opposition, hope and change seem to have run their course. The novelty of the fresh cannot emerge so long as we cling to the stale. I am struck by the contrast between this current malaise in thinking about the future and the grand anti-imperial and anti-colonial visions of the past. By turning, as I do in my current work, to the early twentieth century anti-colonial projects in India, I attempt to return to that earlier moment to re-examine its relation to our present in ways that might open to radically different futures. But I look to the earlier moment without nostalgia and without collapsing the differences between the two historical moments. I hope, rather, to recover exactly those moments that will make possible the thinking, and enacting of, different and differently shared futures. The colonial past, in effect, still gives me the tools and the impetus to think about the present. To show that what seemed familiar was odd and newfangled; or conversely that what seemed novel was in fact quite traditional, gestures towards revising the history of the present. A crooked or zigzagging intellectual trajectory – evidence of the pains of self-revision – is inevitably contingent and, above all, conjunctural, revealing not only the history *of* an individual but also the layers of history deposited *within* an individual. That said, I am convinced that there remains room – as illustrated by the child in the story of 'The Emperor's New Clothes' – for visions that are fresh, idiosyncratic and transformative.

Notes

1 This echoes Geoff Eley, *A Crooked Line: From Cultural History to History of Society* (Ann Arbor: University of Michigan Press, 2005); as well as the title Partha Chatterjee had originally chosen for his book, *Nationalist Thought and the Colonial World: A Derivative Discourse* (Minneapolis: University of Minnesota Press, 1993). Some portions of this essay appeared originally in Mrinalini Sinha, 'Belonging to the World: A Tribute For Edward Said', *Politics and Culture 1* (2004): http://aspen.conncoll.edu/polandcult/arts.cfm?id-51

2 Dilip Simeon, *Revolution Highway* (New Delhi: Penguin, 2010).

3 Vijay Prashad, *The Darker Nations: A People's History of the Third World* (New York and London: New Press, 2007).

4 Ramchandra Guha, *The Last Liberal and Other Essays* (New Delhi: Permanent Black, 2004).

5 Jairus Banaji, 'For a Theory of Colonial Modes of Production', *Economic and Political Weekly*, 7 (52), 23 December 1972; some of his important essays from that time have been reprinted in J. Banaji, *Theory as History: Essays on Modes of Production and Exploitation* (Leiden: Brill, 2010).

6 Carry Nelson and Lawrence Grossberg, eds, *Marxism and the Interpretation of Culture* (Urbana-Champaign: University of Illinois Press, 1988).

7 Bernard Semmel, *Imperialism and Social Reform* (Cambridge, MA: Harvard University Press, 1960); and *Democracy versus Empire* (New York: Anchor Books, 1969).

8 For an account of the post-1989 conjuncture, see Aditya Nigam and Nivedita Menon, *Power and Contestation: India Since 1989* (Delhi: Orient Longman, 2007).

9 Edward Said, *Orientalism* (New York: Pantheon Books, 1978).

10 Edward Said, *Culture and Imperialism* (New York: Knopf, 1993).

11 For a review of some these historiographical developments, see David Ludden, ed., *Reading Subaltern Studies: Critical History, Contested Meaning and the Globalization of South Asia* (London: Anthem Press, 2002); Seema Alavi, ed., *The Eighteenth Century in India* (New Delhi: Oxford University Press, 2002); and Kumkum Sangari and Sudesh Vaid, eds, *Recasting Women: Essays in Indian Colonial History* (New Delhi: Kali for Women, 1989).

12

Some Intimacies of Anglo-American Empire

Antoinette Burton
b. 1961

In 1944 my father, then a private in the US army just a few months past his nineteenth birthday, was wounded in the Battle of the Bulge. As he remembers it, he and some fellow infantrymen from G Company had got themselves separated from their unit and were roaming the Belgium countryside looking for shelter from a relentless barrage of German artillery. Just as they were crossing the threshold of an abandoned Belgian house, a mortar exploded on the other side of the dwelling and its remnants came cascading toward them. In my mind's eye I imagine that the force of the explosion helped propel them inside the house. They retreated to the basement, where they waited for hours, recovering from their wounds and gathering the strength to get up and out. Not all of them got back to the regiment. In the wake of the mortar exploding, the last man among them had not made it through the door of the house. My father was first or second in that fatal line. He was saved by chance; at random; miraculously. His escape from death on that battlefield explains how I came to be here and why I became a British Empire historian.

My father's war experience made him an anglophile, an avocation he came to share with my mother. It left a lasting imprint on my childhood, which was lived mainly in suburban Philadelphia. Desperately wounded, with searing hot shrapnel embedded in his knee and in his hand, he was sent to an army hospital in France. After surgery, he was sent to recover at an army depot in Litchfield, England. He regularly took the train to Birmingham, where he would walk the city as therapy for his recovering knee. There he met a young English girl named Margaret. The story I was told as a child was that she was a nurse who helped him through his recovery. But later in life he told me that he met her in a park, during one of his long walks across the city. In an almost unbelievable echo of many stories of the American GI encounter with native Britons in wartime, she asked him if he had a light. They struck up a friendship that became something more. She took him home to meet her father, Archie, and her brother; her mother had died in the war during an air raid. My father had many fond memories of Archie, who I imagine as a kind of middling-class Brummie, though I really know nothing more about him than what I have written here. Whoever he was, he sowed a deep fondness for England and English people in my father that was to shape both of our lives.

David and Margaret did not follow through on the GI–English Rose narrative and marry. My father could not do so because she was not a Catholic. He was, and he knew his parents would not approve of that kind of mixed marriage. And so, after a brief posting to Germany, he left England for the States. I believe that he and Margaret may have exchanged a few letters but the relationship ended there. Though he went to college on the GI Bill, got a PhD in History and taught the subject for 50 years at St Joseph's University in Philadelphia, my father was not a British historian. He did, however, become a student and a lover of all things English. His work on Theodore Roosevelt – he wrote a biography of him called *Confident Imperialist* in 1968 – led him to Roosevelt's relatives, including Alice Roosevelt Longworth, whom he met in 1970. She, in turn, led him to her father's friendship with the English Ambassador to the US in Roosevelt's time, Sir Cecil Spring Rice, whose many relatives he also met and of whom he also wrote a biography. As my father was not afraid of admitting, he had a mild insanity on the subject of England. Not Britain, but emphatically England – as in 'oh to be in England now that April's there', a phrase he repeated with particular relish every spring.

I grew up listening to my father's war stories, many of which featured close shaves, as above, and gruesome accounts of how good friends were violently killed in the theatre of war.[1] We also listened endlessly to a 33rpm record of *Beyond the Fringe*, the British stage revue that ran in London and New York in the 1960s starring Alan Bennett, Peter Cook, Jonathan Miller and Dudley Moore. Their irreverent skits included 'So You Want to Know about the War?' – a hilarious send-up of English patriotism, class snobbery and war itself (with lines like 'then, unavoidably, came peace'). There was one bit that particularly tickled our funny bone:

> Squadron Leader to Flight Officer Perkins: 'I want you to lay down your life, Perkins.'
> 'Right sir!'
> 'We need a futile gesture at this stage. It'll raise the whole tone of the war.'
> 'Yessir!'
> 'Get up in a crate, Perkins.'

'Sah!'
'Pop over to Bremen.'
'Yessir!'
'Take a shufti.'
'Right sir!'
'And don't come back.'
'Yessir!'
'Goodbye, Perkins. God, how I wish I were going with him.'
'Goodbye Sah! – Or perhaps it's au revoir?'
'No, Perkins.'

We laughed at the absurdity of it, but we remained puzzled by the word 'shufti'. It had no resonance at all for either of us. We spent hours pondering it, though I do not think we ever looked it up in the dictionary, I imagine because we thought it was too colloquial. I recently Googled it. 'Shufti' is from an Arabic word meaning 'look', so 'take a shufti' means 'have a look' – as simple as that. It apparently made its way into British soldiers' parlance as a result of their involvement in the Middle East during the First World War. But that was the only trace of empire to be found in that *Beyond the Fringe* script.[2]

My father was a man of humble origins, born and raised in Oil City, Pennsylvania, the son of a railroad coal shoveller with an eighth grade education and a housewife with Swiss roots who had converted to Catholicism to please her husband and the big Irish family she married into. But he could recite Shakespeare chapter and verse – 'once more unto the breach, dear friends once more, or close up the wall with our English dead' – and he routinely did so on our long drives between home and the Catholic girls school I attended, Mater Miseracordia. While I gained an appreciation for English culture on these short daily journeys, I did not get a sense of empire from my father. To the extent that he thought about it at all, he approved of it – in large part because it offered so many pathways into amusing word-plays, another of his avocations. He loved saying 'Injah!' for India; he loved Churchill; and he brooked very little criticism of empire's racism or sexism. That made for some interesting conversations between us as adults. Meanwhile, I found my way towards British imperialism through more circuitous routes.

Encased as I was in a middle-class white Catholic enclave growing up, I encountered few histories or traces of empire either at home or abroad. My mother Gerri is a second-generation Italian American. She grew up on the New Jersey shore where the culture was predominantly Irish Catholic and Italians were required by the Irish clergy to attend mass in the basement of the parish church while the real service went on upstairs. This was a powerful memory for her and she was as outraged by it as she is proud of her Italian heritage and her parents' all-American immigrant story. Yet she threw herself into my father's anglophilia, pushing him to take up a sabbatical in England

and moving our family (myself and two sisters, all under the age of 9) to Petts Wood in Kent for six months in 1968. I went to the local Catholic school, Manorfields, which I remember mainly as cold and as the site of inedible school dinners. I have no memory of my classmates except one girl whose arms were foreshortened and whose hands emerged from her shoulder sockets. My mother called her 'a thalidomide baby' and she tried to explain to me what that meant, mostly in chemical terms, as I recall. My father's research took us to England again in 1972, when I was 11, and that experience made a huge impact, though empire simply did not intrude. What I do remember was heated debates between my parents and their English friends about the pros and cons of joining the Common Market. As one very English lady friend said, overlooking the sumptuous high tea table she laid every Sunday (perhaps for our benefit?): 'I suppose we'll all have to eat garlic now.' My mother never flinched.

Confident Imperialist notwithstanding, I passed through most of my secondary and tertiary educational life basically unaware of empire. As an undergraduate at Yale I was mainly focused on surviving the environment as both a student and a woman. The class of 1983 was only the tenth coed class to graduate and I think it's safe to say that women students were still curiosities – for some professors, anyway. It was not until I got to graduate school that empire revealed itself to me. I arrived at the University of Chicago in the fall of 1983 to study the intersections of religion and science under the late great Irish historian and patriarch, Emmet Larkin. Much to his dismay, and thanks in part to my continued alienation as a woman among a majority of male students at Chicago, I discovered women's suffrage history. I abandoned Darwinism for feminism and did my MA thesis on Millicent Garret Fawcett's political thought. Larkin was not sure she had any, so the game was afoot. But it was chance that ultimately led me to India and empire. I had a summer pre-dissertation fellowship to go to the Fawcett Library, then located in the basement of the City of London Polytechnic. Now called 'The Women's Library@LSE', the Fawcett was a delightfully shambolic place in the late 1980s. David Duggan, the archivist and friend to so many first-generation feminist historians, acknowledged its peripheral location – in the East End and in the very dank basement of the Polytechnic – by meeting all visitors at the door with the greeting: 'Congratulations, you've found us.' In the back, in a morass of uncatalogued papers that were so dusty and rusty that I took to wearing overalls to the archive, I literally stumbled across a pile of material on the Contagious Diseases Acts after their repeal at home in 1886. That stash was mainly about the CD Acts in India, it involved the feminist social reformer Josephine Butler, and it set me on a course of imperial history from which I have not yet returned.

That research trip to London was eye-opening outside the archive as well as in it. Passing through Heathrow, security was very tight: as they did at least into the early 1990s they went through your baggage with a fine toothcomb, even taking the caps off my pens, citing the threat of IRA terrorism. 1986 was also the year that the US bombed Libya. It was the first time I had encountered anti-American feeling in Britain, and it made me feel quite hot under the collar. I realized that I had grown up in and out of England bathed in complete ignorance of America's role in the world beyond Woodrow Wilson at Versailles. My insulation from critiques of the US had a lot to do, of course, with my class position and racial privilege, but it was upsetting to hear such negative views of American foreign policy nonetheless. I realized what American imperialism was at that very moment, and for the first time. Henceforth empire has been a palimpsest for me: a way of thinking the hyphen in the concept 'Anglo-American' critically, and a way of registering the relentless impact of the imperial present on the writing of contemporary British Empire history.

As I have written about at length elsewhere, my increasing exposure to feminism and postcolonial theory was key to sustaining that critical posture.[3] So were my observations of the experience of an African American friend and fellow PhD candidate from Chicago who was doing her research in London the same time I was. She wanted to write on blacks in Britain but she could make no headway in the archives; she felt her inquiries about materials on the subject were rebuffed because she was not white. This was compounded by her experiences on the streets of London and in her local wine shop, where the proprietor constantly tried to sell her Jamaican rum when what she wanted was Chardonnay. This, together with the serious harassment, both subtle and overt, that she faced on the tube and in her daily life in London, exposed me to forms of prejudice I had only read about in novels. I had never witnessed face-to-face racism. She was traumatized and I was shocked; and she was traumatized that I was shocked. This was not my parents' England.

Meanwhile I did my dissertation research on British feminism and Indian women, which became my first book, *Burdens of History*. I took up my first job at Indiana State University in Terre Haute, Indiana, where the 1990 Gulf War reached directly into my world history classroom. Basra, which I had planned to talk about as a major centre of ancient civilization, was now on everyone's map as the target of US bombing raids. Young working class Hoosier men, black and white, were being pulled out of school because they were called up for National Guard duty, some before the final exam could be administered. Student evaluations of my course – which featured women and gender alongside the textbook narratives of world history – came back with 'burn women's studies' emblazoned across them. My education in race and class in the US heartland continued as I realized I had Holocaust deniers and the grandchildren of Klansmen sitting in my lectures. In the midst of this, I returned to England for extensive research several summers in a row, at a time when the country was embroiled in debates about the role of figures like Mary Seacole in the national curriculum. In 1993, the black British teenager Stephen Lawrence was brutally murdered by white youths in a case that has had reverberations for nearly two decades now and speaks volumes about the history of race and racism in post-imperial Britain. I wrote *At the Heart of the Empire*. I went to see Tom Stoppard's *Indian Ink* at the Aldwych Theatre. I edited the 2003 collection, *After the Imperial Turn*.

Born as I was after the official end of empire, my experience of it has been refracted through the postcolonial outcroppings of Britain's imperial history to be found in the everyday life of the multi-racial United Kingdom. I came of age intellectually during an extended historical moment when, each in his own way, Stuart Hall and Edward Said were exploding the canonical historiographical scene. Despite the evidence everywhere of imperial and post-imperial impact – whether in the form of economic decline, the rise of the Pakistani grocery or the popularity of films like *My Beautiful Laundrette* – Britain's imperial pasts, let alone its postcolonial citizens of colour, were yet to be recognized as legitimate aspects of its 'national' history. My work and that of others in this volume (Catherine Hall, Minnie Sinha, John Mackenzie, Philippa Levine) was part of a fractious debate about the right and proper place of empire in Britain's Island Story. Some of those debates happened at the Institute of Historical Research, London; some at the American Historical Association meetings; some at the North American Conference of British Studies; some at the Berkshire Conference of Women Historians; and still others at sessions of the Canadian and the Australian Historical Associations. Others happened in department hallways and living rooms and classrooms on both sides of the Atlantic. I remember heated arguments with various interlocutors in the Senate House tearoom and in the pubs and coffee shops that surrounded the British Library (this, while it was still housed in the British Museum). These discussions seem a long time ago now, in part because they have been supplanted if not surpassed by a wide variety of 'new' British imperial histories, the majority of which are not concerned with the impact of empire at home. The turn to the transnational and the global has thrown the kind of empire history I sought to write in the 1990s into bold relief *and* into shadow, as the impact of the post-9/11 world has made new forms of empire viable. Though we cannot as yet perhaps fully appreciate the exact cause and effect, these new imperial forms have also made new ways of writing, thinking and teaching empire possible. And necessary.

While I was not conscious of it at the time, I see now that my response to the strife and violence of the neo-imperial world order of the twenty-first century that I have had the privilege of merely watching from the safety of Urbana, Illinois, was to turn away from writing about British imperialism per se.[4] My friendship and collaborations with Tony Ballantyne propelled me towards the intersection of imperial history with global frames. *Bodies in Contact* (2005) and *Empires and the Reach of the Global* (2012) were intended to reach undergraduate students in world history courses. *Moving Subjects* (2008) aimed to link questions of mobility and intimacy with histories of empire in a global age. In my own monographic work I moved away from histories of empire towards histories of colonial and postcolonial Indian women. I wrote *Dwelling in the Archive*, and then *The Postcolonial Careers of Santha Rama Rau* and *Brown Over Black* in fairly quick succession. In those latter two I was trying to figure out what postcolonial history, as subject and method, might look like beyond Britain proper. Rama Rau's career as an author and a translator of India to the West was most successful in the US; and the figures in *Brown Over Black* tracked Indian postcoloniality to Africa and back again. I purposely sought an India-based publisher, Three Essays Collective, for *Brown Over Black*, because I wanted a different kind of readership, one as political as it was academic, if not more so. For reasons I only partly understand, I wanted to shake off my past as an empire historian and find new audiences.

By 2012, then, I had travelled a fair distance from my dissertation and from the exclusively Western marketplace of ideas as well. But the Anglo-American empire has never been far from my mind. How could it be? The noise in my head from the wars in Afghanistan and Iraq has been loud and persistent. It drove me to do an edited collection of primary sources from the Victorian Anglo-Afghan campaigns for use in undergraduate classrooms and, most recently, to develop a synthetic narrative account of British imperialism from Afghanistan to inter-war anti-colonialism called *The Trouble with Empire*. I see that book as an attempt at anti-imperial empire history – the only kind that I, as a witness to the spectacular collapse of the imperial formations I was trained to think of as the right and proper objects of study and critique, can live with. This is not nostalgia, I hope, but *realpolitik*.

I had not, in fact, intended to contribute an essay to this volume, believing that I had said my autobiographical piece in the introduction to *Empire in Question* (2011). Writing that text certainly made me curious about the ways that their life stories had impacted all the empire historians I have read and known. It led indirectly to a conversation with Dane Kennedy about his own empire stories. That led to our speculation about what it would be like to collect some of those personal histories and create an intergenerational archive that could help students appreciate the links between imperial history and empire writing. In the winter of 2015, as we were wrapping up this collection, the revanchist forces of ISIS accelerated in the wake of neo-imperial collapse; a transnationally apparent, rageful hunger for the global caliphate rushed in to fill the vacuum. My father, for his part, fell deeper and deeper into dementia, returning him to the trauma of his wartime wounds in a classic case of PTSD, six decades delayed. I realized anew that history is a war against forgetting, and that when it comes to empire, amnesia is a dangerous game. So I decided to join up rather than stand down. Whether as a historiographical project or as a series of events unfolding in distant and not so distant lands, imperial history hurtles along with all insensate speed. I for one feel overwhelmed and perpetually fascinated by it. I also feel an obligation, an urgency, even, to explain how empire shaped me, and to account in some measure for *How Empire Shaped Us* as well.

Notes

1 See 'Unit', in David H. Burton, *Animating History: The Biographical Pulse* (Philadelphia: St Joseph's University Press, 2007), pp. 283–320.

2 I refer here to the 1962 album (Capitol Records, 'Alexander H. Cohen Presents Beyond the Fringe'). For a broader discussion of the comedy revue and its imperial referents see Stuart Ward, '"No Nation Could be Broker": The Satire Boom and the Demise of Britain's World Role', in S. Ward, ed., *British Culture and the End of Empire* (Manchester: Manchester University Press, 2001), pp. 96 ff.

3 Antoinette Burton, *Empire in Question: Reading, Writing and Teaching British Imperialism* (Durhan, NC: Duke University Press, 2011).

4 The insularity of Urbana, Illinois, from US empire is itself a matter of contingency and debate, of course.

13

Homes and Native Lands: Settler Colonialism, National Frames and the Remaking of History

Adele Perry
b. 1968

The second line in the English-language version of Canada's national anthem, 'O Canada', proclaims the singer's allegiance to 'Our home and native land'. The anthem itself is a precarious sort of national object, reflecting Canada's multiple and uneven claims to nation, ongoing location within formal and informal empire, and particular history of the liberal, modern, settler state. As an official anthem, 'O Canada' was not formally adopted until 1980, after a century of variant local uses, inevitable quarrels, and solemn state deliberations including a special joint committee of two levels of the federal government that met between 1964 and 1967.[1] 'O Canada' was first composed in French, and has official versions in English and French and a regularly used bilingual one. Unsurprisingly the French version is different from the English one, referring not to 'home and native land' but to 'Terre de nos aïeu'. This version gestures to lineage and its connection to place, while the English anthem makes a more plain-faced manoeuvre of settler colonialism by making the settler literally 'native' and displacing migrants from the equation.

I grew up in British Columbia, Canada's westernmost province, in the 1970s and 1980s. In the schools I attended we sang both 'O Canada' and

Britain's imperial anthem, 'God Save the Queen'. The patriation of the Canadian constitution would be concluded in 1982, but if the singing of anthems by school children is any measure, idioms of nation and idioms of empire continued to co-exist, and, in different ways, still do in Canada. Our current prime minister, Stephen Harper, has a particular penchant for the monarchy, and in 2011 reintroduced the word 'royal' back into the names of Canada's armed forced and ordered that portraits of Queen Elizabeth be displayed prominently at foreign embassies.

When I was young we did not sing any of these songs very often. The British Empire was pretty much gloss. The queen was on our money, and the names of our towns and cities could eerily echo the metropole. There were lived and meaningful ties: my family had relatives in Scotland who mailed us socks, tea towels and alarmingly sweet candy every Christmas. But we lived in North America, and nowhere else. We had a certain distrust of colonial institutions, like the Brownie group my mother would not let me join because it was, she explained, 'fascist'. My first journeys outside of Canada were to adjacent American territory, travelling by car to Portland, Oregon for my father's union convention, taking the ferry from Victoria to Anacortes, Washington, and later the Greyhound bus to Seattle to see the King Tutankhamen exhibit. Mainly, we stayed in Canada, and coveted American chocolate bars that could not be purchased on our side of the border and watched television from Seattle, where the announcers spoke of places with Indigenous names that sounded familiar: Snohomish, Skagit and Clallam.

Those place names were familiar because they shared our history of colonialism, of the assertion of non-Indigenous rule over Indigenous territories in the middle decades of the nineteenth-century. The material relations and logics of settler colonialism structured and animated our lives. In much of Canada, the right of state and, by extension, of settlers to own land is secured through the mechanism of treaty. British Columbia's history of recognizing and negotiating Indigenous title is different. With the exception of a handful of treaties negotiated between Governor James Douglas and Coast and Straights Salish people in the 1850s and a chunk of Canada's Treaty Eight that crosses the Rocky Mountains, the British Columbia I grew up in was un-ceded territory. With the exception of peoples and territories that have been successful in the modern treaty negotiation process begun in 1990, it remains as such.

It was through these histories and the mechanisms they bestowed that my family owned land, whether the standard city lot, thirty-six feet across and laid out on the grid that reorganized space around the British Empire and paid for on the so-called market through punishing 1980s mortgage rates or the rural so-called 'Crown Land' we pre-empted through the legal processes of colonization first established in the mid-nineteenth century. The latter my parents did as part of a co-operative established in the early 1970s and named Illahe, the word for land in Chinook Jargon, the West Coast trade language that used to communicate across linguistic and cultural barriers. That the co-op took an Indigenous name and that the cabins we built and lived in during the summers had (and have) no power, running water or road access gestures to a different sort of aspirational politics, one formed in a particular social space and informed by twentieth-century counterculture. But this aspirational politics is not any less a colonial one.

Our lives as settlers were shaped by a particular politics of whiteness, one that was animated primarily in opposition to Asians. People from Europe and Asia arrived in what would become British Columbia at essentially the same time and following roughly similar patterns with almost entirely male migrants, arriving in occasional numbers beginning in the last half of the eighteenth century and in more meaningful waves beginning in the 1850s. By the 1880s British Columbia had developed a sustained, rigorous and frequently violent politics of anti-Asian activity, one that translated into a range of restrictive immigration policies that taxed, banned and restricted migration of people identified as Chinese, Japanese and South Asian, or, as we called them in an effort to differentiate them from the other kinds of Indians, Indians from India. As historian Henry Yu explains, until the years following the Second World War Canada sustained a kind of 'racial apartheid akin to the forms in other British settler colonies such as Australia, New Zealand and South Africa – enshrined in laws in areas as disparate as voting rights through housing titles and labour relations'.[2] By the 1970s and 1980s this history of anti-Asian policy and practice was challenged and frayed around the edges, but it was hardly over.

The twinning of Indigenous dispossession and regulation with anti-Asian politics produced a particularly racialized form of settler colonialism, one British Columbia shared with parts of North America's west coast and the Antipodes. These were the social relations that made the second line of 'O Canada' catch my attention. The phrasing of the song almost invites singers to change the lyrics, to adjust them to proclaim that 'Our home's on native land', and in doing so make it a critique of settler colonialism rather than a proclamation of national fealty. I did this silently as a non-Indigenous and white child in public school gymnasiums, and critics of Canadian settler colonialism have continued to do so, riffing off the reworked anthem to draw attention to the injustices of Canada's particular history of empire. A quick Google search for 'Our home on native land' and 'Canada' brings up 5,710 hits that link to popular articles about Canadian history, documentary films about Indigenous people, scholarly articles about Indigenous self-government, photographs of protest placards and clever and memorable images of upside-down maple leafs accompanied by the reworked anthem.

The stakes of reworking the language of nation and empire are high. As a historian, I think we risk making a fetish out of settler colonialism, and perhaps have already done so of the framework of the 'British world'. Settler colonialism is usually defined as a form of colonialism where colonizers 'come to stay' and 'establish new political orders for themselves rather than exploit native labour'.[3] Framing the uneven and complicated histories of the Americas and the Antipodes in these terms downplays the ongoing significance of Indigenous labour and resources to these colonial projects and overstates the permanence of newcomers, who often did not stay, at least for very long. It can make little sense of the more than two centuries where the fur trade – which sought Indigenous resources and labour, and had little concern for land, per se – was the primary mechanism of colonialism in northern North America. The usual framing of settler colonialism also overstates the development of responsible government and self-rule, which had and indeed still have an uneven history in the places we most generally consider settler colonies: Canada, Australia, New Zealand, the United States, and, less often, South Africa and Israel. Available frameworks for thinking of settler colonialism can also misrecognize or minimize the vigorous persistence of Indigenous life, the fact that, as anthropologist Audra Simpson explains, 'There are still Indians, some still know this, and some will defend what they have left. They will persist, robustly', even in what Simpson calls 'the teeth of constraint'.[4]

But settler colonialism remains an indispensable tool for explaining the kinds of places I grew up in and continue to live and work in. Settler colonialism may never wholly remake the political, economic, or social worlds of the spaces it inhabits, but its logics do heavy lifting despite its manifest partialities and failures. If nothing else, settler colonialism works to naturalize the presence of non-Indigenous people in Indigenous space, to manage Indigenous presence as some sort of problematic or celebratory anomaly. At the same time it works to settlers' (especially white ones) claims to the territories they inhabit seemingly inevitable, legitimate and even destined. In the British Columbia I grew up in, we did not often question our lives lived within Indigenous spaces and predicated on Indigenous dispossession. Instead, we talked about the beauty of the place, the deliciousness of the fish we caught from the ocean. Ours was a heavily astheticized vision of place and space, one amenable to putting ourselves in the middle of, to making ourselves its subject, critics, and beneficiaries and always, the centre of its stories. When I read memoirs and fiction from settler South Africa or Australia, this is what I find most familiar: the focus on land, imagined as almost or wholly devoid of Indigenous peoples and histories, and non-Indigenous person's relationship with and love for it.

I was not much of a high school student. This cannot be blamed on the individuals tasked with teaching me history in the Vancouver public high schools I attended. One went on to win awards for developing curriculum around Louis Riel, the Metis leader and diplomat tried and eventually hanged for treason in 1885. Another teacher was Marcy Toms, a founding member of one of Canada's first self-styled 'women's liberation' groups and a vocal socialist and feminist. As a classroom teacher she was sharp-minded, rigorous, and committed to making a diffident group of hippy kids and punk rockers aware of the wider world they lived in. She gave us weekly quizzes on current affairs and showed us *1900,* Bertolucci's epic film of oppression and revolt in peasant Italy.

I spent the year after high school as a participant in Canada World Youth, an international development programme funded by the Canadian government. We spent three and a half months in Nova Scotia, and my flight there was the first time I went east of the Rocky Mountains. The second part of the programme was held in Jamaica. The months I spent in Clarkstown, a small town in the north coast Parish of Trelawney, provided me with a very different vision of the British Empire and its lived and enduring histories. I attended church for the first time there, and the plaques on the walls of the Anglican Church were adorned with plaques honouring British plantation owners. Slavery had been abolished over a hundred and thirty years ago, and Jamaica was an independent nation forged in a postcolonial moment. Church services were usually led by black, Jamaican women lay preachers. If settler colonialism worked to make my race and colonial status hard to see, Jamaica made me hyper-visible as a young, white woman in a black country. Canadian banks and bauxite mines in Jamaica and busloads of white, Canadian tourists on air-conditioned buses made clear that Canada's place in a global economy predicated on the poverty of the global south and the wealth of the global north. I had no way to square this with the enduring fact that Canada had its own global south within its borders.

I became a student in my home town of Vancouver in 1987, at a university named for an explorer, Simon Fraser. I gravitated towards history and women's studies, and to social history as a way of imagining, researching, and writing and engaging with the present. I did not encounter a lot of material that interpreted Canadian history as colonial history, and what I did I did not much understand. An anthropology professor assigned a large introductory class Hugh Brody's iconic *Maps and Dreams: Indians and the British Columbia Frontier* (1992) and I remember reading it with disinterest. The only work by an Indigenous author that I can recall studying was one from another part of the Americas, the widely circulated *I, Rigoberta Menchu: An Indian Woman in Guatemala* (1984). I took a course on African history, a course on European women's history, a course on the history of Iran, and it was there that I encountered work that linked gender, space and empire. I also took Canadian history, sometimes framed as an avenue for women's or working-class history, and sometimes framed within the concerns of the contemporary nation-state.

In 1991 I entered the Graduate Programme in History at York University in Toronto to study Canadian history. The status of Canada as a legitimate area or 'field' of historical scholarship and of Canadian universities as an appropriate place to conduct doctoral studies were by then secure, but not of any long duration. By the 1920s Queen's University, McGill and the University of Toronto offered doctorates, but for much of the century they were rarely pursued and less frequently rewarded with academic positions.[5] This story is necessarily familiar to historians of empire, and had endless variations around the British Empire. Like the Australian context analysed by Ann Curthoys, historians' commitment to the nation reflected not the Canadian nation's longstanding stability, but its relative short, insecure and fractured history.[6] The imperial relations of historical knowledge and authority played out differently in French Canada, which had distinct and pressing relationships to both wider Anglophone and Francophone worlds, and to the recuperative and potentially radical work of history for its authors and audiences.[7] By the latter half of the twentieth century, Canada's proximity – geographic, and for English-speaking Canada at least, linguistic – to the increasingly powerful informal empire of the United States created another layer to the complicated layers of empires, nations and their relationship to Canadian histories. Historians of Canada, who lived, worked and were trained within Canada had at least two powerful, Anglophone juggernauts to define themselves and their work in opposition to.

The narrative of a small, colonial and/or postcolonial nation writing its histories amid the constraint of an imperial world that denied its authority to do so is powerful narrative, and it is one that does not easily accommodate critical analyses of the layers of empire that produced Canada and countries like it. Our aspirant nationalisms are necessarily predicated on an ongoing and demanding displacement of Indigenous subjects and claims, and the situation of settler ones in their place. This is true of the vernacular sorts of nationalism encoded in the anthems that I began this essay with. It is also true of the more nuanced arguments for Canadians (imagined as implicitly non-Indigenous ones) to train their own students (also imaged as non-Indigenous) and write their own histories. Certainly Indigenous peoples played roles – sometimes important or causal ones in studies of the fur trade, eighteenth and nineteenth-century war, or resistance to Canadian expansion in the late nineteenth century – in these histories. But Indigenous people seemed to disappear slowly from the pages of Canadian history around 1812 in central Canada, and around 1885 in Western Canada. After that Indigenous people were ephemeral, lingering, anomalous, and denied the complexity of modernity, at least until the development of contemporary Indigenous protest. As historian Mary Jane Logan McCallum argues, much of Canadian history makes it appear 'as if Native people retreated from "planet earth" only to appear again, angry and tardy, in 1969'.[8]

This was the layered and at times contradictory moment in which I came to York in the early 1990s. Questions of French–English identities had been and were still absolutely central to Canadian history, generating its defining intellectual questions and producing some of its most sustained attention, its most difficult conversations, and its lasting initiatives. Left nationalist interpretations of Canada's powerlessness in relation to informal American imperialism continued to circulate. Discussions of region were also on the table, and had been long before one of my professors, Ramsay Cook, influentially argued that Canadian history be best understood as a series of 'limited identities'. By the 1990s, questions of gender were there too. As historian Donald Wright has argued, the professionalization of history during the middle decades of the twentieth century was an intentionally gendered project. By excluding women, historians distinguished themselves from amateurs, buffs and dabblers.[9] In the late 1960s and, more critically, the 1970s, women historians associated with second wave feminism had mounted a sustained challenge to the logic that worked to formally and informally exclude women from the practice of academic history. They would go on to produce careful studies that backed up experiences of unfriendly classrooms and cruel letters of reference.[10] But still, when I entered the graduate programme in History at York it was with a substantial cohort of female students. The particular whiteness of Canadian history had not generated the same sort of attention, and still has not. In 2006, Franca Iacovetta noted that Canadian historians are 'overwhelmingly white, more specifically, mostly Anglo-Celtic in English Canada, and, in Quebec, anglo- and francophone, with no concrete discussion of implementing strategies for trying to diversify the profession'.[11] With the exception of the striking of a standing committee on Equity and Diversity within the Canadian Historical Association in 2009, this remains mainly true. The subject of Indigenous history has had a deep and lasting impact on Canadian historiography as a whole, but, as McCallum has powerfully argued, Indigenous scholars remain few and poorly acknowledged within the profession.

The Canadian history I was trained in was rarely narrow. Like other relatively small national scholarships, it could not much afford to be. A commitment to social history demanded wider engagements. Canadian social history emphasized the possibility of excavating subaltern pasts and was inherently comparative, drawing especially heavily from British, American and French scholarships. When we studied Indigenous history, immigration history or women's history, we never just looked to the nation, but sought and found our points of connection and comparison where they presented themselves. What I learned was emphatically not the history of high politics or of states. Things imperial had an insecure and modest place within the new social history as it was being written and taught. Histories of empire seemed old, stuffy and artificially isolated from the politics and societies that made them.

It was not the history of the Colonial Office, Governor Generals or the Commonwealth that made me a kind of accidental or at least sideways historian of empire, if I am that. In the English-speaking world in the late 1980s and 1990s, and certainly in the Canadian parts that I lived in, feminist politics were marked by powerful and often divisive conversations around race, and the limitations of mainstream feminism to speak to and about women of colour. This produced powerful analyses of black and Indigenous women, and it also generated calls for white women to examine their own racial location and privilege, their own complicated histories as racialized subjects by authors such as Ruth Frankenberg in the American context and Vron Ware in the British one.[12] It was this that sent me to the archives with the intention of researching a thesis on white women in mid-nineteenth-century British Columbia. I had not gone to York with the intention of working on British Columbia history, which, like most regional fields within Canadian history, is practiced most seriously at universities located within that particular region. But like so many historians, I found myself writing about home.

The home I found in the archive did not yield what I expected it to. It never does, and this is surely one of the reasons why historians hang on to the romance of the archives: the archive trips us up and disciplines us in unexpected ways. I went to Victoria, where I had spent a good part of my childhood, rented a room from the Godmother of my best friend. I went to the British Columbia Archives every day and worked among the other grad students, the genealogists, and the land claims researchers, staying late and taking off my shoes when nobody else was there. I read missionary archives and handwritten, microfilmed correspondence between London's Colonial Office and local officials in Victoria and New Westminster. I read newspapers, which parsed, often in gory and aggressively racialized detail, the mechanics, or at least some of the mechanics of daily life in an unstable settler colony. I read whatever letters and memoirs I could find. I went to archives in Ottawa and Toronto and then to London in what was my first trip to Europe. At the British Library I could not locate anything about British Columbia in the card catalogue until I realized it was listed under 'Columbia, British'. At the old Public Records Office I sat with the other scholars of a far-flung and radically changed empire and former empire who had all come to bring their difficult histories home.

That the history I was finding in these archives was a history of empire was unavoidable. The archives spoke about Indians and Natives and Settlers and Colonizers and often, Whites. There were governors and missionaries. Everywhere there were Indigenous people, and generally presented in local, specific terms, as known and intimate subjects of place and its stories. The insecurity and partiality of whiteness was undeniable. Here the historiography of British Columbia and the fur trade was useful, especially that by scholars such as Sylvia Van Kirk and Jean Barman who had probed the gendered histories of these subjects. So was the history of the western United States that went under the banner of the 'New Western History'. Germinal analyses of Indigenous women written by Indigenous authors and scholars in the Canadian context such as Janice Accose provided critical grounding. What would later be known as the 'new imperial history' had yet to take on that particular form, but the works on gender and empire by scholars such as Antoinette Burton, Catherine Hall and Mrinalini Sinha were mapping the gendered histories of empire in striking ways. Ann Laura Stoler's early periodical literature on race-making and colonial societies in the Dutch and French Indies suggested ways of reading the endless anxieties of race and gender that marked nineteenth-century empire. Histories of Australia and New Zealand made critical steps in exploring how settler colonies were particular if hardly exceptional sites of racialized and gendered histories. Patricia Grimshaw, Marilyn Lake, Charlotte Macdonald and others helped point to the possibilities of thinking of what were often labelled frontier pasts as ones better understood as settler colonialism.

The dissertation became a book, *On the Edge of Empire: Gender, Race, and the Making of British Columbia, 1849–1871* (2001), and its footnotes and the journeys it has travelled speak to this process of transformation, of reimagining Canadian history as imperial and more particularly settler colonial history. This was not my process alone, and there is no way it could be. As I was thinking about seeing western Canadian history as imperial history so were historians Sarah Carter, Elizabeth Vibert, Daniel Clayton and Cole Harris. In different ways, so were historians Lisa Chilton and Sheila McManus, who were students at York at the same time. My analysis of the possibilities of thinking about empire in general and the British Empire in particular are very different than Philip Buckner's, but it is no accident that his calls to think of a 'British World' with Canada figured clearly within in it occurred at approximately the same time.

I have continued to work on histories of this empire that made me, researching and writing about histories of vernacular colonialism in the nineteenth century with a particular focus on northern North America, where I continue to live and work. I have been trained, employed and funded within what is essentially a state system. My career as a historian is a wage of empire.

I began teaching at the University of Manitoba in 2000. Winnipeg is a different sort of settler place than British Columbia. Here the fur trade has a longer history than settlement. Here was a powerful history of Indigenous resistance, one that is awkwardly integrated into provincial and regional identities, including a yearly day off in honour of Louis Riel. Here treaties were a central mechanism of colonization and relationship, and they remain powerful touchstones. Advertisements on the sides of city buses remind us that 'we are all treaty people'. I live with my family on an old Metis river lot, one that was never quite wholly remade by the grid brought by the British surveyors that arrived in the Red River settlement in 1869.

In a range of ways my work tries to put what are usually registered as Canadian histories into a more rigorous conversation with those generally seen as imperial ones, and in doing so, provide a context for histories of Indigenous peoples and their colonizers. I remain unsure if this work has succeeded in rethinking histories of settlement and disposition or whether it has simply revamped imperial perspectives and subjectivities and in doing so, given them a new kind of shelf-life. My 2015 book, *Colonial Relations: The Douglas-Connolly Family and the Making of the Nineteenth-Century Imperial World* deals with Demerara, Red River, Vancouver Island and Oregon. These were all places with thick, enduring and variegated histories, ones those conventional archival approaches are not always equipped to navigate with much precision or intellectual nuance. Does framing these histories primarily as ones of empire work to calcify the elision of Indigenous and black histories that lies at the core of settler colonialism and anti-blackness? Does putting histories of colonialism and related histories of whiteness at the centre of our optics denaturalize them or does it only serve to sever these histories from their most powerful interlocutors and critics?

The past few years have been rich and complicated times for those of us who study places like western Canada and for those of us who live here. There has been a flowering of a robust, rigorous and transborder Indigenous scholarship, associated not with conventional disciplines, including History, but with Native and Indigenous Studies departments and organizations such as the Native America and Indigenous Studies Association, founded in 2007. The winter of 2012–13 witnessed a reinvigoration and redirection of Indigenous activism around a movement that became known as Idle No More. This has brought to new prominence a set of questions that cut to the quick of Indigenous and non-Indigenous peoples' relationship to Canada. Indigenous people have asked difficult questions about Canada and its particular history of empire: about the power and limits of treaties, about the staggering numbers of murdered and missing Indigenous women and girls, about the history of residential schools, about the possibilities of solidarity between Indigenous people and racialized migrants.[13] It is this activism that has put the word settler into wide circulation in English Canadian popular discourse. It is this engagement that demands that non-Indigenous people take seriously the extent to which our history and our relative prosperity is predicated on the routinized dispossession of Indigenous peoples, lands and resources.

As I finished this essay I attended Winnipeg's third annual Idle No More New Year's Eve Round-dance. This one was held in honour of the more than 1,200 Indigenous women and girls, either murdered or missing, and who are a potent and painful symbol of the ongoing and deeply gendered violence that settler colonialism imposes on Indigenous communities in Canada. The round-dance is a longstanding practice for a number of North American Indigenous peoples, and Idle No More remade it as a critical medium of community-building and protest. In the winter of 2012–13 we danced in shopping-malls, in city streets and in front of the Parliament house in Ottawa. The 2014 New Year's Eve dance was held at the intersection of Portage and Main, a central intersection in Winnipeg's core and an iconic location in modern Canadian mythologies of westward expansion and capitalist prosperity. In laying claim to this intersection, we asserted the city's status as an Indigenous space and called attention to the ongoing inequalities and violence visited on the more than 12 per cent of Winnipeggers who are Indigenous.[14]

This round-dance attracted fewer people than the one two years ago. But there were still enough of us to shut down the intersection with the help of the city police, no doubt mindful of ongoing criticism of their responses to violence against Indigenous women and girls. The songs sung in Anishinaabemowin at the round-dance are worlds apart from 'God Save the Queen' or from 'O Canada'. And once you hear the second line of 'O Canada' as a recognition that 'our home is on native land' it is hard to hear it any other way. Recognizing settler colonialism necessarily reframes the nation and its histories. So does recognizing the robust Indigenous histories that were there, all along, and are here, visibly, vibrantly, never easily and often painfully, now. These histories belong to the particular spaces that made them, and to empire. I want a scholarship that takes the complicated history of Indigenous and non-Indigenous, local and global, and speaks directly and incisively to the complicated present of the fractured and compelling place where I have lived my life on unequal ground. This is how empire shaped me, and this is how I hope history can help unmake empire.

Notes

I would like to thank Lisa Chilton, David Churchill, Karen Dubinsky, Ryan Eyford, Franca Iacovetta, Peter Ives, Steve Penfold, Jocelyn Thorpe, Donald Wright and especially Mary Jane Logan McCallum for the many conversations and comments on the draft of this paper.

1 There is a summary available at http://www.thecanadianencyclopedia.ca/en/article/o-canada/, accessed 27 December 2014.

2 Henry Yu, 'Global Migrants and the New Pacific Canada', *International Journal* (Autumn 2009): 1016.

3 This is from Lorenzo Verancini, '"Settler Colonialism": Career of a Concept', *Journal of Imperial and Commonwealth History*, 41, 2 (2013): 313.

4 Audra Simpson, *Mohawk Interruptus: Political Life Across the Border of Settler States* (Durham, NC: Duke University Press, 2013), pp. 12, 7.

5 See Chad Reimer, *Writing British Columbia History, 1784–1958* (Vancouver: University of British Columbia Press, 2009); Carl Berger, *The Writing of Canadian History: Aspects of English-Canadian Historical Writing since 1900*, 2nd edn (Toronto: University of Toronto Press, 1984).

6 Ann Curthoys, 'We've Just Started Making National Histories, and You Want Us To Stop Already?', in Antoinette Burton, ed., *After the Imperial Turn: Thinking with and through the Nation* (Durham, NC: Duke University Press, 2003), pp. 70–89.

7 Ronald Rudin, *Making History in Twentieth-Century Quebec* (Toronto: University of Toronto Press, 1997); Serge Gagnon, *Quebec and its Historians: 1840 to 1920,* trans. Y. Brunelle (Montreal: Boreal, 1982).

8 Mary Jane Logan McCallum, *Indigenous Women, Work, and History: 1840–1980* (Winnipeg: University of Manitoba Press, 2014), p. 10.

9 Donald A. Wright, *The Professionalization of History in English Canada* (Toronto: University of Toronto Press, 2005), chapter 5.

10 Linda Kealey, 'The Status of Women in the Historical Profession in Canada, 1989 Survey', *Canadian Historical Review*, 72, 3 (September 1991): 370–88; Ruby Heap, 'The Status of Women in the Historical Profession in Canada: Results of 1998 Survey', *Canadian Historical Review*, 81, 3 (September 2000): 436–51.

11 Franca Iacovetta, 'Towards a More Humane Academy? Some Observations from a Canadian Feminist Historian', *Journal of Women's History*, 18, 1 (2006): 145.

12 Ruth Frankenberg, *White Women, Race Matters: The Social Construction of Whiteness* (Minneapolis: University of Minnesota Press, 1993); Vron Ware, *Beyond the Pale: White Women, Racism, and History* (London: Verso, 1992).

13 See The Kino-nda-niimi Collective, eds, *The Winter We Danced: Voices from the Past, the Future, and the Idle No More Movement* (Winnipeg: ARP, 2013).

14 Statistics Canada, 'Aboriginal Peoples in Canada: First Nations People, Métis and Inuit' – http://www12.statcan.gc.ca/nhs-enm/2011/as-sa/99-011-x/99-011-x2011001-eng.cfm (accessed 7 July 2015).

14

Empire Made Me

Clare Anderson
b. 1969

I live and work in Leicester, a city in the English Midlands that is well known for its cultural diversity, and a place where the aftermath of empire and Britain's multi-directional imperial connections are ever-present in our daily lives. Leicester could not be more different from the small, East Anglian village where I grew up in the 1970s and 1980s, or from the Scottish capital city, Edinburgh, where I attended university in the 1990s. My large, extended farming family has no personal connection with empire, as far as we know, and empire did not feature explicitly in my life as a child, teenager or student in my early twenties. However, despite or perhaps because of this I became an historian of the Indian Ocean world. This chapter will work through the personal and political forces that first drew me to its study, and that continue to shape my intellectual engagement with history, colonialism and postcolonialism.

I was born in 1969, and grew up on a farm in the village of Houghton, which lies on the River Ouse in Cambridgeshire, a county in the east of England, near the small town of St Ives. Houghton is extremely picturesque; there is a Norman church, numerous thatched cottages, and a clock tower in the village centre. It is mentioned in the Domesday Book, and surrounding fields bear the marks of ridge and furrow farming. During my childhood, village life was punctuated with the seasonal rhythms of harvesting, Maypole dancing, cricket, well-dressing,[1] feast week and Remembrance Sunday. A statue of the locally famous nonconformist Potto Brown (1797–1871) stands in the village square, in honour of his philanthropy in founding the village chapel and two local schools.

Empire did not feature explicitly in my life as a child. My father was too young to fight in the Second World War, though he served his national service as a doctor's assistant in the Royal Navy on the Isle of Wight afterwards. His older brother had seen wartime service, travelling the world in the navy, though he never talked about it. My mother was born after the war, her father having served in the Home Guard. Nobody, as far as we are aware, undertook any kind of East India Company or colonial service, or migrated to the settler colonies. However, as an adult I have come to realize that empire had been a presence in my early life, but that it was never discussed as such. I remain uncertain as to whether this was the result of ignorance about empire in this small, rural place; or whether it was because of the difficulties of finding a vocabulary to talk about the discomfort of the loss of imperial dominions and possibly the erosion of national distinction or pride, in the aftermath of the war. Ann Laura Stoler has usefully described the inability to find the right words to speak of empire as 'colonial aphasia'.[2]

Why in the absence of family or personal connections, or discussions of colonization or decolonization, do I say that empire made me? It is because although it was never made explicit, I did encounter what we might loosely term 'the imperial' in several areas of my life. I mentioned earlier that a statue of local hero Potto Brown, born at the turn of the nineteenth century, takes pride of place in the centre of my home village. It was put up shortly after his death, at the end of the nineteenth century. At school, by the age of ten we had studied his life and work, and celebrated his philanthropy in education and the Church. What we did not learn then, and what I discovered only recently, is that Potto Brown was a nonconformist Quaker, and was so active in anti-slavery agitation in the 1830s that his home became the movement's local headquarters. He hosted John Scoble, the secretary of the Anti-Slavery Society, and met the American anti-slavery and peace activist Elihu Burritt, who had been appointed American Consul in Birmingham (England) by President Abraham Lincoln, and later described his trip to Houghton.[3] His son later wrote: 'The St. Ives people were great supporters of the movement, and it was said that any lecturer speaking on any subject at a meeting could always elicit cheers from his audience if he referred to the abolition of slavery.'[4] This might not appear worthy of note to scholars of metropolitan, radical, activist political circles, but it seems to me enormously important in suggesting just how connected one small East Anglian village was to global political concerns and debates in the aftermath of the abolition of slavery in the British Empire.

There were other imperial, and global, connections too. Like everybody we knew in the 1970s, my family was fiercely patriotic. Our village celebrated the Queen's Silver Jubilee of 1977 with enormous gusto. In my Brownie uniform, I sat on the back of a tractor and trailer (driven by my granddad), with my pack, in a circle, arms straightened above our heads and hands clasped together. We were candles on a celebratory cake. (I was fiercely jealous of Sunday School, which did Noah's Ark, and was much more interesting, I thought.) This brings me to my next point: Girl Guiding. It is well established that Sir Robert Baden-Powell's Scout movement, which began in the first decade of the twentieth century, informed by Sir Robert's army experiences in India and Africa, promoted character, fitness, patriotism and loyalty to empire, initially amongst boys and, within a year or so and through Agnes and Olive Baden-Powell, girls.[5] The Brownies and Girl Guides were an important part of my growing up, and what I now know to have been my socialization as a young woman. We learned how to sew, cook and camp. We unquestioningly obeyed particular hierarchies, and pledged our loyalty to God and the Queen. And – I remember this distinctly – we studied the Commonwealth. I massively enjoyed working towards my Commonwealth badge, for which I chose to study the Caribbean island of Antigua. To be sure, this did not necessitate any kind of understanding of the Atlantic Triangle or enslavement, but rather was underpinned by a celebration of the emergence of the Commonwealth of Nations. Britain, of course, lay at its heart. We were, it seemed to me at that time, one large and fundamentally equal family.

Some of the highlights of my childhood and early teenage years were repeat coach trips to the Commonwealth Institute in London. The Institute was located on Kensington High Street in London, about seventy miles from where I lived. Though I was not aware of it then, it was the legacy of the Imperial Institute, which had been established in 1887 following the Colonial and Indian Exhibition, held in London during the previous year. The Commonwealth Institute opened in 1962, funded by the Foreign and Commonwealth Office.[6] I have thought long and hard about why I so enjoyed these trips, and I have dug deep to remember them. Memory of course is a tricky thing, and I am loath to make any attempt to describe how I think the displays were mounted, or what I think I felt or experienced there, for fear of being contradicted by historic guidebooks, catalogues or photographs. However, I am confident in saying that for a child growing up in a small, mono-cultural village, the Institute represented the geographical expansiveness and richness of other places and cultures, and the seemingly limitless possibilities of travel and study. My story of visiting the Commonwealth Institute is not, I am sad to say, a story of any kind of personal awakening to post-imperial politics and power. Rather, it is a tale of what I experienced as the chance to escape from life in a small, English country village, albeit imaginatively. Indeed, the nuances of Argentinian claims to the Falkland Islands (Malvinas) escaped me when war broke out in 1982; and I had no understanding of the historic connections between Britain and India when Prime Minister Indira Gandhi was assassinated two years later, though I distinctly remember the event.

I often tell this story: I applied to Edinburgh University because the careers tutor at my comprehensive school told me that it was unlikely I would achieve the grades necessary to win a place at such a prestigious institution. But I did, and so it was to the capital of Scotland that I headed in autumn 1989: the first person in my large, extended family to read for a degree. Margaret Thatcher was still Conservative prime minister (at least for a few months more), though the Labour Party would not win an election for almost a decade. 1989 was otherwise a politically memorable year, in Britain if not overseas. A deeply unpopular community charge (poll tax) had been rolled out across Scotland in 1989, the Berlin Wall fell in November, and student grants had been frozen and replaced with loans.

My first year university flat was on Antigua Street (number 12, above a fish and chip shop), which struck me at the time as a curious coincidence from my days as a Girl Guide. I noticed a further Commonwealth presence on the streets of Edinburgh's Georgian New Town, as Jamaica Street for instance split in two lanes and fed into India Street. Strange as this may sound to twenty-first-century readers familiar with the history of the British Empire, it was some time before I came to appreciate how important empire, imperial trade, enslavement and sugar plantations had been to the development of the city's wealth and prosperity. These issues were not openly acknowledged at the time.[7] This realization dawned as I met and worked with two extraordinary scholars who have had a huge impact on the development of my work and career. First was Ian Duffield, who had joined his political activism with his research through his work in Africa and on pan-Africanism, and later on the black presence in early colonial Australia. Second was Crispin Bates, then a young man fresh out of Cambridge, excited by the intellectual possibilities of engagement with history, subaltern studies and postcolonial theory.

It is difficult to overemphasize just how important Ian and Crispin were (and remain) in and to my personal and scholarly life. They opened my eyes to the ongoing economic, social and cultural relevance of a history that I had not learned in school. As we journeyed together across colonies and continents, beginning with undergraduate study of imperialism in 1990, and extending eventually into the completion of my doctoral research in 1997, a history of global power and exploitation unfolded, leaving me with a set of uncomfortable questions about the history and legacies of empire for the geo-politics of the late twentieth century. I chose the Indian Ocean island of Mauritius as the focus of a PhD project that I initially envisaged as a history of crime and punishment in a colony entirely populated through migration, including African and Indian slaves and Asian indentured labourers. I had specialized in Australian penal colonies and social theories of punishment during the final (fourth) year of my History/Sociology degree programme, and under the tutorage of eminent penologist David Garland (another massive influence on my work) I had become interested in the many absences of empire within the development of social theories of punishment. During my first term of postgraduate registration, I ventured to the Public Record Office in Kew (now renamed The National Archives) and was astonished to find Colonial Office papers indicating that Mauritius had been the site of a penal settlement for convicts from India. This became the focus of my research, and I spent the next three years piecing together a social, cultural and economic history of the penal settlement during the period 1815–53, using Colonial Office papers as well as India Office records, and the Mauritius Archives.[8] The necessary use of records from across multiple archives in writing histories of forced mobility and migration has been a defining feature of my subsequent work.

I submitted my PhD for examination at the end of August 1997, and moved to Leicester the following day (waking up in my new flat to news of Princess Diana's death). I took up what was initially a temporary lectureship in the Department of Economic and Social History.[9] I was rather overwhelmed to be the replacement for the eminent scholar of South Asia, Clive Dewey, who had gone overseas as a research fellow. Leicester could not have been more different to Edinburgh. If poverty in the latter had largely been hidden away from central view in suburban housing 'schemes', Leicester's was concentrated in some of the tightly packed, city centre, red-bricked terraces that are so typical of the English Midlands. Leicester also brought me for the first time into everyday contact with what Jordanna Bailkin has called the afterlife of empire.[10] In a city rightly celebrated for its tolerance and diversity, it was impossible to ignore the significance of postcolonial migration and displacement – including of people from the Caribbean (especially the small islands), South Asia and East Africa – and their enormously creative social and cultural impacts.[11] Famously, a few years later the 2011 census revealed that Leicester is one of three British cities outside London where although they are the largest single group, white Britons are in a minority overall.[12]

I would like to pause here to stress the profound impact that higher education has had on my personal life, and how university and my personal background have shaped my research career. Edinburgh University took me out of a village setting and into city life. It brought me into contact with people from hugely privileged social backgrounds, many connected to wealthy and/or intellectual metropolitan circles, which were very different to my own. It opened my eyes also to some of the complexities of social injustice, which had not been discussed in my family when I was growing up. These included the unravelling of apartheid in South Africa and, closer to home, Section 28 (which in 1988 banned the 'promotion' of homosexuality in schools) and Scottish claims to Independence within the context of a seeming denial of the nation's implication in Britain's imperial expansion. Initially, though, I was most interested in the social dynamics of gender, because they seemed to have most resonance for my own life. I undertook voracious reading and study of a range of feminist history and theory, and I have since spent time trying to figure out how gendered experience (including of sexuality) triangulates historically with that of 'class' and 'race'. I was and remain keenly aware of their personal and political dynamics; and I know that the working through of the historical significance of gender, class and race in many ways represents my efforts to make sense of the formation of my own (now) distinctly bourgeois life, as a white, professional woman and a migrant to (and near twenty-year resident of) a postcolonial English city, where I am a member of what is sometimes called an 'ethnic minority'.

How has this interplay between the personal and the political related to the development of my specific research interests? They might be summarized as an attempt to bring the peripheries of empire into its centre, and to place ordinary people at the heart of historical process and change. My postdoctoral research was initially dedicated to exploring Indian convict transportation to sites in the eastern Indian Ocean, including to penal settlements along the littorals of South East Asia and the Andaman Islands in the Bay of Bengal. I began to explore the connections between Asian, metropolitan and imperial convict flows, and my work expanded to include research on transportation from and between the Caribbean, Cape, Mascarene Islands, India and Australia. I also started to see how penal settlements were linked with enslavement and Indian indentured labour. Despite the many theoretical difficulties implied in the task, I have always been mindful of foregrounding convicts' agency in my research, most recently in a biographical project called *Subaltern Lives*. Here, I attempted to use the experiences of a range of ordinary people who were transported to or who were associated with penal settlements as a kaleidoscope into convict transportation, as well as into larger questions of society and social change in the Indian Ocean world.[13]

I am certain that my fascination with mobility, and my respect for people who inhabit the margins or periphery of society, comes out of my own journey across economic, social and cultural worlds. I have also found that my interpretation of the experience of penal transportation has changed with alterations in my family life. In the years since I became a mother, first in 2003 and then in 2005, and again in 2008 when my father died, my understanding of the meaning of the mobility invoked by penal transportation has undergone a profound change. As a young woman, I interpreted it partly as an opportunity to leave behind often-distressed circumstances and to forge a new life in a place where new identities were up for grabs. I now find reading histories of family separation unbearable: whether they relate to men and women leaving behind babies, children and sick or elderly parents; or desperate letters and petitions written in the hope of news or reunion in the face of serious illness. This brings me to my next point. Though many historians seek a personal distance from the archive, through their 'objective' handling of documents, others take a self-acknowledged positionality in their work. Pioneering feminists, for instance, have researched social and cultural history with real meaning for their lives, including those where race struggles intersected with those of gender.[14] Sociologist Liz Stanley has coined a brilliant expression for such feminist historical practice, and its acceptance that all research represents a choice among many and will always be selective and partial: *The Auto/Biographical I*.[15]

I spent four years in the Department of Sociology at the University of Warwick, from 2007 to 2011. It was at this time that I became centrally focused on questions of history and method described above, as well as two further, interrelated issues, greatly stimulated by my fellowship in Warwick's recently established Global History and Culture Centre.[16] These were: the bringing together of subaltern history with transnational or global history, and the critical interrogation of the aftermath of empire. I was fortunate enough to enjoy an extremely collegial working relationship with a fourth key influence on my research: David Arnold, who was also at Warwick, and a member of the Centre at this time. My work grew to call for an engagement with the scattering of archives of mobility across national repositories, and histories of colonies/nation states decentred by histories written from multiple, connected archives. It also urged taking seriously ethnographic work, not through the production of conventional oral history, but in research on people's understandings of imperial history and its relationship to the societies in which they (and we) live.[17]

These interests developed most keenly in collaboration with two eminent Indian scholars who live and work in Gujarat: historian of science, Madhumita Mazumdar, and anthropologist Vishvajit Pandya. Over a four-year period, after a chance meeting at a conference at the University of Sussex, together we undertook a research project on the Andaman Islands, which had been the largest penal colony in the British Empire, excepting Australia. We sought scholarly integration of the history of the Islands' Indigenous peoples, and convict, refugee and other migrant settlers; and attempted to bring together historical research with anthropological/ethnographic method. Using an archive base spread across three continents, our research narrative interrogated how society, culture and political economy in the Andamans have been historically constituted. Critically, it offered also interpretations of how history is understood in the Islands today, and how it has been deployed (and contested) in the making of nation, community and identity. For me, this Global North/Global South collaboration has made an important political point, not just through the bringing together of equals in the practice of scholarly research and writing on empire, but in engaging with the aftermath and meaning of Empire in people's lives today.[18]

The ongoing significance of empire in both respects has been central to the development of my research methodologies, not just through the near-identical structure of the academy in Britain and South Asia, which has made my work with Indian scholars possible, but through the centring of ethnographic and anthropological work in an historical project. In bringing this chapter to a close, I want to discuss how writing with and through the archives of the Andamans, in a South Asian context, my professional became linked to my personal life in unanticipated and unexpected ways.

My story relates to my study of the 'local-born' community in the Andamans, that is to say the men and women who are descended from transported convicts and who live in the Islands today. Because the convicts came from all over India, and were forced into culturally unfamiliar living, working and marriage practices, many mainland forms of social difference and distinction, including caste and gender relations, were transformed. Today the Islands are known as 'mini India'; a place of 'unity in diversity', or what scholars might call a cosmopolitan space.

I had pieced together a history of the local-borns using the archives of empire in Britain and India, and as the project unfolded I became curious to find out how local-born people made sense of their convict past. Between 2010 and 2013 I undertook a series of interviews in the Aberdeen Bazaar area of Port Blair, where many local born families live. Many of the elderly residents had lived through the Japanese occupation of the Andamans during the Second World War, and had witnessed the transition to Indian Independence that started in 1947 and ultimately led to the political assimilation of the Andamans as a Union Territory of the Republic.

The elderly residents of Port Blair had been born at about the same time as my father and his brothers; and though there were significant differences in the communities to which our respective families belonged, and between our cultures, I was struck by the familiarity of local-born refrains about the past and the present. In the small East Anglian village where I grew up, the war was a vital social reference point for many people. At that time, many established families also expressed discomfort about 'incomers', people who did not 'belong' to the village, and their negative impact on country ways of life. As people spoke to me about their nostalgia for the old days, and of their worries that new migrants to the Islands did not understand or respect the Andamans' unique culture, I was reminded of the concerns and laments of people in my home place.

As our work in the Andamans progressed, I could not but think of my own upbringing, and also as a person now living away from my home place, my implication in what was experienced by others as change or loss. In both my home place, and the home place of the people I was researching, this was the passing of an era as the pace and way of life shifted. I know that I am part of this social upheaval, for through my education and social and geographical mobility I constitute some of the shifts that bring together the sighs of elderly people across distant continents and oceans. And though I am able both to understand and to rationalize it, this fact remains nonetheless profoundly discomforting.

Notes

1 A summer custom of parts of rural England, where water wells are decorated with flowers.

2 Ann Laura Stoler, 'Colonial Aphasia: Race and Disabled Histories in France', *Public Culture*, 23, 1 (2011): 121–56.

3 *Potto Brown, the Village Philanthropist* (St Ives, Hunts: Albert Goodman, 1878), 118, 161–3; *A Jubilee Memorial of the Union Chapel, Houghton, Huntingdon, Prepared at the Request of the Church by the Pastor, Henry Bell*

(Cambridge: Cambridge University Press, 1890), 14–15; *Reminiscences of Bateman Brown, J.P.* (Peterborough: The 'Peterborough Advertiser' Company Ltd, 1905), p. 126. I thank Gerry Feakes for lending me copies of these rare books. Claire Midgley discusses anti-slavery in St Ives in *Women Against Slavery: The British Campaigns 1780–1870* (London: Routledge, 1992).

4 *Reminiscences of Bateman Brown*, 126.

5 Michael Rosenthal, 'Knights and Retainers: The Earliest Version of Baden-Powell's Boy Scout Scheme', *Journal of Contemporary History*, 15, 4 (1980): 603–17; Michael Rosenthal, *The Character Factory: Baden-Powell and the Origins of the Boy Scout Movement* (London: Pantheon Books, 1986).

6 The Institute closed in 2002 when some of its collections were donated to Bristol's British Empire and Commonwealth Museum. The museum has since closed, and the collections were deposited with Bristol Museums, Galleries and Archives.

7 In the larger British context, now explored in Catherine Hall, Nicholas Draper, Keith McClelland, Kate Donington and Rachel Lang, *Legacies of British Slave-ownership: Colonial Slavery and the Formation of Victorian Britain* (Cambridge: Cambridge University Press, 2014).

8 The India Office was then based at Blackfriars, and is now incorporated into the Asia, Pacific and Africa Collections of the British Library. The Mauritius Archives are in Coromandel, just south of the capital Port Louis.

9 The department no longer exists; it merged with the Department of History in 2003.

10 Jordanna Bailkin, *The Afterlife of Empire* (Berkeley: University of California Press, 2012).

11 Andrew Brown, 'Here, everyone is a minority', *The Guardian*, 2 January 2010: 25; Esther Addley, 'Real lives: Side by side', *The Guardian*, 1 January 2001: 2.6; Judith Vidal-Hall, 'Leicester: City of Migration', *Index on Censorship*, 32:2 (2003): 132–41.

12 Alice Philipson, 'White Britons a minority in Leicester, Luton and Slough', *The Telegraph*, 10 January 2013; 'Into the Melting Pot', *The Economist*, 8 February 2014.

13 Clare Anderson, *Subaltern Lives: Biographies of Colonialism in the Indian Ocean World, 1790–1920* (Cambridge: Cambridge University Press, 2012).

14 I must note here Catherine Hall's pioneering work, including, co-authored with Leonore Davidoff, the classic *Family Fortunes: Men and Women of the English Middle Class, 1780–1850* (London: Hutchinson, 1987), and the more recent exploration of Britain and Jamaica, *Civilising Subjects: Metropole and Colony in the English Imagination, 1830–1867* (Oxford: Polity, 2002). Other hugely important works published in Australia, and engaging with Indigenous rights, are Anne Curthoys' *For and Against Feminism: A Personal Journey into Feminist Theory and History* (Sydney: Allen and Unwin, 1998); and *Freedom Ride: A Freedomrider Remembers* (Sydney: Allen and Unwin, 2002).

15 Liz Stanley, *The Auto/Biographical I: The Theory and Practice of Feminist Auto/Biography* (Manchester: Manchester University Press, 1992).

16 See especially a recent collection of essays, edited by the Centre's founding director, Maxine Berg, *Writing the History of the Global: Challenges for the 21st Century* (Oxford: Oxford University Press, 2013); and the Centre's homepage at http://www2.warwick.ac.uk/fac/arts/history/ghcc/ (accessed 4 August 2014).

17 For a working through of these themes in the Indian Ocean context, see Clare Anderson 'Subaltern Lives: History, Identity and Memory in the Indian Ocean World', *History Compass*, 11, 7 (2013): 503–7.

18 Clare Anderson, Madhumita Mazumdar and Vishvajit Pandya, *New Histories of the Andaman Islands: Landscapes in the Bay of Bengal, 1790–2012* (Cambridge: Cambridge University Press, 2015). I acknowledge with gratitude the support of the Economic and Social Research Council (ESRC, for the project 'Integrated Histories of the Andaman Islands,' 2009–13 (award no. RES-000-22-3484). Our project was one of the first pilots in international collaboration, which has since been rolled out across the ESRC's various funding schemes.

15

Paths to the Past

Tony Ballantyne b. 1972

My engagement with the imperial past begins not with a political awakening or a transformative intellectual experience, but rather with my family. I am the youngest child of a large family and was raised in Caversham, a working-class suburb in the city of Dunedin in southern New Zealand. My parents were not academics: in fact, because of the timing of their own births they had limited education. My mother Joy, who was born in 1929, left school early at the outbreak of the Second World War to help milk cows on the small family farm in Ohai, 250 kilometres south-west of Dunedin. My father Garth was born the year before and despite having a father who was a teacher, he had a relatively limited formal education, studying book-keeping at a technical college before entering the work force as a clerk.

By the time I was born in 1972, our family had grown to eleven children and it must have been under financial pressure for some time. My father had ended up as a labourer working the nightshift in a printing factory, hard physical graft that was not well paid. In order to help support the family, my mother worked part-time, moving between jobs in catering and working as a cleaner. Their economic situation meant that work, thrift and being skilled with your hands, so that you could preserve, bake and cook cheaply, make and repair clothes, and maintain an old and rickety house, were crucially important.

So my parents were not especially educated. But they were avid readers: mystery and crime novels in my mother's case; pulpy thrillers, whodunnits, adventure stories and sports books in my father's. They were not especially interested in history per se, or at least, the 'big stories' of national history, but they had a strong interest in the family past, in stories about our ancestors who migrated to Southland and Otago, the southern provinces of New

Zealand, and who built families, farmed and mined, and quickly made homes in this new land. This knowledge was not formally kept in a family tree; it was only partially inscribed in the Paterson Family Bible that we had. Nobody in the family was a devoted genealogist, and our family histories were not fortified through any involvement in the ethnic associations (such as the Caledonian Societies), which were common in Otago. Rather our family histories were much more fragmentary, transmitted through a set of condensed stories. These included the death of our great-great-grandfather Francis's second wife Jessie Douglas as the *Henrietta*, the vessel that conveyed them from Glasgow to Dunedin as assisted migrants, sailed into Otago Harbour in September 1860, and the story of my great-grandfather John Ballantyne carrying all of his possessions in a handcart when he walked 175 kilometres from Dunedin to settle at Waikaka in the late 1860s. There were many more stories about more recent generations, narratives that were used to place and explain the characteristics of a large web of aunts and uncles (both fictive and real) and innumerable cousins who were scattered across the small towns of Southland: Gore, Brydone, Waikaka, Waikoikoi, Ohai, Woodlands, Scott's Gap and Manapouri. Although I went to school and played sport alongside Māori children in south Dunedin, Māori were not especially prominent in these older family tales, reflecting the relatively small numbers of Māori who lived in inland rural Southland. Māori connections were important for one strand of our family, however. Amy Robinson, my great-grandmother, grew up in the central North Island, where her father, Thomas Joseph Robinson, ran a Native School at Awahou. Amy moved south, marrying my great-grandfather James Paterson of Waikaka, but was deeply imprinted by her formative years living in a predominantly Māori community and surviving the calamitous Tarawera volcanic eruption of 1886. The importance of those histories to Amy was signalled by her giving three of her children Māori names drawn from the traditions of the Te Arawa people her family lived amongst.

Thus I grew up in a family where value was attached to talking, family stories, and reading. Education was very important: my parents believed that education had an intrinsic significance, but they also understood that it was an effective way for their children to gain a level of material comfort and security that eluded them. This commitment also reflected the values that they imbibed in their childhoods. Both of them were born in the late 1920s into families that were strongly shaped by the Protestant traditions, especially Presbyterianism. By the 1950s they were not practicing Presbyterians, but they sent the older children to Sunday School, believed in God and had a cultural outlook that was deeply imprinted by Presbyterianism's emphasis on thrift, time discipline and its fundamental egalitarianism, which encouraged an innate scepticism about 'airs and graces': 'don't trust the rich' was an earnest piece of advice my mother gave me when I was 12.

All of this suggests that I was raised in a family that was strongly imprinted by the distinctive form of colonial culture that developed in southern New Zealand. Otago was established as a so-called 'systematic' colony in 1848 organized around the principles of Edward Gibbon Wakefield. The Otago scheme was driven by an association of Free Church of Scotland laity and was envisaged as transplanting Presbyterian values – thrift, hard work, the primacy of the Bible, the cultural centrality of literacy – to the most distant edge of the empire. In reality the dominance of the large Presbyterian community was tempered by close everyday interactions with and accommodations to English Anglicans, Methodists and Baptists, and a significant number of Catholics (especially after the influx of new colonists following the discovery of gold in 1861). While the Ballantynes were of good Presbyterian stock from Castleton and then Jedburgh in Roxburghshire, our family tree laced together Anglicans, Baptists and Brethrens (the Robinsons, Crappers and Dewes), Lowlands Presbyterians (Blakies), Irish Protestants (the Kings and Fishers) into the Scottish Presbyterian families that we primarily identify with, the Patersons (from Lesmahagow) and the Ballantynes.

These family stories were the most significant connections I felt to the colonial past when I was growing up, although I probably did not think of them as being about empire. I studied history at high school but New Zealand was less prominent in our syllabus than the history of twentieth-century wars and British political history. I was better at Geography and ultimately more interested in sport, especially cricket. I read widely about the history of cricket, especially about the infamous Bodyline Ashes series of 1932–3 and, in my final year of school, I also read C. L. R. James's *Beyond a Boundary*. It was through this reading, more than my formal schooling, that I began to develop an interest in empire and colonialism. That sport loomed large was hardly surprising given that rugby, cricket and horse-racing were key parts of our family life. But it also probably reflected the centrality of sport in New Zealand's racial politics in the 1970s and 1980s, when New Zealand's sporting contacts with South Africa were divisive and the struggle against the Springbok (the South African rugby team) tour of New Zealand in 1981 catalysed deeper critiques of Pākehā racism and the legacies of colonialism.

I enrolled for a BA at the University of Otago in 1990 with no firm vision of my career path; I probably imagined that I would follow many of my siblings and their partners and become a schoolteacher. In my first year I did not take the very popular New Zealand history course and perhaps this choice was motivated by a scepticism regarding the celebrations of the nation's sesquicentenary, manifesting my developing unease towards nationalism. More positively, taking medieval British and European courses was driven by my enthusiasm for medieval and early modern British history, which at least partially reflected the persistent cultural influence of Britain and British history in New Zealand. Those areas continued to be my primary interests in my second year of study when I was admitted into the Honours programme. The compulsory course that I was required to take as an Honours student that year was a revelation. In the first half, we were introduced to a range of key passages in the development of historical thinking, reaching back to significant pre-Enlightenment and important non-Western traditions, by Professor W. H. 'Hew' McLeod, the world-leading authority on Sikh history. The second half of the course was a hands-on research exercise using early missionary manuscripts from New Zealand, directed by Otago's new appointee in Māori history, Michael Reilly. Michael encouraged us to immerse ourselves in the rich body of manuscripts held by the Hocken Library; but in framing the research exercise he prompted us to understand missionary texts in light of Ranajit Guha's argument that colonial texts were often encoded by the rebel consciousness of the colonized. This class not only pointed me towards my first fleeting engagement with subaltern studies, but Michael also stressed the importance of reading missionary texts against Māori traditional knowledge, encouraging us to read the important study of genealogy and tribal formation in Jeff Sissons, Wiremu Wi Hongi and Pat Hohepa's *The Pūriri Trees are Laughing*. Reading that work was a very important experience because it not only conveyed the complexity of traditional politics, but also communicated some of the distinctive features of Māori ways of narrating the past. Working through the missionary manuscripts in light of these texts and creating an argument of my own was a compelling experience, one that encouraged me to think about the possibilities of postgraduate study for the first time.

A key component of the fourth and final year of my Honours degree at Otago was writing a 20,000-word dissertation. For this exercise I returned to those same missionary manuscripts and I decided to explore missionaries and the problem of sexuality. The spur for this was two-fold: first, I had read parts of volume one of Foucault's *History of Sexuality* for our Honours seminar in the preceding year and I was eager to return to those missionary texts in light of Foucault's arguments about the productive workings of power; second, and following on from the first, I had read a sequence of important works by New Zealand scholars – the political scientist Robert Chapman, the historian and poet Keith Sinclair, and the historian Judith Binney – that identified missionaries as the progenitors of the corrosive form of Puritanism. Missionaries were difficult cultural ancestors and for these Pākehā scholars, religion was central to understanding both the stultifying weight of the Puritanism that they saw as a powerful thread in Pākehā culture and the undermining of traditional Maori culture in an age of empire and colonialism. Such arguments were very much alive in 1993: Jane Campion's much-lauded *The Piano* was a potent indictment of the repressive nature of colonial culture and the Protestant ethics that were transplanted to New Zealand.

So although listening to family stories meant that I grew up with narratives of empire, it was this initial foray into research that really set me on the path to be a professional historian and I have returned to those missionary manuscripts repeatedly: they are the foundation of my recently published *Entanglements of Empire: Missionaries, Māori and the Question of the Body*. Of more immediate importance, however, is that my dissertation was integral to me gaining a Prince of Wales Scholarship to pursue doctoral work with Chris Bayly at Cambridge. I had formulated a project that was designed as a comparative history of colonial knowledge, focusing on a seemingly unlikely pair of sites, Punjab and New Zealand. The rationale for the project was that the two colonies shared similar chronologies of cross-cultural engagement, annexation and colonial warfare; but I also chose them because I already had a good grasp of New Zealand historiography thanks to my excellent teachers and mentors in Erik Olssen and John Stenhouse, and under Hew McLeod's tutelage I had developed a decent grasp of the modern history of Punjab. I was also very lucky that I had developed a broad sense of colonialism, having taken papers on colonial America and Australian history and having been taught South African history by John Omer-Cooper. In the twenty-two months between completing my Honours degree and arriving in Cambridge I worked as a tutor in World and Pacific history and as a research assistant in the Otago History Department; I also took night classes in *te reo Māori* (Māori language) at Otago Polytechnic; and I worked through a reading list of relevant works that Chris Bayly had given me while visiting New Zealand in 1994.

Newly-married to a fellow Otago student, Sally Henderson, I arrived in England in September 1995, staying initially with Sally's uncle and aunt at Felixstowe, where they were on a teacher exchange. Felixstowe felt reasonably familiar and comfortable: its seaside penny arcades, promenade and terrace houses all conformed to the sense of England I had formed in New Zealand. And having grown up in a family for whom the Sunday lunchtime screening of *The Big Match* – showing highlights of English Football League matches – was a key part of our weekly routine, it was exciting to see an Ipswich Town home game at Portman Road. This was part of an initial delight to be in England, where so much of the culture that I had consumed as a child and teenager had emanated from, including the TV shows my parents loved (from *Professionals* and *Z-Cars*, through *Coronation Street* to *Are You Being Served?* and *It Ain't Half Hot Mum*), the music that my older brothers were devoted to (David Bowie, Roxy Music and T-Rex), and where the novels I loved as a young reader were set (especially those by Enid Blyton, Michael Hardcastle, Robert Westall and Susan Cooper).

This façade of familiarity was quickly punctured when I arrived in Cambridge. The town was beautiful, packed with architectural landmarks and history, but I never felt at ease there. Suddenly I was 'a colonial' – a term that I encountered routinely – and my accent frequently drew wry comment. Many of my fellow students in the History Faculty appeared confident of their projects and trajectories: they knew why their projects were important, they had clear plans, and the British students seemed to possess an innate grasp of how Cambridge worked. These perceptions were undoubtedly a product of my own uncertainties and the strong sense of otherness that was central to how I thought of myself while I was at Cambridge. Questions of class became more important for me as my own anxieties around my social origins were exacerbated in the face of the wealth of most colleges and the University itself and in light of the tremendous class-privilege of so many of the students. Unlike some American students and many from the former colonies, I found the trappings of Cambridge difficult to embrace: I did not row, I did not like port and sherry, I did not enjoy formal dinners, garden parties and May Balls. I did enjoy many aspects of British culture – the newspapers, the cricket and football, the popular music, and the heritage – but I longed for the easy informality of New Zealand life. I missed Dunedin greatly and almost from the moment I arrived in Cambridge I looked forward to returning to New Zealand.

Fortunately, as a postgraduate student, I would be a member of, and live in, Wolfson College. By Cambridge standards Wolfson was a new college, with a large population of international postgraduate students: it was poorer, but more socially-mixed than the traditional colleges. But it was still Cambridge; academic gowns were worn to dinner at Formal Hall, grace was said in Latin, and clear hierarchies encoded the operation of the College. I ended up at Wolfson because of the influential scholar of Hindi, Stuart McGregor: Stuart was a New Zealander and had corresponded over the years with Hew McLeod. This connection pointed to one of the real benefits of being based at Wolfson: it had a significant number of South Asianists as Fellows, its President was then Gordon Johnson (a notable member of the so-called 'Cambridge School' of Indian history), and it had a large number of South Asian students. So life in college, where I had good friends who were from Secunderabad, Dhaka, Ambala and Jallandar, and taking Hindi classes through the Faculty of Oriental Studies greatly extended my knowledge of South Asia, which was further enhanced by my archival work in Delhi and Punjab in 1996.

But it was Chris Bayly's supervision that made my time in Cambridge a transformative experience. The range and depth of his knowledge, his willingness to spend time with his students, and the seemingly endless lists of articles and books, old and new, he would encourage me to read not only greatly enriched my thought and writing, but offered a valuable model of engaged supervision. I met Chris very regularly, normally spending an hour with him in his rooms at St Catharine's College discussing what I had been reading or writing, before heading off to the Eagle pub for a pint. Conversation would then open out and I learnt a great deal about the connections that shaped scholarly work and would always come away with further things to read and think about. Chris was also central in the intellectual life of that part of the Cambridge History Faculty that took non-European history seriously: during my time in Cambridge, he co-chaired the

Commonwealth and Overseas History Seminar (now renamed the World History Seminar) with A. G. Hopkins (who was my secondary advisor) and frequently convened the South Asian seminar. Through those regular gatherings I encountered a host of new ideas as well as hearing papers from scholars who had played key roles in shaping imperial history as a field, including Ronald Robinson and David Fieldhouse.

My Cambridge experience gave me a strong sense of the development of the imperial history tradition as well as the range of new work on empire and on India that was flourishing in the mid-1990s: in a short span of months I read Bayly's *Empire and Information*, Bernard Cohn's *Colonialism and its Forms of Knowledge*, Mrinalini Sinha's *Colonial Masculinity*, Tom Metcalf's *Ideologies of the Raj*, and Eugene Irschick's *Dialogue and History*. It was clear that the old imperial history tradition embodied by Robinson and Fieldhouse had been pushed aside and there seemed to be a range of exciting new possibilities as a result of the innovative perspectives that had gained traction through the cultural turn and as established scholars took up new questions.

In some ways that explosive burst of scholarship was unsettling; the field seemed to be moving so quickly and I was very unclear where my work would sit. During the course of my dissertation research, my project shifted from being a comparative history of colonial knowledge to a kind of connected history, reconstructing the ways in which the Aryan idea developed in colonial India and was transplanted and reworked in a range of locations across the empire including England, Scotland, Ireland, Southeast Asia and New Zealand, where there were protracted debates over Māori origins and where some influential colonial ethnologists argued that traditional Māori religion was a degenerated form of popular Hinduism and tapu was a transplanted form of caste. In reconstructing the multiple translations and reworking of Aryanism, I began to think of the empire as a web-like structure, consisting of multiple networks that not only linked metropole to the colonies, but which also directly linked colonies, even those as seemingly disparate as India and New Zealand. This analytical metaphor of the 'webs of empire' has been widely used since the publication of my book based on the dissertation, *Orientalism and Race* (2002), but as I finished the dissertation I was very uncertain about how this project placed me. Where would my PhD, which moved between so many sites and historiographies, take me? Although I was confident of my understanding of my research sites, I was concerned that other historians would not see my work as 'grounded' in one place, one culture, one language. Would South Asian historians see me as a South Asianist and would New Zealand historians see me as a New Zealandist?

These concerns were largely allayed when I successfully applied for a Junior Lectureship in History at the National University of Ireland, Galway/ Ollscoil na hÉireann, Gaillimh. Although the advertisement had stipulated a range of possible fields of expertise (including Russian history), I was appointed to teach the history of the British Empire and colonialism. I taught courses on the history of the Pacific as well as surveys of the British Empire and Indian history and graduate seminars on historiography and colonial knowledge for the very successfully taught MA on Culture and Colonialism. Teaching and working in Galway further enriched and complicated my understandings of empire. In the History Department, my colleagues Nicholas Canny and Steven Ellis were central protagonists in the debates over how the early modern history of Ireland might be studied; whether Ireland might be seen, as Ellis suggested, as an integral part of the history of the Tudor state or, as Canny argued, as a key colonial laboratory within England's nascent Atlantic empire. At the same time, there were widespread discussions about the usefulness of postcolonial theory for interpreting Irish history. The nature of colonialism and cultural imperialism were invested with a political and cultural urgency in Galway that seemed largely absent in Cambridge: these were pressing debates as they bore on key aspects of the Irish national story and cultural identities. And in Galway there was a particular concern around these issues because of the importance of the Irish language in the university's mission: the university is close to the Connemara Gaeltacht, its History Department was committed to teaching as much of its programme as possible in Irish, and the university as a whole was invested with a special statutory responsibility for the cultivation of the Irish language.

Life in Galway itself was very social. On the back of the 'Celtic Tiger', the university was expanding and there was a group of young international faculty in commerce and the humanities as well as some recently-appointed locals. Like me, many of these newcomers were struck by the warmth of Galwegians and the sociability of the locals stood in stark contrast to our experience living in Cambridge. Against the backdrop of a robust local culture (embodied in the popularity of traditional Irish music and the importance of the Irish language in the West), I began to explore Ireland's imperial connections in the nineteenth century. The immediate outcome of this was that I expanded my fleeting discussions of Anglo-Irish scholars who contributed to the development of comparative philology, ethnology and folklore studies in my nearly-completed book manuscript *Orientalism and Race*, which was based on my PhD. My research on Irish knowledge networks also allowed me to make a small contribution to the debates that were playing out around the millennium about whether Ireland was a colony and its precise position in Britain's empire.

After two years, Sally and I left Galway to move to Urbana-Champaign, Illinois, where I had been appointed as an Assistant Professor of Transnational History. Those earlier uncertainties about the legibility of a mobile multi-sited approach to imperial history suddenly seemed misplaced, as increasingly humanities scholars were interested in the possibilities of transnational scholarship. When I arrived at Illinois, it was clear that the precise nature of transnational history was subject to multiple and contesting interpretations amongst the faculty. These played out in a variety of forums, including the host of reading groups that were integral to the robust and rich intellectual life of the Illinois department. I was involved in campus level discussions around the possibilities of 'global studies' and within the History Department I worked very closely with Antoinette Burton in exploring the possibilities of teaching world history at undergraduate level. Those exchanges around the pedagogy and politics of world, global and transnational history catalysed the ongoing collaborations between Antoinette and myself. This collaboration was underpinned by key commonalities in our visions of the project of British imperial history – especially around the value of critical histories of empire and the value of cultural analysis – as well as a shared commitment to pushing against Eurocentric visions of both empire and world history. Antoinette's work and friendship was also a key catalyst for me beginning to write a revisionist cultural history of modern Sikhism which particularly explored the connections between Punjabi migration and the encounter with British imperial power. That project, which traced the reverberations of these imperial connections in contemporary Britain, drew upon a lot of the material I had gathered during my archival research in Britain and India and the material around Sikh popular culture that I began informally collecting while I lived in Cambridge. I imagined that manuscript – which was ultimately published as *Between Colonialism and Diaspora: Sikh Cultural Formations in an Imperial World* – as staging an encounter between Hew McLeod's meticulous histories of the development of the Sikh tradition and Antoinette's path-breaking work on the centrality of India in the making of imperial Britain.

This peripatetic career trajectory seemingly came to an end in 2002, when we returned home to New Zealand and I took up an appointment teaching World and South Asian history back at the University of Otago in my hometown of Dunedin. This was effectively Hew McLeod's old position and it was wonderful to be able to extend our department's commitment to teaching the histories of India. On my return, Hew was an important mentor and my many discussions with him were integral to the completion of *Between Colonialism and Diaspora*, which appeared in 2006. Until Hew's death in 2009, he was a key link for me into the international Sikh studies community and since his death, I have done much less work focused on Sikh history.

But India has remained a significant element of my work as I have been committed to exploring the shifting connections that have linked New Zealand to Asia, especially India and China. On my initial return to Otago, it was an obvious move to apply the transnational analytical strategy that I developed in *Orientalism and Race* as a starting point for rethinking the history of colonial New Zealand. From the mid-1980s a sequence of works by Claudia Orange, James Belich, Anne Salmond and Judith Binney had constructed a powerful reassessment of the colonial past that framed New Zealand's history as a bicultural national story. These readings generally paid limited attention to imperial connections and emphasized the primacy of Māori–Pākehā relations in shaping the nation. Initially I wrote a couple of historiographic essays that critiqued this approach by highlighting the ways in which it depended on the excision of these Asian connections, but I have subsequently drawn on extensive archival work to explore some key passages in the changing place of South Asia in the development of New Zealand.

By 2004 I had completed the first draft of the manuscript of *Between Colonialism and Diaspora* and I was looking for a new long-term project to work on from Otago. Initially I thought a global history of Theosophy would be a good project in light of my work on India, the prominence of some New Zealanders in the early development of Theosophy as a global movement, and the early emergence of Dunedin as a significant centre for Theosophists within Australasia. I set this aside, however, for another project that applied my interest in imperial knowledge production to the context of southern New Zealand. In October 2002 and October 2003, I took leave and Sally and I travelled around Otago and Southland, visiting many of the small towns where we had family connections. With hindsight, it was these trips that first suggested to me the possibilities that might come from training my attention on this region, which I knew well and which possessed rich archives detailing changing patterns of imperial connections.

During 2004 I worked my way into this new research area, writing an essay that effectively staged a collision between the scholarship on colonial knowledge in South Asia and the local archives I had begun to explore. This convinced me that it would be useful to try and write a history of the connections between knowledge and the colonization of southern New Zealand; something that was further confirmed through a series of conversations that I had with Mike Stevens, a young Māori historian from the local Kāi Tahu people who had recently completed an Honours degree in History at Otago. Mike decided to stay at Otago for his graduate work and I was the primary supervisor for his brilliant PhD that explored the interplay between cultural continuity and change through the lens of the long-standing Kāi Tahu practice of muttonbirding. Mike is a lecturer in our department, and my ongoing conversations with him, which now span a decade, have been crucial in shaping my appreciation of the history of the south.

So this project on colonialism in Otago and Southland has shifted my primary research focus back to New Zealand, but I continue to understand these sites within a global and imperial frame. The importance of empire remains central to my work, standing at the heart of my re-reading of the early histories of missionary work and cross-cultural debate in my *Entanglements of Empire*. But most of my archivally based work now explores the histories of southern New Zealand and the ways in which the region was continually remade by empire and colonization during the nineteenth century. I continue to work on the history of knowledge production and hope to finish a sequence of books exploring those dynamics in the coming years, but the question of place itself increasingly stands alone as a focus for my speaking and writing within New Zealand.

My argument that I have developed in recent years, which suggests places were and are made by institutions and cultural practices shaping and lacing together the trajectories of capital, goods, things, animals and people into knot-like junctures, owes a great deal to the work of the geographer Doreen Massey, but it was also borne out of more personal realizations. I only slowly recognized that the histories of my colonial ancestors, and those of my wife's ancestors as well, were stories of movement; ships and voyages were the key transition points between the old and new worlds in these stories. And once they arrived in the colony these families rarely stayed fixed: families moved from Sussex to the New South Wales to Riverton to Fairlight to Glenorchy to Quarry Hills to Invercargill; or from Castleton to Jedburgh in Roxburghshire before coming to Dunedin, to the goldfields of Central Otago, back to Dunedin, to Waikaka, to Portobello, to Mosgiel, to Sawyer's Bay, to Caversham. These people who are frequently designated as 'settlers' were, in fact, unsettled and mobility was integral to the dynamics of colonization and fundamentally shaped the nature of colonial society. Tracing their routes, where they paused and where they stayed will be an important concern of my future work as I increasingly realize that the stories I grew up with are a rich starting point for thinking about the nature of empire, the shape of colonial society, and how my own family was embedded within the dynamics of colonization.

16

Conversations with Caroline

Caroline Bressey
b. 1974

Though I have looked at the photograph countless times, the clarity of Caroline's portrait is still striking. Her gaze demands you pause and look at her, address her, and acknowledge her incarceration. A plain backdrop frames her. In other pages of the album, some of her fellow patients cover their face before the camera's gaze or a hand belonging to an out-of-frame body holds them up before the lens.[1] Caroline's gaze meets the photographer and, through the camera's lens, us, directly. She sits, or has been seated, on a chair, the back of which can just be seen curving behind her right arm. Her face, described as 'coal-black' and 'very mannish' by British newspapers that reported her presence in court in September 1905, appears extraordinarily smooth, a softness that contrasts to the hardness of her stare.[2] She wears what appears to be a tailored tweed jacket, no sign of the Inverness cape she wore to the hearing at the Mansion House before she was sent to Stone Asylum for the City of London's pauper patients in Dartford, Kent. Caroline's blouse has a large, perhaps ruffled, bow or collar, but the details have been bleached out, or failed to fix, during the development of the print. Her tightly curled hair is cut very short. Newspapers reported that her 'mannish' appearance was enhanced by the white felt 'wideawake hat' she wore in court, but her short hair style would also have been a key part of performing her identity when she lived and worked in England as Paul Downing.[3]

Like many other women whose lives passing as men in the early twentieth century were revealed to the public, Paul Downing's life working as a male labourer came to an end following an encounter with the police and then local medical authorities.[4] Police Constable Bailey arrested Downing on Blackfriars Bridge as she chased down omnibuses and hailed the conductors, asking if they had seen her missing wife.[5] Taken to Bridewell

Place police station, in one of the divisions in the City, a usual search for weapons and property revealed nothing suspicious, and Downing's clothing and manners gave Bailey no cause to suspect he was interacting with a woman. The property found on Downing at her arrest included a pipe, tobacco pouch, a knife and comb, some collars and ties and a Bible.[6] These innocuous personal items were key to the authenticity of Paul Downing's identity but were no reason to hold an individual in a police cell if you were not aware of the deception. Downing's 'strange conduct' on Blackfriars Bridge, however, was reason enough to have her sent to the Bow Infirmary (formerly London's Bow Workhouse) where she was admitted onto the male ward.[7] Downing lasted three days here before her 'masquerade' was revealed. Her life as Paul Downing was taken from her and, after a hearing at the Mansion House, she was transferred to the female ward of the City of London asylum. The Asylum opened in 1866 with a capacity for 250 pauper patients. By 1872 the Asylum was full and so an expansion was undertaken, increasing the potential number of patients to 583 by 1895.[8] In 1900, the Senior Assistant Medical Office Arthur E. Patterson assessed that the majority of rate-paid patients admitted to Stone Asylum had been, like Caroline, 'found wandering' within the jurisdiction of the City of London. They came to Stone, via the City, from all parts of England, and from all quarters of the globe.[9] Among this diverse household of strangers, Paul Downing was forced to revert to a life as Caroline Brogden, a 'Negress' from North Georgia who had travelled through the United States and lived in France, as well as Spain and Belgium according to some reports, before coming to England, where she had worked as a labourer on a chicken farm and most recently as an odd job man in south London for a Bermondsey undertaker.[10]

Newspapers reported that Caroline refused to reveal anything of her former life, but the authorities believed her strong American accent confirmed her birthplace and concluded she was around thirty years old. In faded ink at the top of her medical record, out of the frame of officially required data collection, someone had added an additional description: 'a woman of colour', and then placed in brackets underneath, 'American Indian Cherokee native'. If Caroline was assumed by those around her to fit the description of 'a woman of colour / American Indian Cherokee native', why were these particular definitions seen to coalesce in her? Such a description places Caroline's body in a complex matrix of histories of empire, slavery, migration, gender, work and class. Though hers is surely an extraordinary story, ordinary women like Caroline rarely find a place in the re-telling of British histories, particularly in the period dramas that were – and perhaps even with the diffusion of channels through digital media platforms remain – a foundational part of the making and remaking of the geographical imagination of the British nation.

For me, the clocks turning back an hour at two am on the last Sunday in October and the resulting darker and colder evenings of autumn still signal the coming of a televised costume drama mini series on the BBC as much as they do the beginning of winter. I remember these programmes as the focus of Sunday evenings with my parents, a working class migrant mother from Jamaica who came to Britain with her twin brother in the 1960s, and my Cambridge-educated middle class English father. Most of the dramatizations I remember us watching were of Dickens: *The Pickwick Papers* (BBC, 1985), *Oliver Twist* (BBC, 1985), *Martin Chuzzlewit* (1994), *Our Mutual Friend* (BBC, 1998), and *Great Expectations* (BBC, 1999). More recent adaptations have included Jane Austin's *Pride and Prejudice* (I have in mind the BBC's 1995 production), Henry Fielding's *The History of Tom Jones, a Foundling* (BBC, 1997), Elizabeth Gaskell's *Wives and Daughters* (BBC, 1999) and the ever-popular Dickens once again with *Bleak House* (BBC, 2009).[11] Although I continued to enjoy these realizations of Victorian London and the outrageous fortunes and misadventures of Dickens' characters during my teenage years, I became increasingly critical of the visions of Britain's past I saw around me, in the urban landscapes of London and its representation on television. Was the world of Dickens so different to the cosmopolitan one I knew, and what of the histories of empire that brought my mother from the Caribbean to Britain's shores? Empire did of course figure in these televised tales. Australia, the West Indies and America were places where characters were deported or migrated to and, off screen, where they made and lost fortunes, forging or losing reputations that had rippling effects on those who they left behind waiting for them, or hoping they never returned, on screen.

There was no doubt a link between these televised constructions of Victorian Britain and my interest in the Victorians at school; I remember writing an essay on the coming of the railways, and developing an interest in local history, prompted by our history teacher taking us out into the suburban streets surrounding our school where she talked us through points of architectural history. Dating buildings by the style of their brickwork is a game I still like to play. But histories of a multi-cultural London and the role of empire in the making and remaking of its many geographies remained stubbornly absent from popular culture and my school history. I did not understand these absences within a framework of Stuart Hall's critical reflections on media representations, since his Open University programmes were late night television I was not watching. My critical framework was formed in the context of fiery political debates at home, listening in to and later arguing with two strongly anti-Thatcherite parents.

When I first began researching black life in London, I was often asked why I chose London to be the site of its focus. It seemed to me that this question was usually inspired by an assumption that if there were black women in Britain (seemingly unlikely), they would have lived in the old slave ports of Bristol and Liverpool (probably as prostitutes) not London (for London's history as a slave port was not well known). Having spent my whole life living in London I had a very personal desire to investigate the city of my birth, the city that is my home and still a city that I love, though with more difficulty than when I was eighteen. Like other kinds of young love, as I grew up I saw and better understood the many faces of the city that were sometimes difficult to reconcile with city loyalty. Though it came in the context of a long and painful history of young men dying in police custody for which no one was prosecuted, the shooting by police of the electrician Jean Charles de Menezes in July 2005 and the gutlessness of the authorities' response was a painful blow to my belief in the city's soul.[12] Becoming trained as a historical geographer, I understood my research as an opportunity to better understand my city, its potential to offer a sense of belonging and my own sense of place. London is a city whose growth and density has terrified and impressed commentators through the ages and is an ideal location for an investigation into the diversity of experiences that must have befallen its numerous immigrants, like Caroline Brogden, and millions of their descendants like myself. As a young woman I began to spend more time walking through the city, and realized that although it seemed many Londoners were proud of the fact their city had always been a diverse and pluralistic community, the urban landscape reflected little of the histories of the millions of immigrants who sweated to support its foundations. Much like the television dramas I had grown up with, the social and political geography of London's urban spaces had largely excluded these complex, racialized imperial and post-imperial stories from public spaces.

I began considering how to formulate these ideas as a research project during my final year as an undergraduate at Cambridge University, where I read Geography between 1994 and 1997. The politics of empire did not largely figure in the curriculum, but issues of race and racism came through strongly in courses such as the Geography of HIV/AIDS, alongside the politics of class in my historical geography classes. As a student at Newnham College, then the home of feminist scholars including Germaine Greer and my own Director of Studies Linda McDowell, I was strongly influenced by the work of feminist geographers and through them was introduced to black theorists such as bell hooks.[13] It was a postgraduate student at Newnham who recommended Dolores Hayden's book, *The Power of Place*, to me. Through the landscapes of Los Angeles, Hayden examines the social and cultural meanings that people invest in places, and thus how urban landscapes are a framework for connecting historical stories and the public memory of contemporary urban life.[14] As a geography undergraduate focusing on historical geography, I found in Hayden's work a method by which I could combine my interests in Victorian and contemporary London. Inspired by her work on LA, I intended my first research project, undertaken as a dissertation for my undergraduate geography degree, to focus on urban landscapes as public history and the representation of black women in the urban landscapes of London. I walked the city again, but, though black women could be found representing empire in the foundations of memorials to Queen Victoria and Prince Albert, I could not find any representations of the Carolines who were part of the multi-cultural Victorian and Edwardian city.

As I read more about the politics of heritage and memorialization I increasingly came to understand how histories of women like Caroline were further marginalized by the location of their biographies within the working class histories of the city. So, to show that black women were absent from spaces of London's heritage I had to prove they were historically present in the city. This research, which initially took place in the archive of the children's charity Barnardo's at Barkingside on the site of the charity's former girls' homes at the eastern end of the Central line, formed the heart of my undergraduate dissertation. Going into the archives to uncover the lives of black women remains the key focus of my research twenty years later. I am still striving to understand how these women's lives fit into the histories of London, how they faced and fought racism, how they maintained their families in the face of crippling poverty, illness and despair, how they were influenced by political and family drama, travel, migration stories, hope, work, conviviality and fun. I am now increasingly interested in the lives of black men in London and also the multi-cultural families and working class networks that the women whose lives I have explored belonged to, whether as friends, colleagues, sisters-in-law, grandmothers, as the local barmaid or a favourite performer. For me, histories of race and racism are inseparable from those of class and sexuality, all embodied in the fragmentary tale of Caroline Brogden.

London is a busy place, filled with people – individuals, families and strangers, friends and those passing through. I can see all the characters I have found in the archives on the streets among them and I maintain a hope that my work contributes something to the remakings of the multi-cultural community of which I am a part and which is the direct and indirect result of Britain's global empire. The debates around ideas of remaking the identity of Londoners is, as Stuart Hall so eloquently argued, always ongoing, always being debated and refashioned – in part because, as the Troubles in Ireland, the wars in Afghanistan and Iraq, the Mau Mau war veterans' compensation claims case and the consequences of all these actions on Britain have shown, imperial history is a chapter that has not been closed. But, in the current political moment in Britain, the fractured tone of the debates about national identity and history feels particularly acute. And for those like myself who believe the multi-cultural city to be a reality that is still too little understood, the attempt to crush the developments that have been made – particularly by the Conservatives and UKIP (the United Kingdom Independence Party) – marks this moment as a particularly grave one. The current tenor of the debate can be seen as beginning when Michael Gove was made Education Secretary for the coalition government that came to power in Britain in May 2010. Gove's announcement of a curriculum review in 2011 was introduced with his lamentation that the national history curriculum schools failed to include Churchill, Queen Elizabeth, Gladstone, Disraeli, Florence

Nightingale and Horatio Nelson.[15] Gove's intentions for school history (and other subjects) generated a tense debate on the role of politics in the teaching of history and, by implication, the role of empire, 'people of colour' and those outside of elite circles in representations of the national past.[16] When an outline of the new proposals was published in February 2013, it became clear to the Historical Association that, among a number of their concerns, the inclusion of women and diverse ethnic groups were 'clearly tokenistic' while 'nods to social, economic and cultural history' were rare.[17] As Martin Spafford, a London-based history schoolteacher, observed, bar 'two Tudor queens, women only enter history in the mid nineteenth century'. In regards to black history:

> According to Gove . . . there were no British people of African or Asian origin until after the Second World War. They are invisible in the primary curriculum and first appear in secondary schools when enslaved. This matters because a 'whitewashed' story of these islands can propagate the lie that the narrative belongs only to some of us while others are excluded. In uncertain times these are dangerous myths for young minds: thereby lies disaster, as we understand so well from recent history. Without understanding our continual and everchanging diversity we cannot know Britain.[18]

Malorie Blackman, the nation's first black children's laureate, concurred, voicing her concerns that the plans would further alienate children from ethnic minority communities.[19] That the outline formally published in February 2013 was an improvement on the initial plans published by the *Daily Mail* in December 2012 illustrates how easy it is for arguments thought to have become core to historical practice, such as the centrality of women's history to historical work, to be questioned, and the key points they sought to engender remain undervalued and contested.[20] The Historical Association argued that Gove's outline completely failed 'to recognise that history is an intellectual discipline underpinned by a rigorous conceptual framework'.[21] Another view would be that Gove's outline reflected the entrenchment and consolidation of the conceptual framework of Thatcherism, given a new opportunity to establish itself in 'austerity Britain'. Stuart Hall, who coined the term Thatcherism, had argued years before Gove's appointment that: 'Little Englander nationalism could hardly survive if people understood whose sugar flowed through English blood and rotted English teeth.'[22] Focusing minds on the dates of kings and a couple of queens is one way to do this. However, Gove's decision to change the examinations taken by fifteen- and sixteen-year-olds presented an opportunity to challenge the conservative intentions of his policies. Two new history GCSEs being developed by an exam board cover significant periods of immigration to Britain since the Roman period and will be available to be taught in schools by September 2016.[23] Whether this will remain a solitary example is no longer within Gove's direct influence; certainly some teachers and commentators celebrated when Gove was removed from the post of Education Secretary in July 2014, but the full consequences of his actions while in post remain unclear.

Official history curricula are not, of course, determinants of all that students will know of history, as my childhood love of Victorian costume drama illustrates. Schools are only one of many transmitters of and for the past. The adaptation of Andrea Levy's award-winning book *Small Island* (2004) for television in 2009 focused attention on the experiences of black people in England during the Second World War to great acclaim. But in both scholarly and popular form, the place of Black histories in the re-telling of English history before the War remains ad-hoc and marginalized. In its fourth season the popular ITV (Independent Television) drama *Downton Abbey* introduced its first 'black character', not a domestic servant, or a journalist, a lawyer, or a labourer, barmaid or butler, but an 'American jazz musician' named Jack Ross. As Filipa Jodelka highlighted, Ross was 'a black character' not a character who happened to be black.[24] The persistent absence of 'Black Britons' in the narrative of British history illustrates the complex politics of belonging in historical narratives and the reluctance of many to examine the intersections of class and race and gender in the histories of Britain. In the 2007 BBC adaptation of *Oliver Twist*, Sophie Okonedo became the first black actress to play the character of Nancy on screen.[25] Okonedo had to justify the decision to cast her in the role, but she argued strongly that 'In Victorian times there were plenty of sailors cavorting with prostitutes at the docks . . . I'm sure a child like me could easily have been born, especially since I'm of mixed race. There were certainly lots of black people in London.'[26]

Okonedo's assertion is undoubtedly true, but in the absence of long and deep histories of migration to Britain, a Nancy who is not white or seemingly 'not English', will always come as a surprise to many. It is also important to remember that, contrary to the contemporary UKIP narrative of London's exceptional multi-culturalism, London is not incomparable or extraordinary, as Laura Tabili's recent historical geography of South Shields illustrates. Based on her detailed research on migration into Victorian South Shields, including white migrants from Germany and Sweden as well as Jewish migrants, Tabili argues that a high level of residential and marital integration existed in the city and extrapolates that migrants were more widespread and integrated relationships of all kinds were more common in England than previously understood.[27] In his seminal publication on the history of black people in Britain, Peter Fryer reflected that establishing how the continuity and struggle of black communities was maintained in Victorian Britain was a question that could only be answered with detailed local inquiry.[28] His call inspired my research in London and some local history groups such as the Northampton Black History Project have also started on this work, but there remains a great need for historical studies focusing on local geographies to illustrate the vast imperial networks that towns and cities in Britain were plugged into.

It is through such studies that individuals such as Caroline Brogden can be placed back into the spaces of their communities and into the dramas of Victorian and Edwardian cities whether or not they can be seen in the literary works of Dickens or Gaskell. There are signs that this is happening. *The Paradise*, 'an intoxicating love story set in England's first department store in the 1870s' (inspired by Émile Zola's novel *Au Bonheur des Dames*), was a BBC drama filmed in the north-east of England which first aired in 2012.[29] Towards the end of the second series, the character Christian Cartwright, a renowned photographer, was introduced. He was played by the black English actor, Nathan Stewart-Jarrett, but as the drama has not been commissioned for a further season, this opportunity to develop a theme of ordinary multi-culturalism has passed.[30] But while *The Paradise* indicates some change, for many such change remains far too slow. After becoming the first black British actress to be nominated for an Oscar in 1996, Marianne Jean-Baptiste spoke out about the racism she faced from the British film industry and her decision to move to the United States to support her career.[31] Nearly twenty years later, the lack of roles considered suitable for black actors in Britain has marginalized a generation of actors, pushing them across the Atlantic to find roles in American dramas. It is hard to remember that for Caroline Brogden, the pull of opportunity was in the other direction.[32]

I feel the pull of a connection to Caroline so strongly in part, I am sure, because of the materiality of the photograph which accompanies her medical notes in the City of London asylum archive. I now find it hard to believe that she is thirty years old in the photograph. Her slim and 'fine physic' is visible, but she looks, to me, to be tired and so much older, though I have found no evidence to contradict the conclusions made by the medical men at Bow Infirmary in London's East End.[33] Compared to the oversized leather-bound medical case book in which her medical records are held, the print of Caroline's picture is small, separated from the dense notes of her doctors by a red ink border.[34] These notes indicate that on her admission in September 1905, an examiner confirmed that Caroline suffered from 'Many delusions telling me she is a man and that she has a wife who married her without her knowledge', and so it was with confidence that Caroline's social condition was recorded as 'Single'. No level of education was ascribed to her, no address of friends or family recorded.[35]

I still struggle with how to meet the strength of Caroline's gaze and how to place her within the broader histories of women I have researched in the archives of Victorian and Edwardian London. For Caroline Brogden's gaze is confrontational and the feeling of anger which I sense resonating along the photographic trace is underlined by my knowledge of the tragic outcome of her unmasking, a knowledge of her fate which she may have feared, but would not have known when her photograph was taken. Caroline died in the asylum on 21 June 1906, the cause of death given as mania and acute pneumonia, which she suffered for six days. A nurse, E. Jones, had been present at her death and Caroline was not restrained. On the death certificate it is confirmed that Caroline was a 'female', single and still 30. I was not named after Caroline or for her, but she is my namesake, we are both made and unmade in our meeting in the archive, and sometimes I feel it keenly. But this is a meeting only I take part in, one that I fill with my own meanings through the initials we share and my understandings of the trans-Atlantic slave trade, the legacies of enslavement in the United States and for the 'Black Atlantic', of empire and queer histories, feminist histories and contemporary political conflicts. Though of course it is also possible that Caroline has tricked me too, that Caroline Brogden was not her name. Perhaps it was an alias given to medical men and those in authority to maintain her privacy, if not her freedom, and that my personalized reunion with my namesake is not that at all. Perhaps it is an encounter with a 'trickster', the author of a masquerade who managed, despite a brutal unmasking and constant surveillance at the end of her life, to maintain her own carefully constructed costume drama.

Notes

1 For more on the two characters I have in mind here see Caroline Bressey, 'The City of Others: Photographs from the City of London Asylum Archive', *19: Interdisciplinary Studies in the Long Nineteenth Century,* 13 (2011): http://www.19.bbk.ac.uk/index.php/19/article/view/625/741 (accessed 5 July 2015).

2 *Daily Telegraph*, 14 September 1905; *Daily Chronicle*, 11 September 1905.

3 *Portsmouth Evening News*, 11 September 1905, p. 3.

4 Alison Oram, *Her Husband Was a Woman: Women's Gender-Crossing in Modern British Popular Culture* (London: Routledge, 2007).

5 In referring to Downing as 'she' I have followed Alison Oram's lead. See Oram, *Her Husband Was a Woman*; *Cheltenham Chronicle*, 16 September 1905, p. 8.

6 *Daily Chronicle*, 14 September 1905.

7 *Derby Daily Telegraphy*, 11 September 1905. The City of London's Bow Workhouse became Bow Infirmary in 1867.

8 Francine Payne, *Stone House: The City of London Asylum* (DWS Print Services, 2007). On paupers before 1862 see Elaine Murphy, 'The New Poor Law Guardians and the Administration of Insanity in East London, 1834–1844', *Bulletin of the History of Medicine*, 77, 1 (2003): 45–74; 'Hospital and Dispensary Management', *The British Medical Journal*, 23 July 1896: 237; Arthur E. Patterson, 'An Analysis of One Thousand Admissions into the City of London Asylum', *British Journal of Psychiatry*, 46 (1900): 473–87. In 1905 private patients accounted for 46 per cent of those at the asylum: 'Hospital and Dispensary Management', *The British Medical Journal*, 11 August 1906: 237.

9 Patterson, 'An Analysis of One Thousand Admissions'.

10 *The Star*, 11 September 1905, p. 2; *Nottingham Evening Post*, 11 September 1905, p. 6; London Metropolitan Archives CLA/001/B/01/015: 90.

11 Many of these have variously been remade and repeated and I have undoubtedly conflated different versions of adaptations in my mind; I cannot really remember watching the *Old Curiosity Shop*, given I was only five when it was broadcast by the BBC in 1979. I have no recollection of watching *A Tale of Two Cities* broadcast in 1980, and it turns out the 2009 adaptation of *Bleak House* began broadcasting in September of that year.

12 Institute of Race Relations (Harmit Athwal, 'The spotlight is back on black deaths at the hands of police', 31 August 2011: http://www.irr.org.uk/news/the-spotlight-is-back-on-black-deaths-at-the-hands-of-police/, accessed 5 July 2015).

13 Newnham was and remains, for now, a women's only college. Germaine Greer resigned from Newnham in 1996.

14 Dolores Hayden, *The Power of Place: Urban Landscapes as Public History* (Cambridge, MA: MIT Press, 1995).

15 *Daily Telegraph* (Michael Gove, 'National curriculum review: children failed by Labour's education reforms, says Gove', 20 January 2011: http://www.telegraph.co.uk/education/educationnews/8269906/National-curriculum-review-children-failed-by-Labours-education-reforms-says-Gove.html, last accessed 5 July 2015).

16 I discuss this in Caroline Bressey, 'Geographies of Belonging: White Women and Black History', *Women's History Review*, 22, 4 (2013): 541–58.

17 The Historical Association ('Curriculum Concerns', 14 February 2013: http://www.history.org.uk/news/news_1722.html, accessed 5 July 2015).

18 Martin Spafford, 'How Michael Gove is dumming down the history curriculum', 1 March 2013: http://www.schoolshistoryproject.org.uk/blog/2013/03/how-michael-gove-is-dumbing-down-the-history-curriculum/ (last accessed 5 July 2015).

19 Susanna Rustin, 'UK's first black children's laureate: new history curriculum could alienate pupils', *The Guardian*, 4 June 2013: http://gu.com/p/3ga8t/sbl (accessed 15 December 2014).

20 Jonathan Petre, 'Gove faces war with equality activists as he axes Labour's PC curriculum that dropped greatest figures from history lessons', *Mail Online*, 29 December 2012: http://www.dailymail.co.uk/news/article-2254705/Gove-faces-war-equality-activists-axes-Labours-PC-curriculum-dropped-greatest-figures-history-lessons-Leaked-drafts-new-history-curriculum-emerge.html; Cathy Newman, 'Will Gove's "posh white blokes" history curriculum ignore women?', *Daily Telegraph*, 9 January 2013: http://www.telegraph.co.uk/women/womens-life/9790633/Will-Goves-posh-white-blokes-history-curriculum-ignore-women.html (accessed 5 July 2015).

21 The Historical Association, 'Curriculum Concerns', 14 February 2014: http://www.history.org.uk/resources/primary_news_1722.html (last accessed 5 July 2015).

22 Tim Adams, 'The Interview: Cultural Hallmark', *The Observer*, 23 September 2007: http://www.theguardian.com/society/2007/sep/23/communities.politicsphilosophyandsociety (accessed 5 July 2015); Jonathan Derbyshire, 'Stuart Hall: "We need to talk about Englishness"', *New Statesman*, 23 August 2012: http://www.newstatesman.com/politics/uk-politics/2012/08/stuart-hall-we-need-talk-about-englishness (accessed 5 July 2015).

23 OCR Exam Board: http://www.ocr.org.uk/news/view/ocrs-new-history-gcses-to-explore-migration-into-britain-down-the-ages/ (last accessed 5 July 2015).

24 Filipa Jodelka, 'The trouble with Downton Abbey's new black character', *The Guardian*, 1 May 2013: http://www.theguardian.com/tv-and-radio/shortcuts/2013/may/01/downton-abbey-new-black-character (accessed 5 July 2015).

25 Serena Davies, 'An Oliver for our times', *Daily Telegraph*, 5 December 2007: http://www.telegraph.co.uk/culture/tvandradio/3669961/An-Oliver-for-our-times.html (accessed 5 July 2015).

26 Quoted in 'An Oliver for our times'. It is worth noting that in this adaptation the actor Timothy Spall also set out to give a more nuanced performance of 'the Jew', Fagin.

27 Laura Tabili, *Global Migrants, Local Culture: Natives and Newcomers in Provincial England, 1841–1939* (London: Palgrave Macmillan, 2011).

28 Peter Fryer, *Staying Power: The History of Black People in Britain* (London: Pluto Press, 1984).

29 BBC: http://www.bbc.co.uk/programmes/p00vhpsv (accessed 5 July 2015).

30 Barbara Hodgson, 'Fans of BBC costume drama Paradise set about reclaiming TV favourite', *The Journal*, 9 June 2014: http://www.thejournal.co.uk/culture/culture-news/fans-bbc-costume-drama-paradise-7234849 (accessed 5 July 2015).

31 Dan Glaister, 'Oscar actress hits out at "old men" of British film industry', *The Guardian*, 15 May 1997: http://www.theguardian.com/film/1997/may/15/news.danglaister (last accessed 5 July 2015); Kate Kellaway, 'Marianne Jean-Baptiste: "Kindness is a religion, and so is honesty"', *The Guardian*, 2 June 2013: http://gu.com/p/3g6t7/stw (accessed 5 July 2015).

32 For examples of discussions on this, see Vanessa Thorpe, 'Britain's black actors must be given a better choice of roles, says star of Spielberg series', *The Guardian*, 27 July 2014: http://gu.com/p/4v9cn/stw (accessed 5 July 2015); Adam Sherwin, 'Black actors leave Britain to escape "lazy stereotypes", says Chuka Umunna', *The Independent*, 31 October 2013: http://www.independent.co.uk/arts-entertainment/films/news/black-actors-leave-britain-to-escape-lazy-stereotypes-says-chuka-umunna-8915673.html (accessed 5 July 2015).

33 Comments on her physical appearance, and that she was around 6ft in height can be found in various newspaper reports. See, for example, *Daily Chronicle*, 14 September 1905 and the *Daily Telegraph*, 14 September 1905.

34 The image can be seen as part of the photographic essay Bressey, 'The City of Others'.

35 London Metropolitan Archives, CLA/001/B/01/015: 90.

17

Dis-oriented in a Post-imperial World

Jonathan Saha
b. 1984

At the age of twenty-one, I visited a hospital in Barasat, a town located just outside of Kolkata. I remember actively supressing my shock at the condition of the building. A damp stairwell, with bare concrete steps. Turquoise paint peeling away from the walls. Rickety-looking, iron-framed beds with catheters and drips propped up beside them. The place did not conform to my past experiences and expectations of a hospital. But I knew that my reactions were also based on a superficial reading of the place. I was aware that my responses were rooted in accumulated images and prejudices about India that I was only partially conscious of. Images of colour, chaos, poverty, decay. Expectations of sensory overload, of contrasts, of 'incredible India', as the tourist slogan runs. I was visiting my elderly grandmother with my dad. She was unwell with anaemia. It would be the first time that I met her.

My dad, although raised a Bengali-speaker, is first and foremost a contrarian. As part of this, he saw no value in the language and (other than Rabindranath Tagore) its literary world. As a result I had never learned to speak it as a child. My grandmother could not speak English, and so when we met it was in silence. Dad disappeared to harass some doctors and sundry members of the hospital staff about her care. In the absence of a shared language, or our unreliable intergenerational translator, we held hands whilst she stroked my arm. It was a brief visit. The intimacy of the moment was dashed as soon as I left the hospital with my dad and stepped onto the street. I was almost immediately descended upon by a small group of mostly middle-aged Indian women. Hair was ruffled, cheeks were pulled, arms were affectionately but roughly rubbed. I was later informed by my dad that these were some aunties, and cousins, and perhaps other interested parties from nearby. At the time, when I looked round for explanation or translation from my dad, I saw him using the opportunity to beat a hasty retreat.

I remember this, my first contact with the Indian side of my family, as an overwhelming one. But it was also frustrating. I was disappointed with myself, at the limits of my ability to communicate. I spent most of my time on the side-lines of conversations, many of which appeared to be about me. Snippets of English occasionally catching my attention, such as 'still a student' out of the mouth of my dad, as he cast me a sideways glance. Looking back, these frustrations were about more than language barriers. I was struggling with the cultural distance between myself and a family, and a place, that I felt I should have a connection with; some kind of innate tie. But I did not. I did not have the cultural knowledge to understand the physical comedy of my determinedly un-Bengali dad attempting to prevent his closest brother from touching his feet in a gesture of respect. It was just unexpected grappling on a doorstep, to my untrained eyes. I felt out of place.

There is no good reason why I should have expected to 'fit in' at Barasat. There is a world of differences between the post-industrial, north-east English fishing-town of Grimsby, where I grew up, and West Bengal. However, perhaps I felt this way partly because my Indian 'heritage' had always been over-determined. Although my mum is white and English, and despite the fact that the closest I lived to India when I was young was Cwmbran in South Wales, it is my Asian background that people are often most interested in. A question that I used to strongly dislike as a teenager and still get asked from time to time is, 'where are you from?' I always knew what was really being asked in this question. It inspired in me an evasive stubbornness not to give my questioner the information that they wanted. After supplying a list of the more-or-less obscure northern towns that I had lived in, I would invariably be asked, 'no, where are you *really* from?', or some variant on this. As Sara Ahmed has brilliantly noted, these are not so much questions as they are statements that already place my origins as outside of an implicit 'here'. I am being asked to give an account of myself, 'an account of how I ended up here, of how I ended up brown'.[1]

Everyday encounters like these reinforced the sense that there was a part of me that was connected to India, and as such, a part of me that did not quite belong in England; or at least required accounting for. This was apparent in the fortunately very few occasions where I have been exposed to racial abuse. One of my most lasting memories of this occurred whilst walking through Grimsby's town centre with a friend whose parents were Iranian. We were confronted by two teenage 'lads', one of whom called us both 'Pakis', before his friend immediately cut in, warning him, 'careful, they might know some of that Chinky-shit!', whilst gesturing kung-fu moves. Although we recognized this as offensive and shocking, at the time my friend and I could not help but find the geographic confusion of racist terms funny in its absurdity. It was this absurdity of racism that I used to use for comic effect among my peers at school. The superficiality of my difference from my white friends was the premise of many of our teenage jokes. We would mock the views of a racist minority by making ironic and ridiculous comments about my background; like claiming I lived in a tepee and ate nothing but curry. I was demonstrating that I belonged by parodying racism and making light of how I could be perceived as different. Nevertheless, I felt the lack of a connection with India and with a culture and a family that I did not know. Although I mocked it, I harboured a sense of being subtly different through the absence, yet spectral presence, of India.

In a sense, then, I am a product of empire. I do not mean in a crude biological or biographical sense. Not through an origins-story that would narrate how patterns of post-imperial migration from the Indian subcontinent led to my mother meeting my father and to them conceiving me. Although perhaps a useful social history, this was not meaningful to me in itself. This history did not provide me with any experiential connection to India, and certainly not to its imperial ties to Britain; of which I was only superficially aware of when growing up. Rather, I am a product of empire in my internalized expectations of Asia and in how my body can be read in Britain. Both have been shaped historically by imperialism and its ideological output, crudely categorized by Edward Said as 'Orientalism'.[2] Against it I have over-emphasized my northern upbringing – and I still do when people make assumptions about my Indian background. Yet, at the same time, I harboured a longing to make a real connection with my imagined India, a figment shaped by empire. This ambivalence, stemming from the largely absent but nevertheless over-determined Asian element of my background, has fostered my interest in the history of British colonial rule in Asia. But not explicitly or directly as a way of understanding my family past; the only 'genealogies' that I have become interested in have been Foucauldian.

This is, perhaps, a more nebulous connection to empire than that of other contributors to this collection. I do not have memories of the British Empire. I was born two years after the Falklands War. I have a fuzzy recollection of watching a ceremony on television marking Hong Kong's return to China. Although through my studies I have become aware of the legacies of imperialism, it was not a past that I was conscious of growing up in. But then again, the nature of imperial memory is never straightforward. I am convinced by the historical anthropologists Karen Strassler and Ann Laura Stoler's argument that memories of empire are not ever-present and being actively supressed. Nor are they best understood, through what they call the 'hydraulic' metaphor, as a reservoir beneath the surface always capable of bursting forth. Rather, imperial memories are actively remade; they are the product of 'memory work'.[3] I do not have my own imperial memories and none were passed on to me either from family or as a result of a continuous, overtly imperial presence in the culture around me. Instead, I have become aware of the unfinished history of British imperialism through events and experiences in which this past has been *made* relevant to me through debate and action. It is this that I wish to emphasize in this essay. Becoming aware of Britain's imperial past and how it has shaped me was not revelatory but an active process of making imperial history relevant.

This happened, at least partially, through political activism. During my first year as a history undergraduate student, a coalition of states led by Britain and the United States of America went to war in Iraq. With thousands of others, I demonstrated on the streets of London against it. It was an important moment in my growing political awareness. At the time, various fringe leftist movements of different hues of socialism and anarchism used the term 'imperialism', then in vogue with the anti-globalization movement, to critique the military intervention. The necessary crudity of the slogan 'no blood for oil!' conjured the image of Machiavellian imperialists sending soldiers to kill and die in order to conquer land and render it amenable to resource exploitation in pursuit of ever greater profits. Although I was against the war, at the time I felt uneasy about labelling it 'imperialist'. The seemingly clear moral connotations of the term I found resulted in kneejerk defensive responses from apolitical, apathetic or ambivalent friends. The situation, I was told, was more complicated. Empire was deemed an out-of-date caricature. It was a folly safely confined to the past. However, looking back, the echoes and parallels were there, if one chose to look. As were direct historical links. The problem was that the imperialism of the past was not recognized as a process that could also be complex. The Iraq war raised historical questions about the legacies of empire, the nature of twenty-first-century global warfare, and the relationship between the two. For me, imperialism went from being an abstract term for understanding the past with, to being an issue of immediate political import.

War in the Near East contributed to an atmosphere of xenophobia at home. Just months into the military occupation, *The Sun* newspaper published the notorious 'Swan Bake' front page headline. In the attached article, the tabloid reporter made the unsubstantiated claim that asylum seekers had killed and eaten 'the Queen's swans'.[4] I remember this article especially, because at the time I was volunteering with refugee organizations in Sheffield, the city where I was studying. As part of this activism, a group of us attempted to raise awareness and counter the type of scare-mongering nonsense that *The Sun* was peddling. It was an up-hill struggle. There was a great deal of animosity towards asylum seekers that we found redirected towards ourselves. It ranged from expressions of a 'little Britain' siege mentality, to out-and-out racism. Underpinning *The Sun*'s article and the wider climate of hostility was an identity structured by difference; 'they' were coming over 'here' and making life harder for 'us'. I was never entirely confident that I was being included in that 'us', and certainly not convinced that I wanted to be. If the invasion of Iraq made the geo-politics of imperialism relevant to me, then working with refugees made me aware of the relevance of imperial cultures and ideologies. The fear and hatred that individuals would openly express about asylum seekers and refugees made it clear to me how exclusionary expressions of nationalism construct their 'Others' partially on the basis of race.

This activism also brought me into contact with people from the postcolonial world. Through these new connections and new friendships, the history of imperial misadventures, old and new, became tangible. Empire was a part of peoples' life-stories and histories. The legacies of the imperial boundaries drawn during the nineteenth century informed the European languages that people spoke. The fallout of liberation wars and national independence struggles had led directly to the flight of some. In others, it inspired a nostalgia for a more stable, almost mythic, colonial past. For the many fleeing war and oppression in Afghanistan, this longer history of empire was entangled with the then on-going military conflict. How imperialism had restructured the world in lasting but deeply fraught ways was made real to me and made relevant. But it was also a difficult experience of confronting my own cultural assumptions and ignorance about global histories. It was a lesson in listening and engaging across barriers, even where we found our views conflicted, and in attempting to make solidarity with people against the stark asymmetries of privilege and social capital inherent to this voluntary activism. However blindly and clumsily I stumbled into these exchanges (which was very), the experience pushed me obliquely towards a central understanding of postcolonial theory; that in order to engage with postcolonial worlds, I needed to first confront my own subjectivity.

These political concerns became entangled with my academic development. Given my interest in imperial economic and political power, in imperial ideologies, and in postcolonial methods – although I was not able to yet articulate it in this language – it is perhaps unsurprising that the writings of the Subaltern Studies Collective of South Asian historians should have been a source of interest, after I had been directed towards them. Their often torturous prose and debates about the ontological status of 'the subaltern' and the epistemological politics of History as a discipline, seemed, in an obscure way, to connect with my wider concerns. These historiographical problems seemed urgent. They seemed to offer a way into thinking about the problems of engaging with marginalized groups without co-opting their own subjective experiences and agendas.[5] Outside of South Asian history, the books that probably had the most profound impact on me were Benedict Anderson's *Imagined Communities* and Frantz Fanon's *The Wretched of the Earth*. Reading Anderson's work felt revelatory. The framework of the nation, that had previously been invisible but implicit in structuring my thoughts, was de-mystified and historicized. I came to see nations as the products of human artifice, a view that helped me to deconstruct the anti-immigration rhetoric that I confronted. Fanon on the other hand was terrifying and exhilarating to read. His exposure of the hypocrisy and violence of European liberal values and claims to objectivity under colonialism chimed with what I had seen in the asylum system; its dehumanizing bureaucratic procedures, callously and carelessly executed, all under the guise of humanitarian support.[6] Through these readings, and others that I encountered during the course of my undergraduate degree, I came to identify my interests as being the history of colonialism in South Asia, particularly the ways in which cultures and societies were remade. This was in part through a distinction that I made with British imperial history, which I unfairly and wrongly considered to inherently privilege the narratives of imperialists. As I developed as a historian, I had to rethink this simplistic separation between colonial and imperial history.

Starting out on my postgraduate career during the opening decade of the twenty-first century meant that I benefited from the developments in the field that had taken root since the literary turn of the 1980s. By the time that I was immersing myself in the historiography, neat and tidy divisions between core and periphery were deemed outmoded. Instead, scholars readily acknowledged the influence that colonial rule had back in imperial Britain and were interrogating the depth, extent and longevity of its impact upon identity-formation there. Of particular concern were normative understandings of race and gender. Rather than being taken as given biological categories, historians had addressed them as categories subject to change over time and as topics necessitating urgent study in themselves. In addition, histories of science and medicine had dispensed with narratives structured by the implicit belief that ideas and practices emerged from Britain and were then disseminated across the colonized world. Instead, historians emphasized the transcultural exchange of ideas and the importance of the colonial world in the generation of knowledge. Insights from post-structuralist thought enabled historians to also study these scientific discourses as the products of power relations. Exposure to this vibrant and diverse scholarship provided me with the critical tools and academic lexicon to understand the contemporary world within the context of an imperial past. It made this past usable to me, enabling me to examine my own subjectivity and to historicize and critique the normative cultural assumptions that have been used to define who and what could be 'British'.[7]

My own journey towards studying the history of British colonial rule in Burma was influenced both by my refugee work and by my academic interests. Before I began my Masters degree at the School of Oriental and African Studies (SOAS), I volunteered with a government backed scheme to re-settle mostly Karen refugees from camps in Thailand to Sheffield in northern England. My ignorance of Burma was total. I once led a party of over twenty of the Buddhist members of this group of Karen refugees to a Buddhist temple in the north of the city, only to find out that it was the wrong branch of Buddhism (Mahayana, not Theravada). We had an awkward cup of tea before we trooped back across the city. During my

Masters and then especially during my PhD I learnt more about the country and its difficult histories from fellow students as well as in my classes. In fact, SOAS in general was a radical change of setting for me. Asian and African histories were no longer marginal subjects requiring some justification but deemed self-evidently interesting and relevant. The student body was also unlike any other I had experienced. This was not only because of its ethnic diversity, which with my wider experience of London, was new to me, but due to the bewildering range of political activities going on. (I remember on the first day of term walking past the Spartacist Society's stall whose banner read 'Iran NEEDS Nuclear Weapons', a public position not adopted by the Islamic Republic itself, and one probably not helpful to its cause.)

I benefited immeasurably from this academic climate and from living in London. It is a city with empire embedded into its built environment, a history immediately recognizable once you are made aware of it. But it is also a city of multiple national communities and layer upon layer of migration. In SOAS itself, postcolonial theory was not merely required reading, it was a prerequisite for chit-chat and bar talk. The postgraduate student body came from across the world, including the children of elites from the Majority World. Its undergraduate population was also more ethnically mixed than anywhere else I had studied or taught before, or since. And yet, historically, this was a pre-eminently imperial institution, originally envisaged as a school for aspiring colonial officials. Both the city and the university were post-imperial worlds that resided in imperial structures. Whilst I was there, my own over-determined Asian background receded in significance. I was in no way as exotic as everyone else around me. I stood out more because of my slight northern accent – and even in that characteristic I found myself outdone by a new friend from Burnley. It was among the friends and colleagues that I made in London that I was most shaped as a historian. Being one among many PhD students and early career historians who were thinking about imperial and colonial history, whilst simultaneously discovering the city made by British imperialism, led to a wonderful sharing of ideas. It was from my fellow travellers, in particular, I was made alert to the ways that imperialism informed gender identities and ideologies, as well as understandings of sexuality, in lasting ways both in Britain and in the postcolonial world.

Another place whose imperial past has been pivotal in shaping me as historian has been Yangon (or, in its more familiar anglicized corruption, Rangoon). I first visited the city in 2008, not long after the monks' protests – dubbed the 'Saffron Revolution' in the global news media – and the terrible destruction of cyclone Nargis. The city was, and still is, replete with colonial-era architecture, in spite of the property development boom following recent, intrepid democratic reforms and economic liberalization. Imposing red brick buildings that were once government offices and institutions, rub-up against inter-war years' residential blocks in which Art Deco features incorporate elements of Burmese aesthetics. The crumbling facades, marked by bursts of green from plants taking root in the masonry, can all too easily evoke romantic sensibilities and a related sense of imperial nostalgia. I had to check myself and remember the histories of colonial control and policing, nationalist agitation and race riots, and devastating imperial warfare, which these structures were also a part of. At the same time, socializing with aid workers from a number of non-governmental organizations at the Strand Hotel – *the* place to get high-tea in imperial times – brought home some of the uncomfortable continuities with the colonial past in Western attitudes and interventions. But the postcolonial history (and, unfortunately, historiography) of Burma/Myanmar also reveals the ways in which the colonial past can be recast in nationalist narratives to further repressive ends. I have learnt that the politics of colonial critique are multi-faceted and that as historians we must be aware of how our arguments can be appropriated and used. The imperial past can also be made relevant in the present in reactionary ways.

Studying Burma has put distance between my ambivalent desire to account for my absent Indian ties and my goals and interests as a historian. It means that there is space between my personal and professional aspirations. But I have found that this is not always recognized. The assumption made by some people is that I must have Burmese family. Well-meaning and interested people regularly ask, 'so, is your family Burmese?' This question is of the same order as 'where are you from?' The questioner has read my body, heard my research interests, and is offering an account that in one-fell-swoop seeks to explain the two mysteries: why I am brown and why I study Burma. On disappointing them by revealing that their explanation is incorrect, the conversation takes one of two paths. Either they want to know where I am in fact from, or, just as often, why I am studying something as 'niche' as the history of Burma. Both questions make me bristle. I have discussed the first question earlier and it is one I have faced many times before. It no longer annoys me as it once did. The second one, however, does irritate me, for two reasons. Firstly, the idea that the history of Burma is niche is premised on the privileging of imperial centres and networks as legitimate subjects of study.[8] Secondly, because implicitly in the structure of the questioning it is clear that the questioner believes that this history would not be niche if I were Burmese, or at the very least had a cousin from there. Beneath this lies the assumption that genealogy explains a person's academic interests. It is similar to the assumption that lay beneath my own expectations when I visited Barasat; that I should have some kind of connection because my dad came from there. His past, my family background, the entanglement of those historical ties with British dominion in Asia, I thought might straightforwardly explain my present. As I hope to have shown here, they do not.

Empire has shaped me in more nebulous and contestable ways. It was less through biological and biographical roots, and more through my ambivalent subjectification within discourses that emerged in the colonial period. This might be because I was born after empire; but I think it has a wider relevance. I do not think it is accurate to conceive of the impact of the imperial past as an identifiable set of legacies with obvious paths to the present and with clear, didactic contemporary lessons (although such as approach has its utility). The memory of empire does not remain just beneath the surface of Britain's collective unconscious, waiting to be uncovered and confronted. Imperialism has shaped my interests and ambitions as a historian. But the imperial past had to be made relevant to me; it had to made into a useful, critical historical framework to confront my own subjectivity. In this sense, interrogating the legacies of imperialism and reflecting on how empire has shaped us, might be more than autobiography. It can be a contribution to what Michel Foucault called a 'history of the present'.[9] It can, and perhaps should, denaturalize accepted ideological understandings and common sense beliefs about identity and belonging – some of which we may still be using to define ourselves. We might be shaped by empire, but through our studies we are striving to find our way out.

Notes

1 Sara Ahmed, 'Being in Question', *Feminist Killjoys Blog*, 2014. Available online: feministkilljoys.com/2014/04/01/beinginquestion (accessed 6 October 2014).

2 Edward Said, *Orientalism* (New York: Vintage Books, 1979).

3 Ann Laura Stoler and Karen Strassler, 'Castings for the Colonial: Memory Work in "New Order" Java', *Comparative Studies in Society and History*, 42, 1 (2000): 4–48.

4 'Swan Bake', *The Sun*, 4 June 2003, 1, 7.

5 Among the essays that have stayed with me are: Shahid Amin, 'Gandhi as Mahatma: Gorakhpur District, Eastern UP, 1921–22', in *Subaltern Studies III: Writings on South Asian History and Society*, ed. Ranajit Guha (Delhi: Oxford University Press, 1984), 1–65; Ranajit Guha, 'Chandra's Death', in *Subaltern Studies V: Writings on South Asian History and Society*, ed. Ranajit Guha (Delhi: Oxford University Press, 1987), 135–65; and David Arnold, 'The Colonial Prison: Power, Knowledge and Penology in Nineteenth-Century India', in *Subaltern Studies VIII: Essays in Honour of Ranajit Guha*, ed. David Arnold and David Hardiman (Delhi: Oxford University Press, 1994), 148–87.

6 Benedict Anderson, *Imagined Communities: Reflections on the Origin and Spread of Nationalism* (London: Verso, 1991); Frantz Fanon, *The Wretched of the Earth*, trans. Constance Farrington (London: Penguin, 2001).

7 It is impossible to acknowledge all the work that has been done. One book that introduced me to many of these historiographic developments was the agenda-setting Ann Laura Stoler and Frederick Cooper (eds), *Tensions of Empire: Colonial Cultures in a Bourgeois World* (Berkeley: University of California Press, 1997).

8 For a longer discussion of this, see Antoinette Burton and Tony Ballantyne, 'Introduction: The Politics of Intimacy in an Age of Empire', in *Moving Subjects: Gender, Mobility and Intimacy in an Age of Global Empire*, ed. Antoinette Burton and Tony Ballantyne (Urbana: University of Illinois Press, 2009), 1–28.

9 Michel Foucault, *Discipline and Punish: The Birth of the Prison*, trans. Alan Sheridan (Harmondsworth: Penguin Books, 1979), 30–1.

INDEX